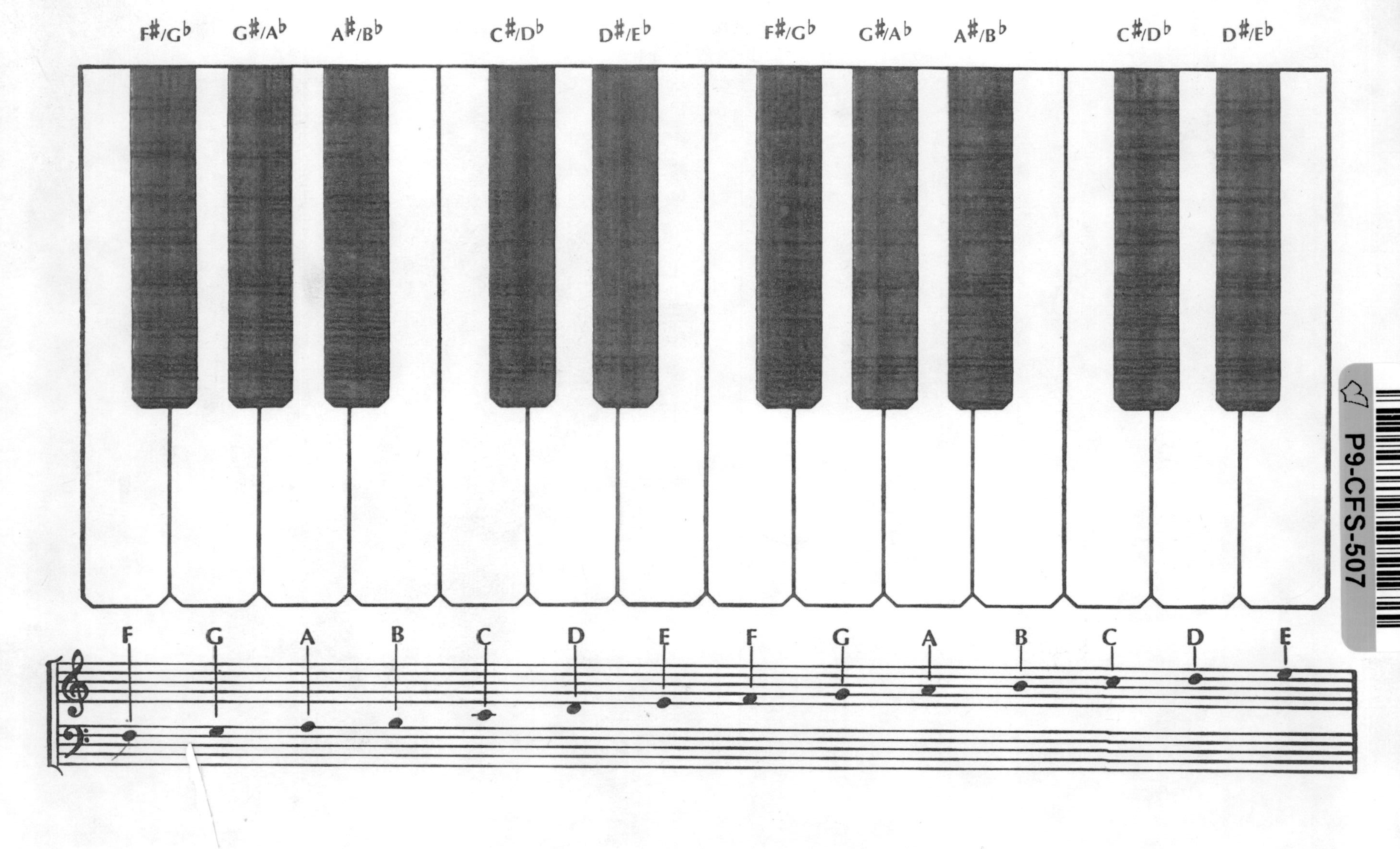
F#/G♭
G#/A♭
A#/B♭
C#/D♭
D#/E♭
F#/G♭
G#/A♭
A#/B♭
C#/D♭
D#/E♭
F
G
A
B
C
D
E
F
G
A
B
C
D
E

# World of Music

CARMEN E. CULP • LAWRENCE EISMAN
MARY E. HOFFMAN
Authors

CARMINO RAVOSA
Theme Musical

JEAN SINOR
Reading Music

DARRELL BLEDSOE
Producer, Vocal Recordings

PHYLLIS WEIKART
Rhythmic Movement

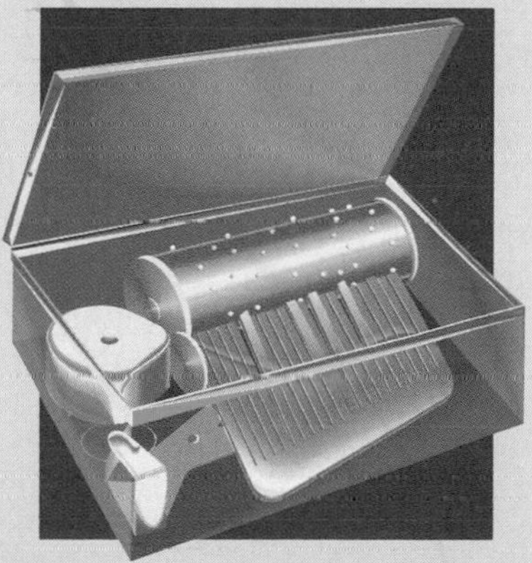

Silver Burdett & Ginn

Morristown, NJ • Needham, MA
Atlanta, GA • Cincinnati, OH • Dallas, TX • Menlo Park, CA • Deerfield, IL

 0-382-18252-9

# CONTENTS

SECTION I

# MUSIC FOR LIVING

# A Song to Begin With

Music can be magic
because of its power.
It can make us feel
glad to be alive.

Here is a song to help
us start the day.

## It's a Good Day

Words and Music by Peggy Lee and Dave Barbour

D Em A7 D
E♭ Fm B♭7 E♭
no-thin' to lose 'cause it's a good day from morn-in' till night.
D7 G E7 A7
E♭7 A♭ F7 B♭7
I said to the sun, "Good morn-in', Sun, rise and shine to-day.
A7 D A7 D
B♭7 E♭ B♭7 E♭
You know you've got-ta get go-in' if you're gon-na make a
A7 D Am A7
B♭7 E♭ B♭m B♭7
show-in', and you know you've got the right of way." 'Cause it's a
D Em A7
E♭ Fm B♭7
good day for wear-in' a grin, and it's a good day for
D A7 D
E♭ B♭7 E♭
play-in' to win, So take a deep breath, and let it all be-
D 1. Em A7 D
E♭ Fm B♭7 E♭
gin, 'cause it's a good day from morn-in' till night. I
2. Em A7 Em A7 D
Fm B♭7 Fm B♭7 E♭
good day from morn-in', such a good day from morn-in' till night.

## Songs in Our Lives

Since the beginning of time, people have used singing to express joy or sadness. Songs are sung in gratitude for a good harvest or to comfort people in hard times. Songs can give us courage when we are afraid or express our excitement when something wonderful happens.

***Willie Nelson***

Songs can tell about love—love for a person, love for a homeland. Songs can express faith and hope, and songs can turn away despair.

We sing to entertain ourselves and to share music with others. We sing to tell stories and to make musical jokes.

***The Bangles***

We sing songs that pass along the heritage of our ancestors. We sing songs of praise and worship and songs that help us celebrate special days.

## A Song for the River

What is the message of "A Friend of Mine"?

# A Storyteller's Song

Sometimes we *sing* a story instead of just saying it.

The writer of this song tells a true story. The grandfather who sailed to America was a real person, all the places exist, and the events in the song really happened.

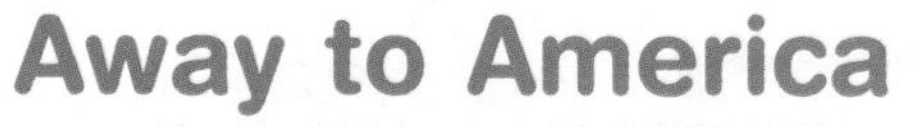

Words and Music by Linda Williams

1. My grand-fa-ther jour-neyed, like so man-y oth-ers, He turned to the West and the
heard of the moun-tains in far Col-o - ra-do, Where ea - gles flew free in the

all he took with him was what he could car-ry, His books and an old vi - o-
moth-er was born there not man-y years af - ter, And all of her sis - ters as

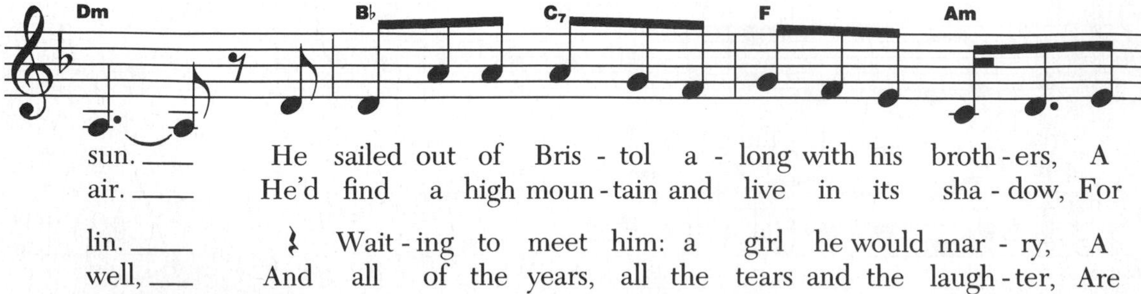

3. Now I've gone away, there was nothing to hold me,
I flew off to London and stayed.
But still I remember the stories they told me,
And think of the journey he made.
Now I miss the mountains when I look around me,
And I really can't tell you when,
But somehow the voice of my grandfather found me
And soon I'll be flying again.
Fly away, come home to America . . .

(Repeat Refrain) Sail away . . .

# An International Heritage

The people of America can trace their cultural heritage to every nation of the world. One person might be able to say, "I am part French, part Russian, part English, and part Navajo!" Another might say, "I am a first-generation American. All my ancestors come from China." Americans come in many varieties. Our music, too, is a rich mixture of international styles.

A Scottish bagpiper

## A Song from Scotland

"Bonnie Doon" was written about 1788. The music is traditional. The words are by the famous Scottish poet Robert Burns. The rhythm in the color boxes gives the song a Scottish sound.

### Bonnie Doon

Scottish Melody Words by Robert Burns

## My Heart's in the Highlands

My heart's in the Highlands, my heart is not here;
My heart's in the Highlands a-chasing the deer;
A-chasing the wild deer, and following the roe—
My heart's in the Highlands wherever I go.

Farewell to the Highlands, farewell to the North,
The birthplace of valor, the country of worth:
Wherever I wander, wherever I rove,
The hills of the Highlands forever I love.

Farewell to the mountains high-covered with snow;
Farewell to the straths and green valleys below;
Farewell to the forests and wild-hanging woods;
Farewell to the torrents and loud-pouring floods.

My heart's in the Highlands . . . .

*Robert Burns*

# A Song from Down Under

The most famous of Australian songs is "Waltzing Matilda." It is the story of a "swagman" who runs afoul of the law and drowns in a "billabong." The song is full of Australian slang.

## Waltzing Matilda

Words by A. B. Patterson Music by Maria Cowan

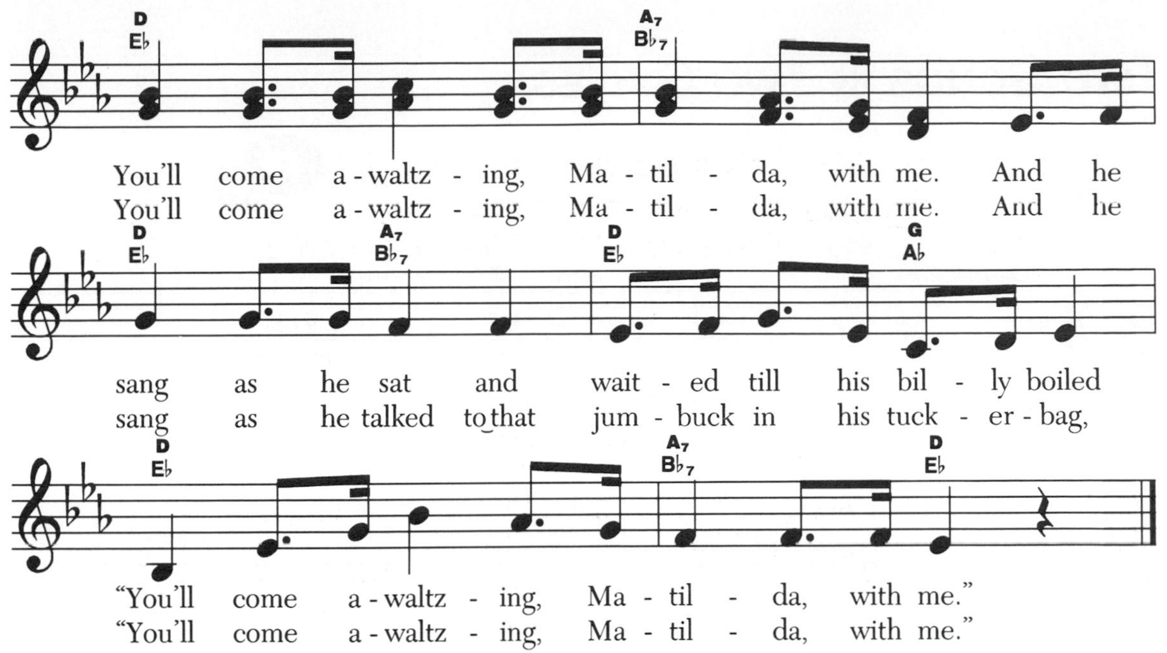


3. Down came the stockman, riding on his thoroughbred,
Down came the troopers, one, two, three.
"Where's the jolly jumbuck you've got in your tuckerbag?
You'll come a-waltzing, Matilda, with me." *Refrain*

4. Up jumped the swagman and plunged into the billabong,
"You'll never catch me alive," cried he;
And his ghost may be heard as you ride beside the billabong,
"You'll come a-waltzing, Matilda, with me." *Refrain*

***"Down Under"*** **. . . . . . . . . . . . Men at Work**

Australian songs tend to be good-natured, easygoing, and often humorous. Even rock bands from Australia like to play songs that are full of mischief.

***Men at Work***

# Two Songs in Two Styles

**CARNIVAL EVENING** ***Henri Rousseau***

Henri Rousseau, *Carnival Evening*, Philadelphia Museum of Art, Philadelphia

# A Song of Freedom

## Waters Ripple and Flow

Guitar: capo 3

Slovakian Folk Song English Words by Marta Novak

C / E♭ — Am / Cm — D7 / F7

1. Wa - ters rip - ple and flow, ___ Rush - ing swift - ly from
2. Faith as strong as the riv - er, Cour - age wide _ as the
3. Riv - er swift - ly flow - ing Heed my yearn - ing ___

G7 / B♭7 — Em / Gm — E7 / G7 — Am / Cm

me. 'Cross the land ___ I love,
sea. For the land ___ I love,
heart. Some - day I will re - turn,

F / A♭ — G7 / B♭7 — C / E♭ — Em / Gm

Run - ning on ___ to the sea. 'Cross the land ___ I
For the right _ to be free. For the land ___ I
Ne - ver to ___ de - part. Some - day I will re -

Am / Cm — F / A♭ — G7 / B♭7 — C / E♭

love, Run - ning on ___ to the sea.
love, For the right _ to be free.
turn, Ne - ver to ___ de - part.

# A Song for Selling Fine Clothes

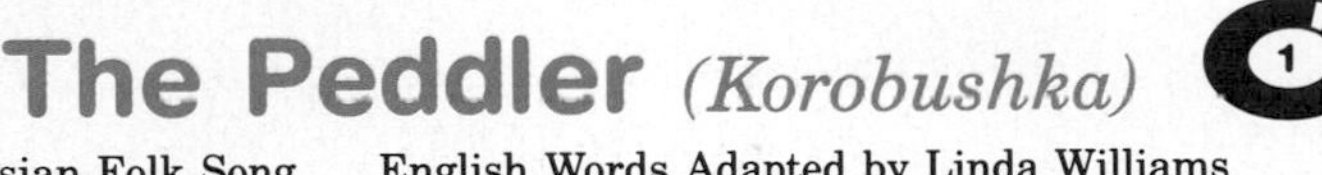

## The Peddler *(Korobushka)*

Russian Folk Song English Words Adapted by Linda Williams

1. Treas - ures have I in my Ko - ro - bush - ka, ___
2. Cost - ly and fine are the wares I bring you, ___
3. Treas - ures have I in my Ko - ro - bush - ka, ___

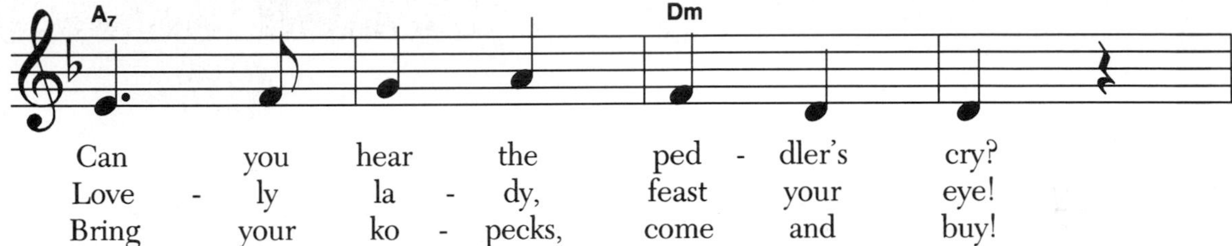


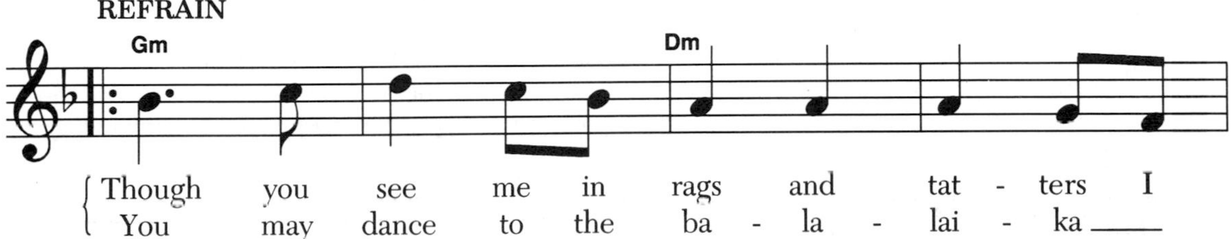

After you learn the song, you can add this countermelody. You can also play it on bells or keyboard.

SONGS OF ISRAEL
Around the Campfire
"Finjan" is the Turkish word for coffee pot.
Finjan
Israeli Campfire Song
Guitar: capo 5
(clap)
A cool des-ert wind blow-ing by, the wood on the
Ha - ru - ach no - she - vet k'ri - rah, No - sif od ki -
fire burn-ing high, We sit in the flick - er - ing
sam lam - du - rah; Ve - kach biz ro - ot ar - ga -
light and send out our song to the night.
man, va - esh ya - a - leh ke - kor - ban;
The song will re - sound as we pass it a - round, as we
Ha - esh me - hav - he - vet, shir - a me lav le - vet so -
pass it a - round, ha - fin - jan
vev lo so - vev ha - fin - jan.
La la la la la la

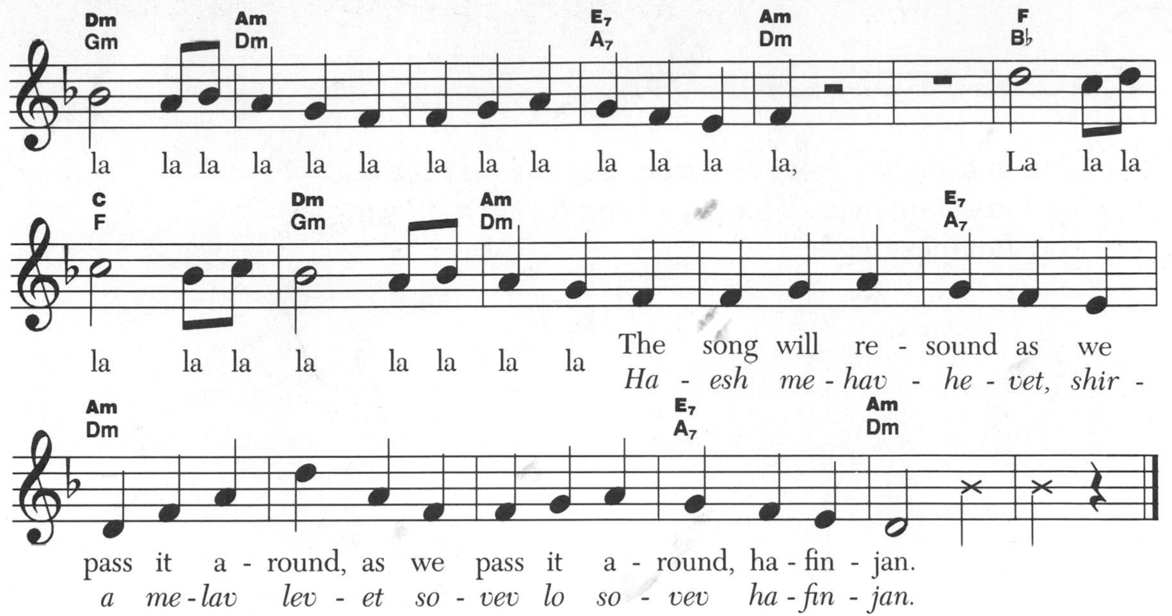


This tambourine **ostinato** will go with the "La la la" section:

(repeat as needed)

## Yibane Amenu

Round from Israel

Countermelody for Bells, Recorder, Keyboard

# A Song from Okinawa

Okinawa is a Pacific Island nation, but the culture and language are Japanese. This love song from Okinawa is in the Japanese style.

## Asadoya

Folk Song from Okinawa

3. Lo! now I have wed another.
Fairer by far than thee.
Sa yui yui
With graceful manners fine,
Dwell we now in happy harmony,
And she is my love, my darling
and all the world to me.

4. And if she bear me a son,
Ruler of this town he will be;
Sa yui yui
And if a daughter fair,
A model of sweet felicity,
And she'll be my love, my darling
and all the world to me.

Honolulu Academy of Art

***Fantasy on Japanese Woodprints* (excerpt). . . . . . . . Alan Hovhaness**

**River-Fog**

Because the river-fog
Hiding the mountain base
Has risen,
The autumn mountain looks as though it hung in the sky.

*—Fukayabu Kiyowara*
*translated by Authur Waley*

# Music from Mexico

Here is a song that can be sung for birthdays, or just as a "morning song." Try singing it in two parts. The harmony part is an interval of a third above the melody.

# A Mexican Farmhand

A "charro" is a peasant or a farmhand. This charro is not well-thought-of by his foreman!

3. "Just one more thing," said *el charro,*
"I would marry your daughter, too," } *repeat*
Firmly the foreman assured him,
"She is taken, Nicolás!" } *repeat*

4. *El charro* cried out, despairing,
"I will throw myself off the cliff!" } *repeat*
Kindly the foreman suggested,
"Then go head first, Nicolás!" } *repeat*

# A Calypso Song

Calypso songs originated many years ago in the West Indies. Plantation slaves were often forbidden to talk, so they sang the news and gossip to one another in rhythmic song patterns as they worked.

## Hold 'em, Joe

Words and Music by Harry Thomas

*Chorus* C F C 1. G7 C
Hold 'em, Joe, Hold 'em, Joe, Hold 'em, Joe, but don't _ let him go.

2. G7 C *Solo* G7 *Chorus* C
Joe, but don't _ let him go. Me don - key want wa - ter, Hold 'em, Joe;

*Solo* G7 *Chorus* C *Solo* G7 *Chorus*
Spring 'round _ the cor - ner, Hold 'em, Joe; Me don - key want wa - ter, Hold 'em,

C *Solo* G7 *Chorus* C *Solo* G7
Joe; Ev - 'ry - bo - dy want wa - ter, Hold 'em, Joe; Fu - ma - la - ca tchim - ba,

*Chorus* C *Solo* G7 *Chorus* C *Solo*
Hold 'em, Joe; Me don - key want wa - ter, Hold 'em Joe; Ev - 'ry - bo - dy want

G7 *Chorus* C *Solo* G7 *Chorus* C
wa - ter, Hold 'em Joe; Me don - key want wa - ter, Hold 'em, Joe. Hold 'em,

Last time go to Coda 1.

F C G7 C

Joe, Hold 'em, Joe, Hold 'em, Joe, but don't _ let him go. Hold 'em,

2.

G7 C Solo F C

Joe, but don't _ let him go. We on a jour - ney, _ he don't walk straight,

G7 C

and that is ___ be - cause he's _ so un - der - weight; That don - key _ of

F C G7

mine, he ___ don't like no weight, Put him on a cart and _ he won't walk

C D.S. al Coda

straight. Me don - key want

Coda

G7 C

Joe, but don't _ let him go!

# A Sad Goodbye

Here is another song from the West Indies. The words are about saying goodbye to a place that will be sadly missed.

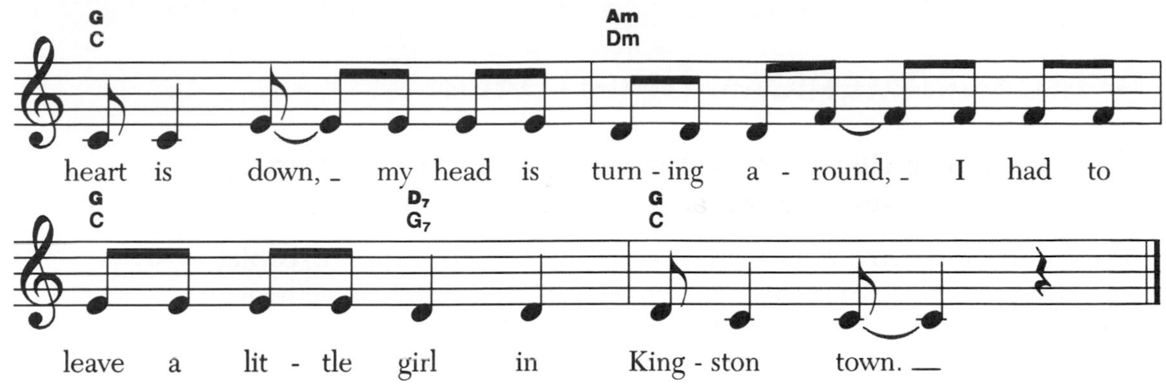


This countermelody goes with the last four lines of the song.

Bells, Recorder, Keyboard

*Harry Belafonte*

# African-American Spirituals

Of all the music that is truly American, the African-American spirituals are among the most distinctive and interesting.

Many spirituals are about characters and events in the Bible. The story that is retold in this spiritual can be found in the Old Testament.

## Didn't My Lord Deliver Daniel?

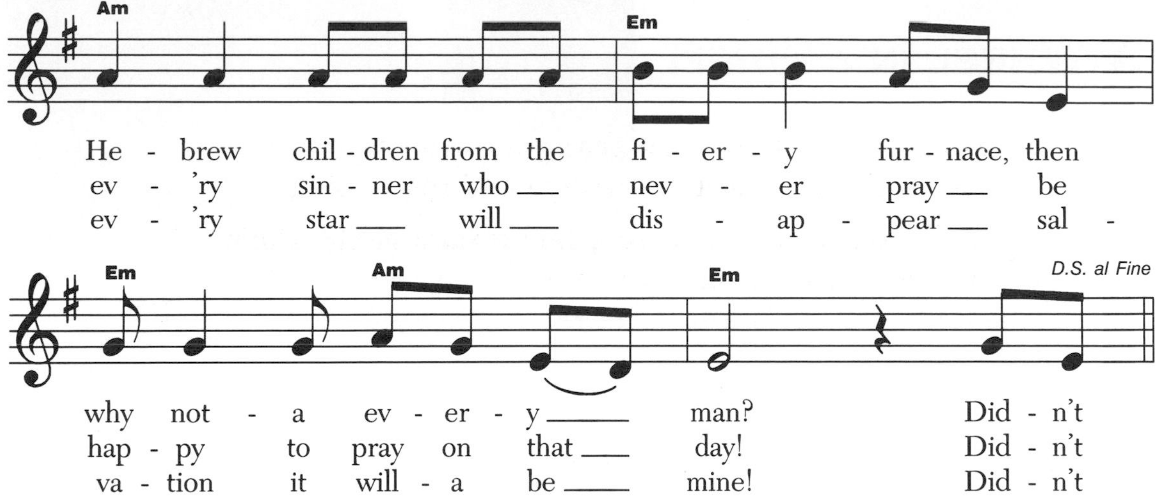


Spirituals make you think of African-Americans, but these songs have become part of our national heritage. All Americans, regardless of their ethnic background, enjoy singing spirituals.

# A Wheel in a Wheel

## Ezekiel Saw the Wheel

**Guitar: capo 3**

African-American Spiritual

*Solo* D/F *Chorus* A7/C7 D/F

E - ze - kiel_ saw the wheel, 'Way up in the mid - dle of the air,

*Solo* D/F *Chorus* A7/C7 D/F

E - ze - kiel_ saw the wheel, 'Way in the mid - dle of the air.

*Solo* D/F *Chorus*

Now the big wheel turn by faith, And the lit - tle wheel turn by the

A7/C7 D/F *Solo* *Chorus* A7/C7 D/F *Fine*

grace of God, It's a wheel in a wheel, 'Way in the mid - dle of the air.

*Solo* D/F *Chorus* A7/C7 D/F

1. Some go to church for to sing and shout, 'Way in the mid - dle of the air,
2. One of these_ days 'bout_ twelve o' - clock, 'Way in the mid - dle of the air,

*Solo* D/F *Chorus* A7/C7 D/F *D.S. al fine*

Be - fore six months they're shout - ed out! 'Way in the mid - dle of the air. E -
This old world gonna reel and rock! 'Way in the mid - dle of the air. E -

# Little Wheel A-Turnin'

African-American Spiritual

Guitar: capo 3

C/E♭ F/A♭ C/E♭ C/E♭ G7/B♭7 C/E♭ F/A♭ C/E♭ Am/Cm C/E♭ C/E♭ G7/B♭7 C/E♭

1. There's a lit - tle wheel a - turn - in' in my heart, There's a
2. There's a lit - tle song a - sing - in' in my heart, There's a
3. There's a lit - tle love a - liv - in' in my heart, There's a

lit - tle wheel a - turn - in' in my heart; In my
lit - tle song a - sing - in' in my heart; In my
lit - tle love a - liv - in' in my heart; In my

heart, ______ in my heart. ______ There's a
heart, ______ in my heart. ______ There's a
heart, ______ in my heart. ______ There's a

lit - tle wheel a - turn - in' in my heart.
lit - tle song a - sing - in' in my heart.
lit - tle love a - liv - in' in my heart.

4. There's a little bell a-ringin' in my heart,
5. There's a little drum a-beatin' in my heart,

A Musical Code
Guitar: capo 5
Swing Low, Sweet Chariot
African-American Spiritual
REFRAIN
Swing low, sweet char - i - ot, Com-in' for to car-ry me home; Swing low, sweet char - i - ot, Com-in' for to car-ry me home.
Fine
VERSE
1. I looked o - ver Jor - dan and what did I see? A band of an - gels com - in' af-ter me,
2. If you get there be - fore I do, Com-in' for to car-ry me home; Tell all my friends I'm com - in' too, Com-in' for to car-ry me home.
3. I'm some-times up, I'm some - times down, But still my soul feels heav'n - ly bound,
D.C. al Fine

# AN ECHO SONG

## Let Me Fly

# An American Indian Song

This song was written by two American Indian college students.

The music of the song is like some of the popular music we are used to hearing. However, the words echo the heritage of the songwriters. In the lyrics, they look to their tribal leaders for guidance and inspiration, as their people have for many centuries.

## Go, My Son

Words and Music by Burson-Nofchissey

Spoken: *Long ago an Indian War Chief counseled his people in the ways that they should walk. He wisely told them that education is the ladder to success and happiness. "Go, my son, and climb that ladder. . . ."*

Go, my son, go and climb the lad - der, Go, my son,
on the lad - der of an ed - u - ca - tion, You can see to

go and earn your fea-ther. Go my son, make your peo-ple proud of
help your In - dian na-tion, then

you. ______ From Reach, my son. Lift your peo-ple up with you.

You can learn to perform "Go, My Son" in traditional Indian sign language. Use the signs illustrated on pages 36 and 37.

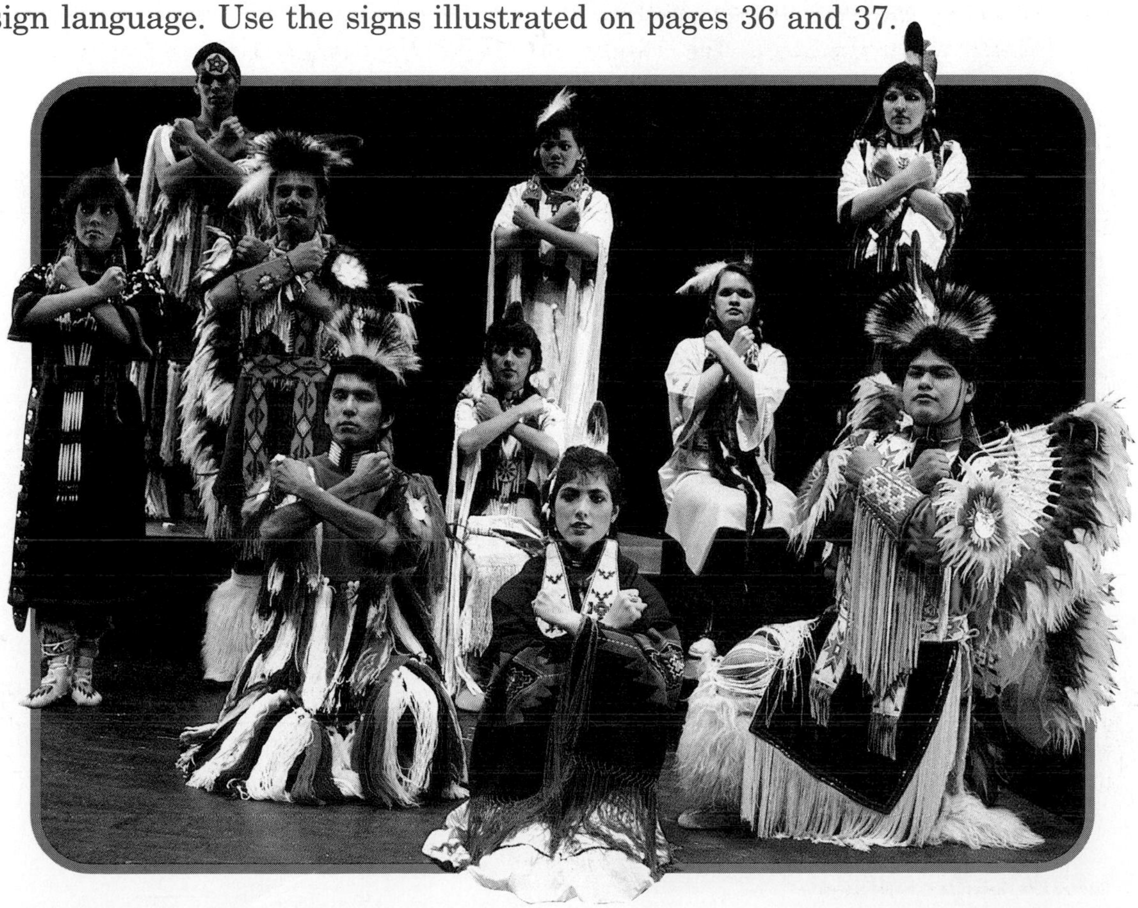

# Signing an American Indian Song

Here are the signs you can use as you sing the refrain of "Go, My Son."

climb

proud

good

vocation

of you

education

Indian

reach

Listen to some traditional American Indian music. In this example, the only tones we hear are the five notes of a pentatonic scale.

"Round Dance Song" (excerpt) .................... .................... Traditional Taos Indian Music

Look at the **melody** of "Go, My Son." How is it similar?

# Music for the Mountain

## Call Chart 1

Here are some of the musical ideas that are used in *Sundance*. There is even a theme made out of the composer's name.

**1.** A strong, heavy pattern of five beats

**2.** A texture of strings, harp, bells and piano, all moving upward

**3.** The recurring pattern of three notes

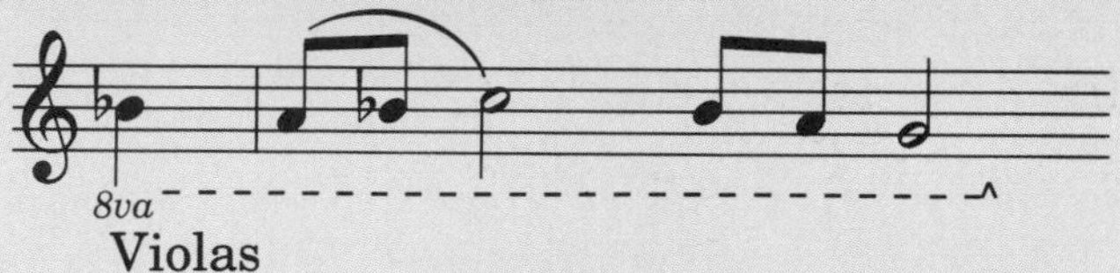


**4.** The "Sundance" theme, introduced by the trumpet

**5.** Brass players creating the sound of the wind

*Blow* through mouthpiece

**6.** The "signature" theme, made out of the composer's name

Now listen to the whole selection.

*Sundance* .......................... Linda Williams

## Meet the Composer

Linda Williams
(b. 1931)

Linda Williams has been writing music all her life. As a music teacher she has written hundreds of songs for her students, many of which have been published. She wrote "Away to America" (page 8) for her students to sing.

She won a national prize for a set of piano pieces while she was still a college student, and she has been a working composer since. Large orchestral pieces like *Sundance* and small chamber works are her favorite projects. She continues to write many songs each year.

Sundance is a small ski resort on Mount Timpanogos in Utah. The American composer Linda Williams sketched the idea for her piece one summer day at Sundance. She wanted to paint a musical picture of the mountain.

# A Nation of Immigrants

The song "Away to America" on page 8 tells the story of one young man who came to America from the British Isles. Immigrants from many countries came to these shores, bringing their customs, their languages, and their songs.

## An Immigrant's Son

American composer George Gershwin was the son of Russian-Jewish immigrants who came to America before the turn of the century. He was born in Brooklyn in 1898 into a home with very little in the way of wealth or social standing. But he would become one of the most successful American composers of his time. George Gershwin was that American ideal, an immigrant's son who made good.

## Meet the Composer

George Gershwin
(1898–1937)

George Gershwin's life was tragically short, but his impact on American music was great. He wrote songs like "I Got Rhythm," "Liza," "Strike Up the Band," and many others. They have become popular classics. He also wrote serious concert pieces, using the catchy melodies, jazzy harmonies, and driving rhythms of popular music.

You are probably familiar with some of Gershwin's concert pieces. They are played all over the world, and have been recorded many times by famous orchestras and concert artists.

His songs for the musical theater are among his most famous and best-loved pieces.

You may already have heard Gershwin's most famous work, *Rhapsody in Blue.* The opening clarinet *glissando* immediately announces that the piece will be full of **jazz** elements.

***Rhapsody in Blue*** **(excerpt)............. Gershwin**

In *An American in Paris,* Gershwin drew a musical picture of a visitor to Paris walking the busy streets.

***An American in Paris*** **(excerpts)......... Gershwin**

All the songs in this **medley** are from famous Broadway shows by George Gershwin.

***Medley*** **("Of Thee I Sing," "Liza," "Strike Up the Band").......................... George Gershwin**

# George Gershwin—Boyhood Years

When George was twelve years old, a piano was brought into his home. It was meant for his older brother Ira, who was to begin piano lessons. But George surprised everyone by picking out songs on the piano, some even with his own catchy accompaniments.

About that time he heard the music of songwriter Irving Berlin. "This is American music," he said, "This is the kind of music I want to write."

"Alexander's Ragtime Band" ......... Irving Berlin

Among the tunes he may have played on the piano were popular songs like "Waiting for the Robert E. Lee." This lively, syncopated song was popular when George Gershwin was about fourteen years old.

## Waiting for the Robert E. Lee

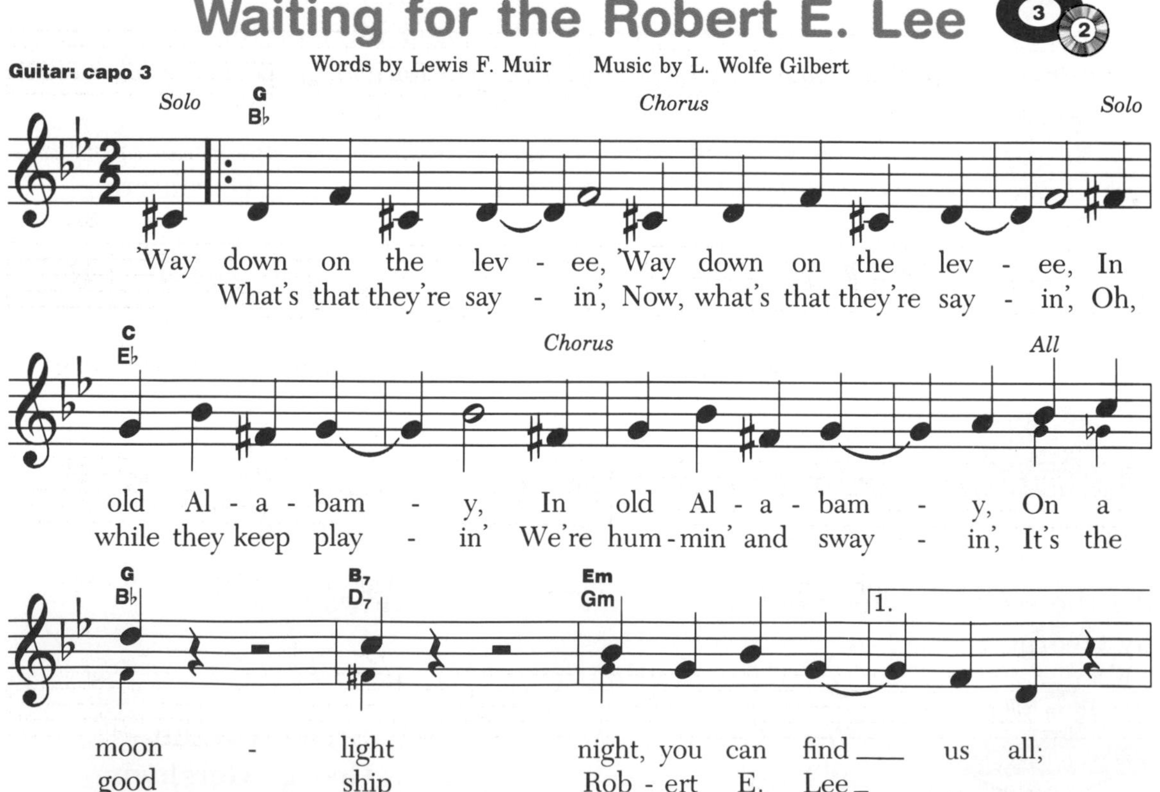

A7
C7
D7
F7
While we are wait - in,' the ban - jos are syn - co - pa - tin'.
2.
Em
Gm
A7
C7
D7
F7
G
B♭
— That's come to car - ry the cot - ton a - way. —
G
B♭
C
E♭
See them step - pin' a - long;
G
B♭
G7
B♭7
Hear us sing - in' a - long. Go take your best gal, real
G7
B♭7
C
E♭
pal, Go down by the lev - ee, I said to the lev - ee! And then
C
E♭
G
B♭
G7
B♭7
join that ju - bi - lant throng, Hear that mu - sic and song:
G7
B7
It's sim - ply great, mate, Wait - in' on the lev - ee,
G7
B♭7
C
E♭
Wait - in' for the Rob - ert E. Lee! —

# The Song Plugger

At the age of fifteen, Gershwin left high school to take a job as a "song plugger." When Gershwin was twenty, he was given a job writing songs for a publisher.

His first "hit" was a song called "Swanee," written in 1919. It sold over two million records.

***George Gershwin***

## Swanee

Words by Irving Caesar Music by George Gershwin

**Guitar**

D D AUG G D
Swan - ee, How I love you, How I love you, My dear old Swan - ee; ___

D D AUG G $A_7$ D
I'd give the world to be A-mong the folks in D - I - X - I -

$A_7$ D D AUG
E - ven now there's some - one Wait - ing for me, Pray - ing for me

G D D AUG
Down by the Swan - ee, ___ The folks up north will

G $A_7$ D
see me no more ___ When I get to the Swan - ee shore. ___

# George Gershwin, Pianist

In addition to being one of America's foremost composer-songwriters, George Gershwin was an accomplished pianist. He wrote many works for piano solo, both popular and serious.

Listen to this old recording of one of George Gershwin's works for piano. The song "I Got Rhythm" appears on page 49.

I Got Rhythm .......................... Gershwin

## Call Chart 2

**Listen to these piano preludes from three different centuries. Notice how they are alike and how they are different.**

**1. Even rhythms, broken chords, one mood throughout**

"Prelude No. 1" from *The Well Tempered Clavier* .. ............................................. Bach

**2. Thick texture, rich harmony, block chords**

*Prelude Op. 28 No. 20*..................... Chopin

**3. Rhythms and harmonies often found in jazz, melody in the style of popular music**

"Prelude No. 2" from *Three Piano Preludes*........ ................................... Gershwin

# Porgy and Bess, An American Opera

George Gershwin's opera *Porgy and Bess* is considered by many to be his finest work.

The story of the **opera** takes place in Catfish Row, a waterfront tenement section of Charleston, South Carolina. It tells how Porgy, a crippled black beggar, finds Bess, falls in love with her, and loses her to another man. She has been lured away to New York, and Porgy is determined to find her.

One of the most famous songs in the opera is this lullaby.

The final scene shows Porgy setting out hopefully to bring her home.

***A scene from Porgy and Bess***

# Call Chart 3

LISTENING LIBRARY
3
2
*Concerto in F,* Themes from Movement 3 .......... .......... Gershwin
1. A
f
2. B (Concerto theme)
3. C
and
4. D
5. E
6. B
7. Coda
tr
ff
LISTENING LIBRARY
3
2
*Concerto in F,* Movement 3 .............. Gershwin

# A Famous Gershwin Song

One of Gershwin's most famous songs for Broadway, this song was written for a 1930 show called *Girl Crazy*.

# Test 1

Here are descriptions of several of the folk songs in your book. The songs come from many nations, but have many elements in common. Each has a distinctive style and purpose, however. Match the descriptions with the songs, and write the letter in the blank.

1. A song that is like a singing commercial for clothing ________
2. A song that imitates flowing water ________
3. A song about a stubborn donkey ________
4. A song about a ghost ________
5. A song sung by a robber ________
6. A song with words by a famous poet ________
7. A song about fireside companionship ________
8. A comedy song about a fieldhand ________
9. A song with a melody using only five tones ________
10. A sad goodbye song ________

A. Finjan
B. Bonnie Doon
C. Waltzing Matilda
D. Jamaica Farewell
E. Asadoya
F. Serenade
G. Waters Ripple and Flow
H. The Peddler
I. El charro
J. Hold 'em, Joe

Use your index to find these songs if you need to look at them.

# What Do You Hear? 1

You will hear eight pieces for instruments. Each will be in the *style* of a song in your book, even though the music is *different* from that song. Circle the title of the song you think is *most like* the music you hear.

*Styles Montage*

1. Hold 'em, Joe — Serenade
2. Serenade — Waltzing Matilda
3. Waters Ripple and Flow — El charro
4. It's a Good Day — Asadoya
5. Las mañanitas — Bonnie Doon
6. Didn't My Lord Deliver Daniel? — In the Moonlight
7. Bonnie Doon — It's a Good Day
8. In the Moonlight — A Friend of Mine

# Test 2

Here are five descriptions of musical selections you have listened to. After each description are two choices of titles. Circle the title of the listening selection that fits the description.

1. A piano piece in a traditional form, with jazzy harmonies

   Men At Work: "Down Under"  Gershwin: *Prelude*

2. A piece that spells the composer's name

   Gershwin: *Concerto in F*  Williams: *Sundance*

3. A piano piece from the 1700s

   Bach: "Prelude"  Gershwin: "I Got Rhythm"

4. A piece that describes a street scene

   Gershwin: *Rhapsody in Blue*  Gershwin: *An American in Paris*

5. Music built on a five-tone scale

   Hovhaness: *Fantasy on*  Chopin: *Prelude*

# WHAT DO YOU HEAR? 2

Songs often create a mood. Usually the words are an important factor. However, music alone, even without words, can create a mood. You will hear eight instrumental accompaniments for songs in your book. Circle the words that best describe to you the mood of the music. You may choose one or more words.

*Moods Montage*

1. Lively Sad Angry Playful Dreamy Cheerful

2. Lively Sad Angry Playful Dreamy Cheerful

3. Lively Sad Angry Playful Dreamy Cheerful

4. Lively Sad Angry Playful Dreamy Cheerful

5. Lively Sad Angry Playful Dreamy Cheerful

6. Lively Sad Angry Playful Dreamy Cheerful

7. Lively Sad Angry Playful Dreamy Cheerful

8. Lively Sad Angry Playful Dreamy Cheerful

Musical Interaction

Tone Color

RHYTHM

SECTION II

# UNDERSTANDING MUSIC

Harmony

FORM

Melody

STYLES

A

C

A

B

A

# RHYTHM—THE HEARTBEAT OF MUSIC

When you find yourself tapping your foot to a piece of music, you are responding to rhythm. It is the heartbeat of music.

As you sing "Dinah," tap your hands on your knees or on your desk. Tap each time you see an x above the note. This is the **beat** of the music.

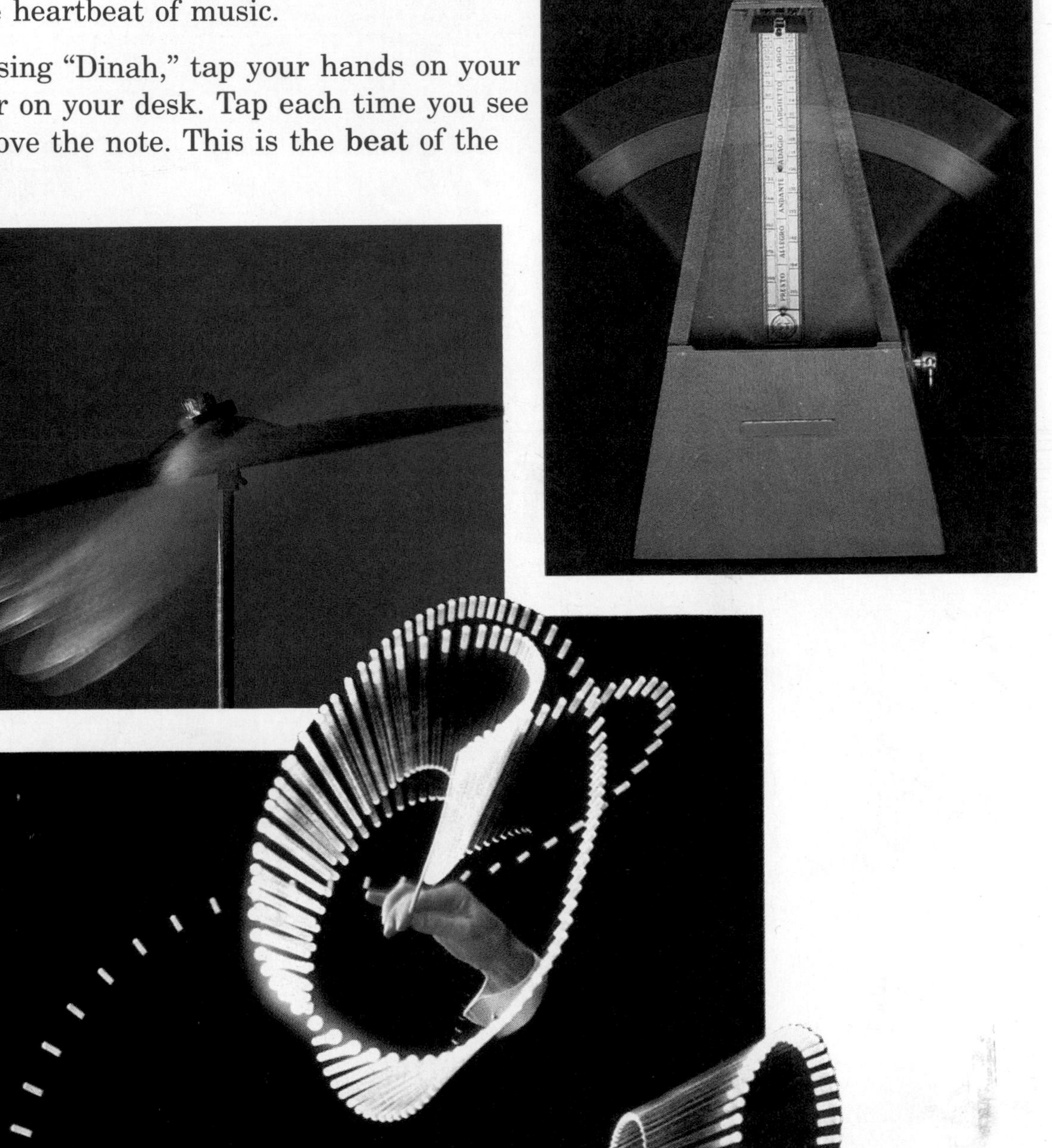

Guitar: capo 5

# Dinah

Words by Sam M. Lewis and Joe Young Music by Harry Akst

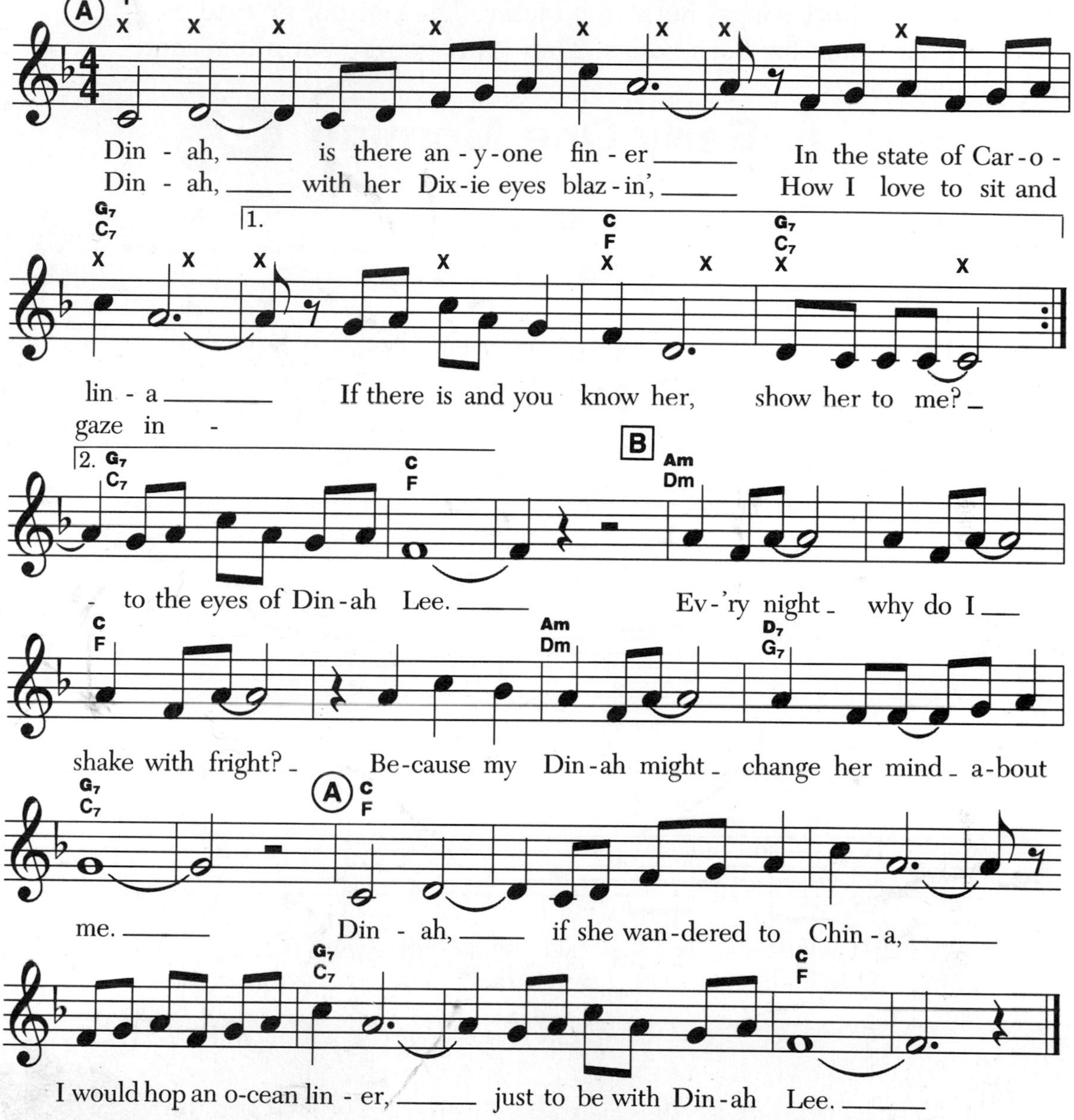

Din - ah, is there an - y - one fin - er In the state of Car - o -
Din - ah, with her Dix - ie eyes blaz - in', How I love to sit and

lin - a If there is and you know her, show her to me?
gaze in -

- to the eyes of Din - ah Lee. Ev - 'ry night why do I

shake with fright? Be - cause my Din - ah might change her mind a - bout

me. Din - ah, if she wan - dered to Chin - a,

I would hop an o - cean lin - er, just to be with Din - ah Lee.



Tap to another version of "Dinah." Keep tapping even during the silences. Keep the beat steady.

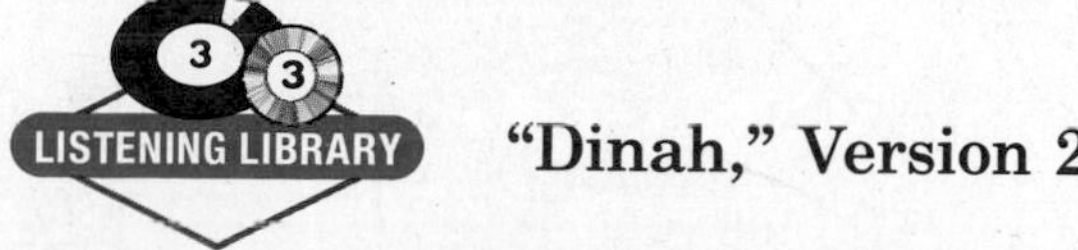


"Dinah," Version 2

When the music stopped and then started again, were you still on the right beat?

# Tempo

Here are two short songs, both in $\frac{2}{4}$ meter. The **tempo,** or rate of speed, is the same for both songs. They can even be sung together, as "partner songs."

## Early One Morning

English Folk Song

D G $A_7$

1. Ear - ly one morn - ing, be - fore the sun had ris - en,
2. One au - tumn af - ter - noon, just as the sun was set - ting,

D G $A_7$ D

I heard a blue - bird in the fields __ gai - ly sing,
I heard a blue - bird on a tree __ pipe a song,

$A_7$ D $A_7$ D

"South winds are blow - ing, Green grass is grow - ing,
"Fare - well! We're go - ing, Cold winds are blow - ing,

D G $A_7$ D

We __ come to her - ald the mer - ry __ spring."
But __ we'll be back __ when the days __ grow __ long."

When you sing them together, the quarter note beat must be steady, even though one song seems to move faster.

## Summer Night, Winter Night

Words and Music by Jean Riddle

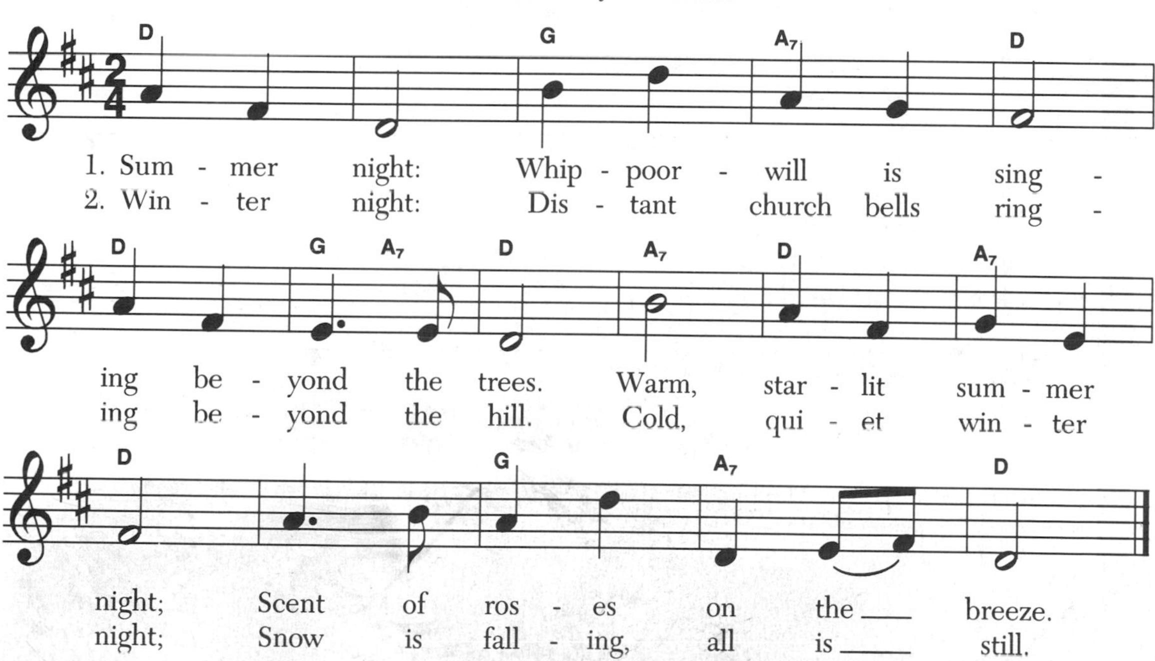




Listen to this piece for **orchestra.** The tempo stays the same, but the first part sounds faster than the second part.

**Overture from *Candide* (excerpt) ........ Bernstein**

# Rhythm and Meter—Mixing Sixes

Begin with a group of six notes.

They can be divided in a number of ways.

1. 2.

Accents tell us how the notes are divided.

1. 6/4 2. 6/4

Play the first pattern on a drum. Play the second pattern on the claves. Have two players play the two patterns together.

The patterns are easier to see when eighth notes are used.

1. 6/8 2. 6/8

Sometimes music in a pattern of six will alternate between accenting groups of two and groups of three.

Try this chant. The words fall naturally into rhythm patterns in groups of two or in groups of three.

## Latin America

Mary Hoffman

6/8

La - tin A - mer - i - ca, Con - ga, Tan - go, Mam - bo, Mex - i - co, E - cua - dor,

Chi - le, Cos - ta Ri - ca, Ur - u - guay, Par - a - guay, Pe - ru, Ar - gen - ti - na,

Sal - va - dor, Pan - a - ma, Con - ga, Tan - go, Mam - bo, La - tin A - mer - i - ca!

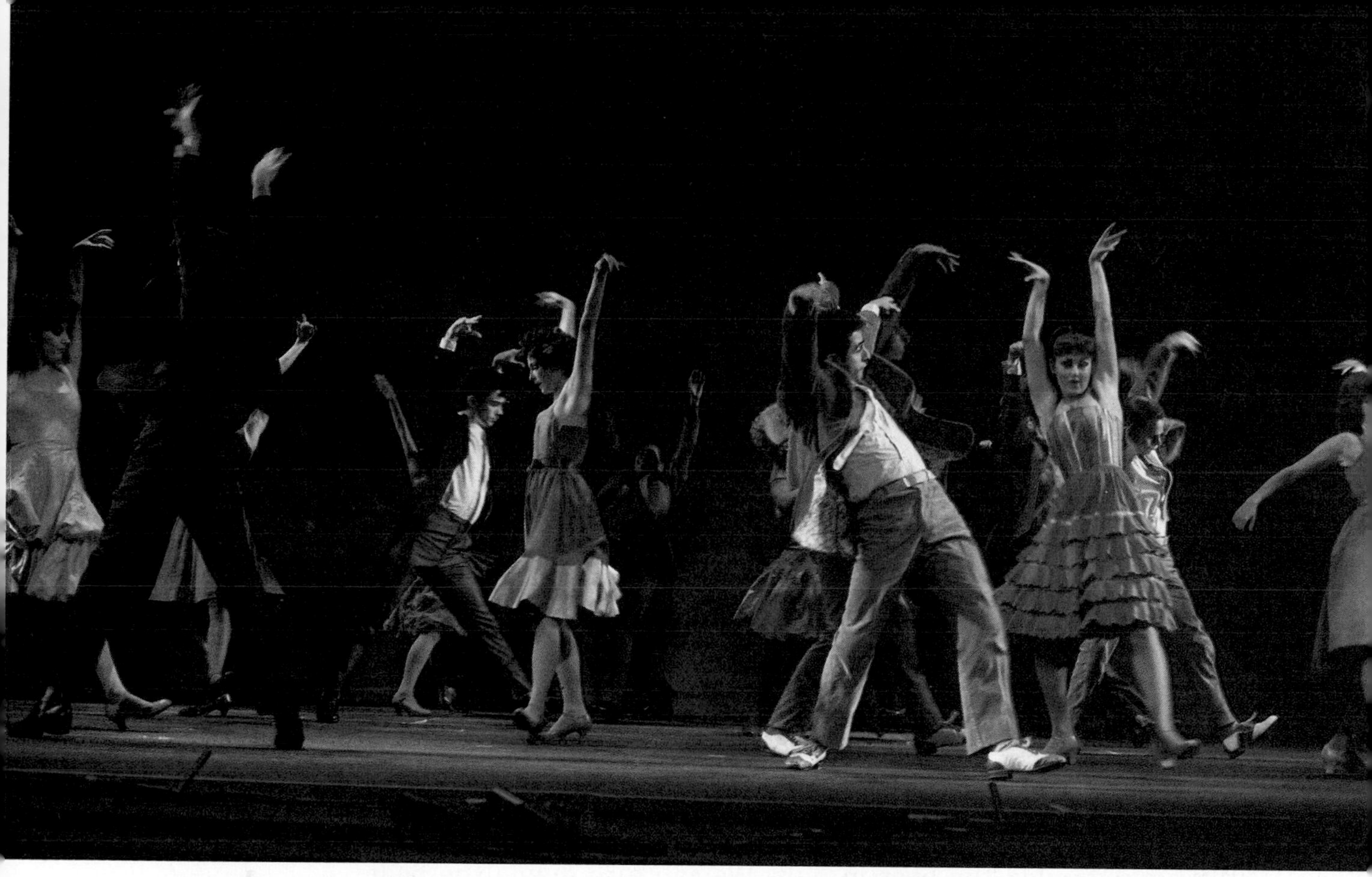

In the musical play *West Side Story,* there is a song about Puerto Ricans living in New York City. This song uses the alternating groups of three and two as in the chant.

"America" from *West Side Story* ......... Bernstein

## Another Way to Mix Twos and Threes

A dance from *Carmina Burana* by Carl Orff also mixes two and threes. However, this time they occur in irregular patterns. The music begins this way:

Try clapping the rhythm pattern, then listen to the way it happens in the music.

"Tanz" from *Carmina Burana* ................. Orff

# Rhythm Patterns—Divide and Conquer

Begin with a steady beat. Tap your knees in a steady *quarter-note rhythm.*

Use football or any other terms and chant while tapping.

pass pass pass pass

Keep a steady beat, but divide it by chanting the word "tackle" on each beat.

tack - le tack - le tack - le tack - le

We have divided the beat in half. We can also divide the beat in half again.

Tap the beat, but this time say the word "interference" each time you tap.

in - ter - fer - ence in - ter - fer - ence in - ter - fer - ence in - ter - fer - ence

Put all the patterns together in order to hear them better. Use words or the tone color of different instruments.

You can find these patterns in the two songs that follow. There are also some other patterns, but as you will see they follow the rhythm of the words.

# Mister Touchdown, U.S.A.

Guitar: capo 3

Words and Music by Ruth Roberts, Gene Piller, and William Katz

After you listen to "Mister Touchdown, U.S.A.," you can make up a football chant to accompany it.

# A Bell Song with Divided Beats

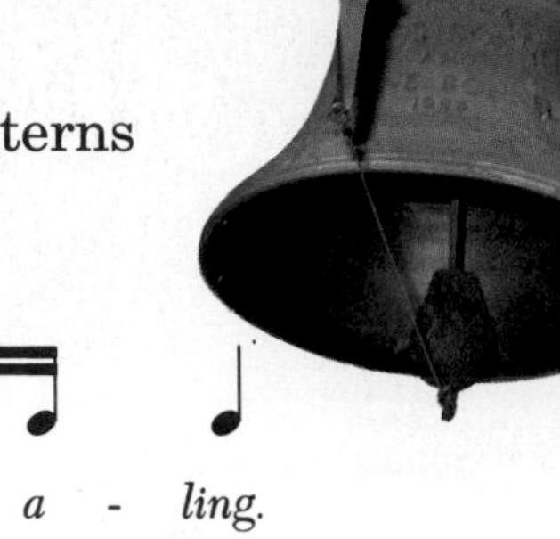

The first line of "Ring, Bells" demonstrates one of the patterns of beat division we have been learning about.

Single beat: Divided beat: Divided again

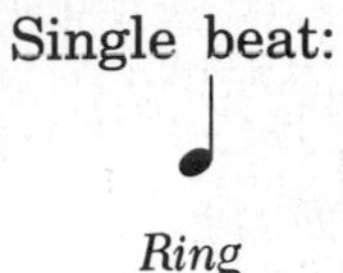

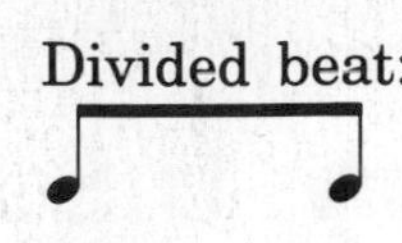

*Ring bells, a - ring - a - ling - a - ling.*

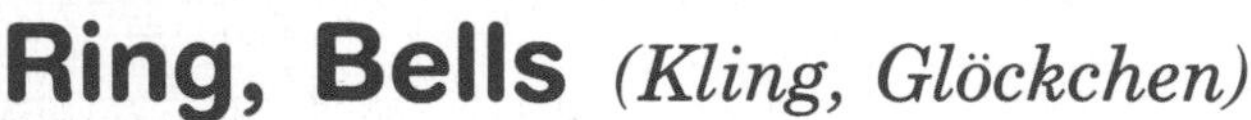

## Ring, Bells *(Kling, Glöckchen)*

Traditional German Carol    English Version by Hilda Trällin    Arranged by Mary Hoffman

Ring, bells, a - ring - a - ling - a - ling, Ring lit - tle bells.
*Kling, Glöck - chen, kling - e - ling - e - ling, Kling, Glöck - chen, kling.*

"O - pen, let us en - ter, Cold the wind in win - ter."
*Lasst mich ein ihr Kin - der, Ist so kalt der Win - ter.*

Maid and in - fant ho - ly, In a room so low - ly.
*Öff - net mir die Tür - en, Lasst mich nicht er - frie - ren.*

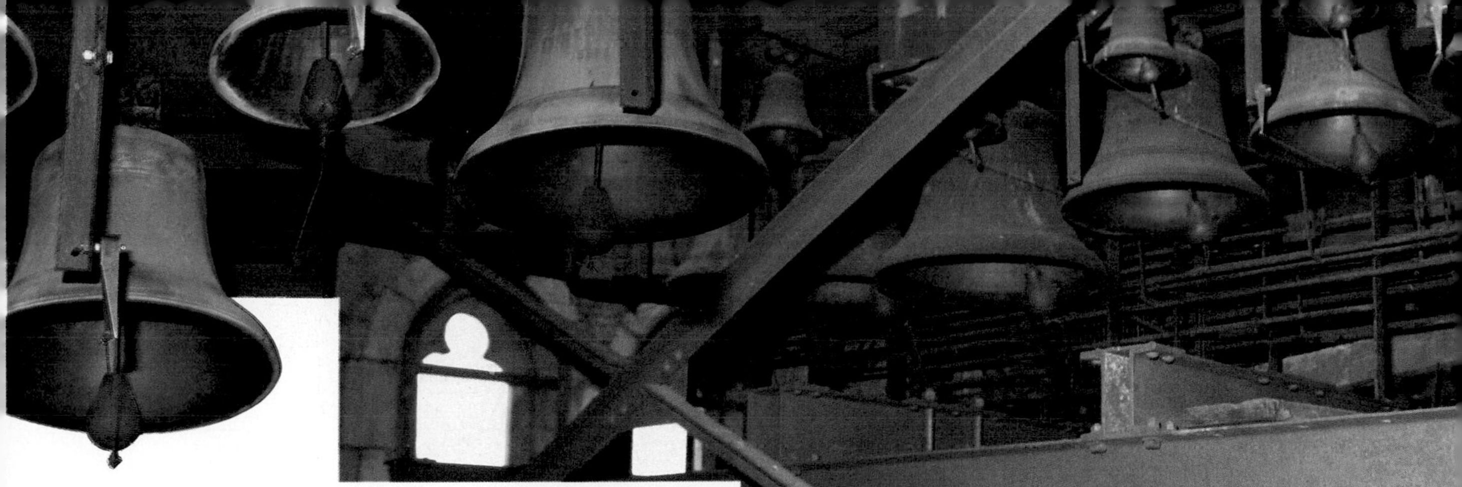

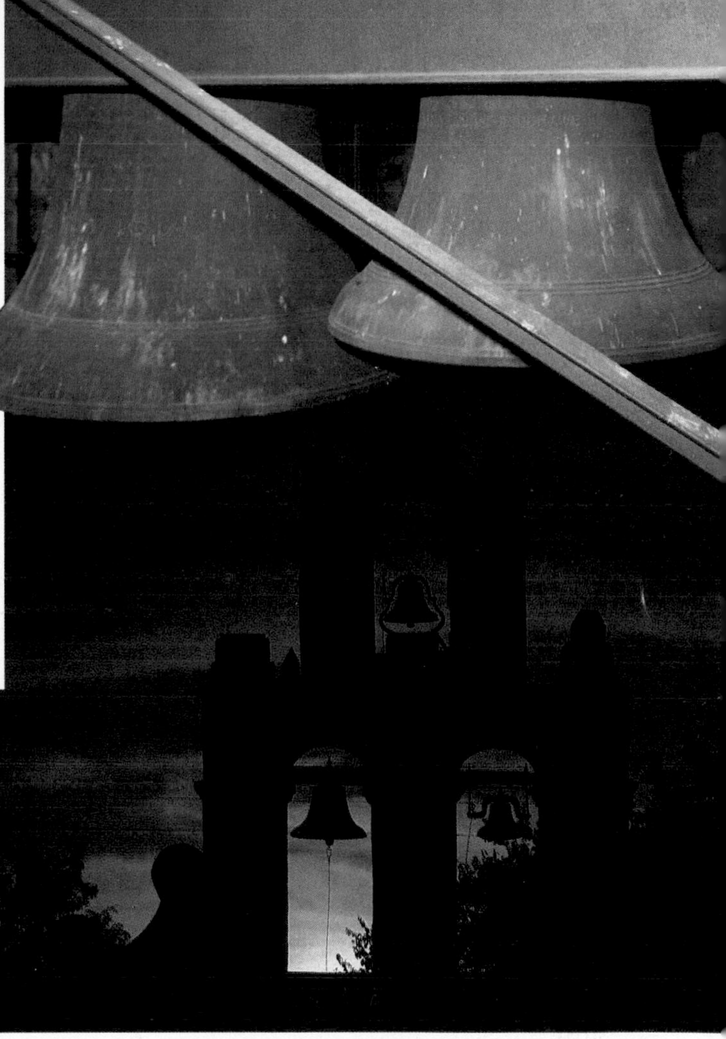

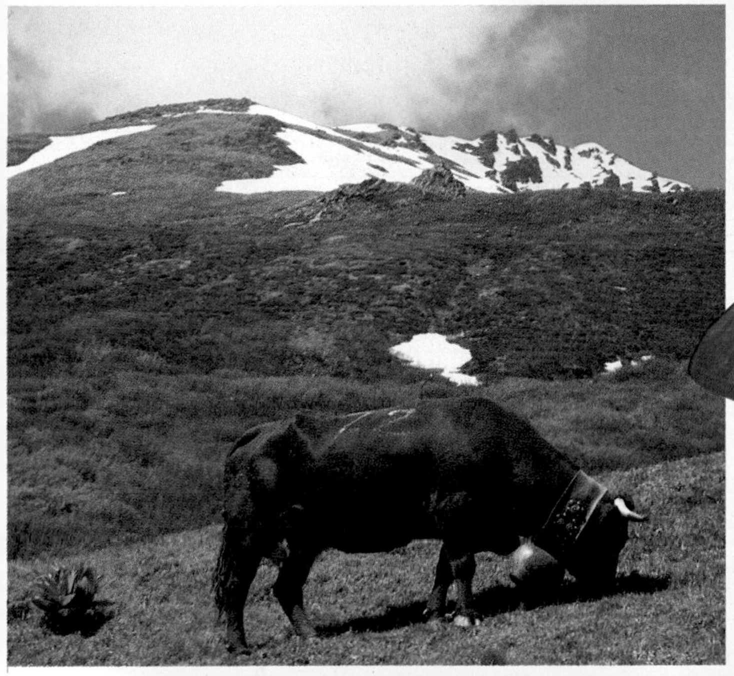

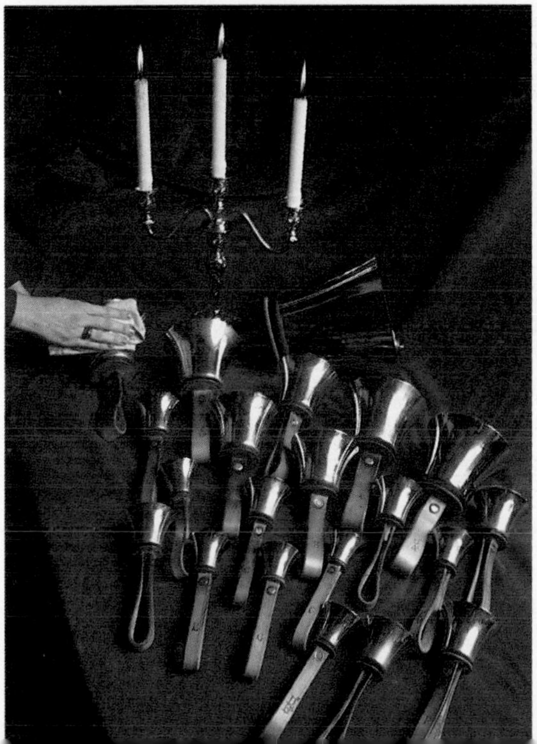

Listen to how one composer imitated the sound of bells in his music.

"Carillon" from *L'Arlésienne Suite* (excerpt) . . . . . . . . . Bizet

## An Off-Beat Song

Play this melody on bells or piano. The strongest tones begin where you expect them to.

Now play this version. This rhythmic device—tones beginning before the beat—is called **syncopation.**

## Comedy Tonight

Words and Music by Stephen Sondheim

1. Some-thing fa - mil - iar, some-thing pe - cul - iar, Some-thing for ev - 'ry-one, a
2. Some-thing con - vul - sive, some-thing re - pul - sive, Some-thing for ev - 'ry-one, a

com - e - dy to - night! Some-thing ap - peal - ing, some-thing ap -
com - e - dy to - night! Some-thing es - thet - ic, some-thing fre -

pal - ling, Some-thing for ev - 'ry-one, a com - e - dy to - night!
net - ic, Some-thing for ev - 'ry-one, a com - e - dy to - night!

Noth-ing with kings, noth-ing with crowns. Bring on the lov - ers, li - ars, and clowns! _
Noth-ing of gods, noth-ing of fate. Weight-y af-fairs will just have to wait. _

Old sit - u - a-tions, new com-pli - ca-tions, Noth-ing por-ten-tous or po - lite; _
Noth-ing that's for-mal, noth-ing that's nor-mal, No rec - i - ta-tions to re - cite! _

_ Trag - e - dy to - mor - row, com - e - dy to - night!
_ O - pen up the cur - tains, com - e - dy to - night!

## Tying It Together

Sometimes syncopation is created with *ties*.

## Circles

Words and Music by Linda Williams

# Dots—An Uneven Rhythm

Remember the sixteenth-note pattern?

*in - ter - fer - ence*

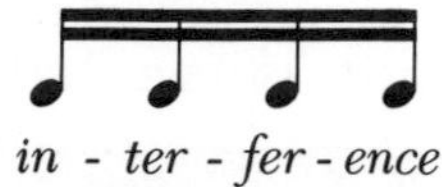

Here is a different chant for the same pattern:

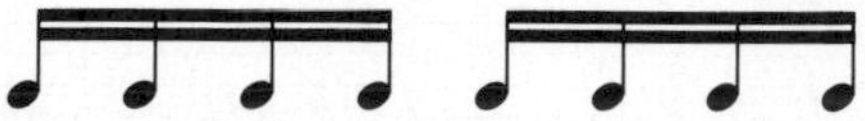
dah dah dah *dee,* dah dah dah *dee*

Now, chant just the first and last sound in each group.

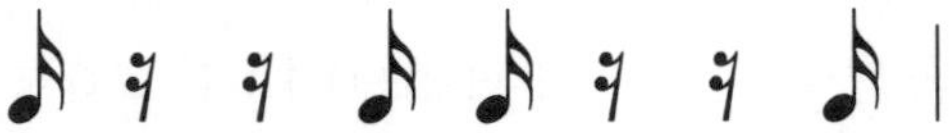
dah *dee,* dah *dee*

There is an easier way to write this rhythm pattern. The dotted rhythm is found in the song "Do, Lord."

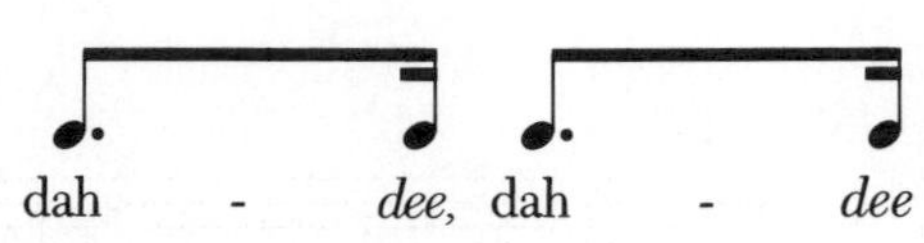

dah - *dee,* dah - *dee*

**Guitar: capo 1**

## Do, Lord

Black Spiritual

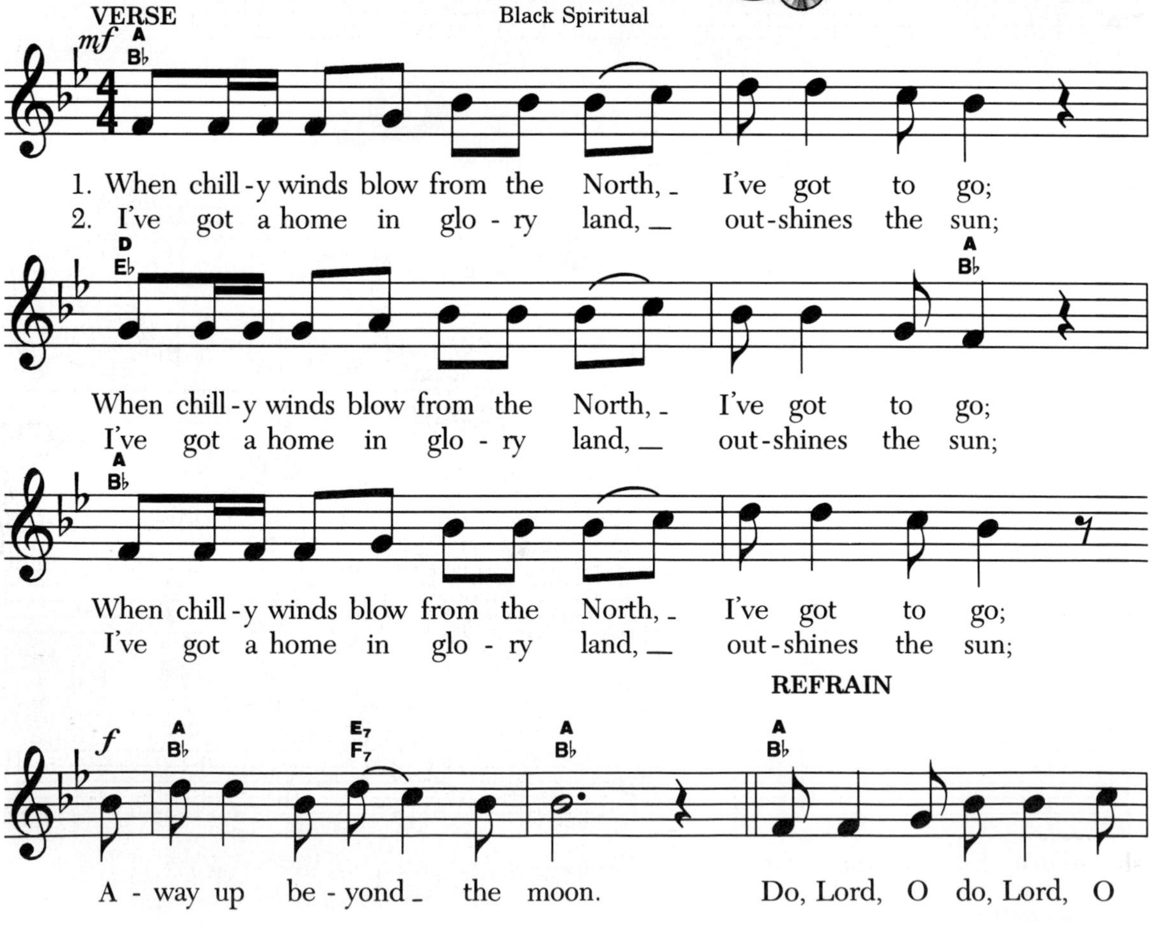
VERSE
*mf*
A
B♭
1. When chill-y winds blow from the North, I've got to go;
2. I've got a home in glo-ry land, out-shines the sun;
D
E♭
A
B♭
When chill-y winds blow from the North, I've got to go;
I've got a home in glo-ry land, out-shines the sun;
A
B♭
When chill-y winds blow from the North, I've got to go;
I've got a home in glo-ry land, out-shines the sun;
REFRAIN
*f*
A
B♭
E7
F7
A
B♭
A
B♭
A-way up be-yond the moon.
Do, Lord, O do, Lord, O

A
B♭
D
E♭
A
B♭
do re-mem-ber me; Do, Lord, O do, Lord, O do re-mem-ber me;
A
B♭
E7
F7
A
B♭
Do, Lord, O do, Lord, O do re-mem-ber me; A-way up be-yond the moon.

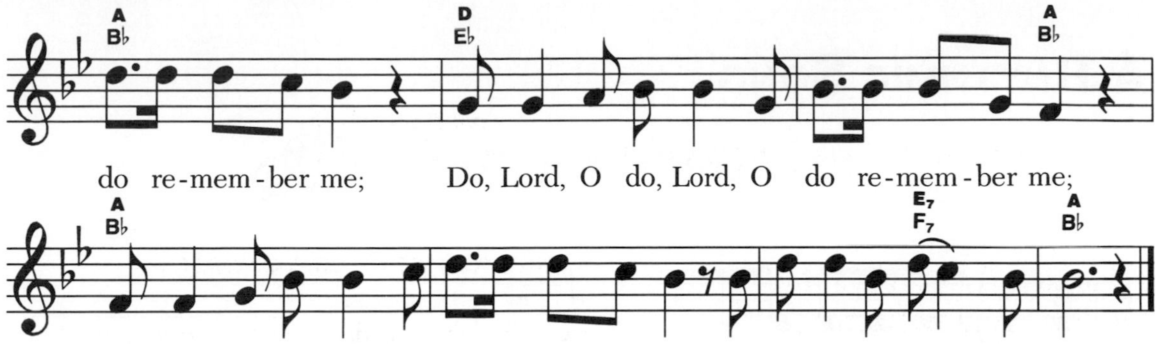

A dotted rhythm is featured in the countermelody to the refrain of "Do, Lord." You can sing the countermelody or play it on a keyboard instrument.

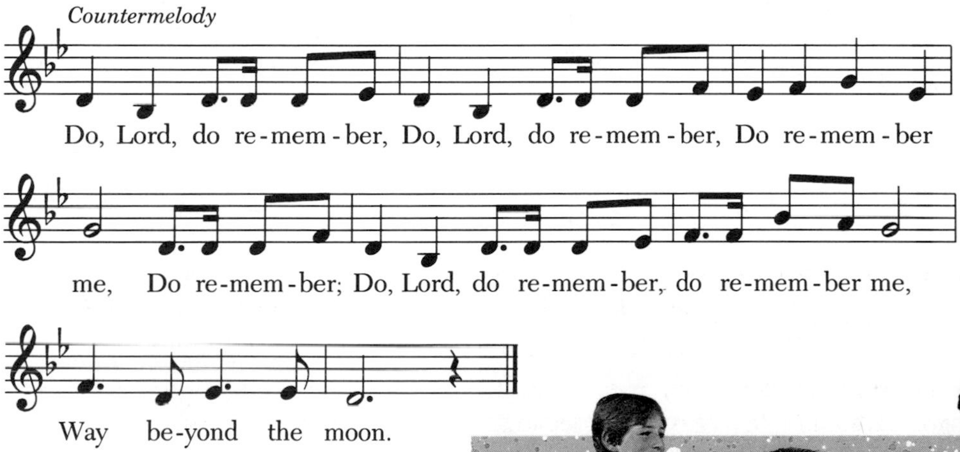
Countermelody
Do, Lord, do re-mem-ber, Do, Lord, do re-mem-ber, Do re-mem-ber
me, Do re-mem-ber; Do, Lord, do re-mem-ber, do re-mem-ber me,
Way be-yond the moon.

Clap

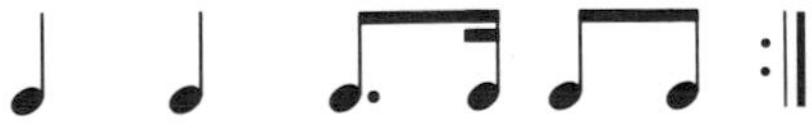

End with

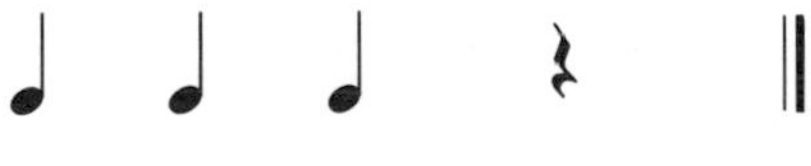

Tambourine

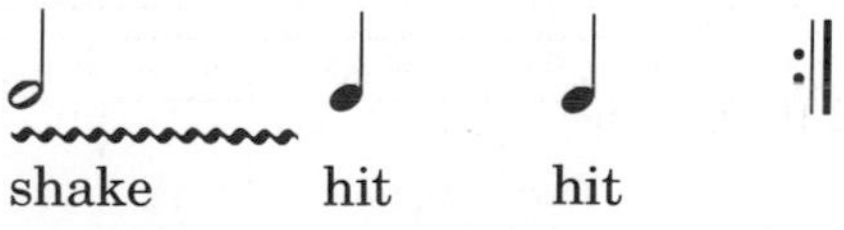
shake hit hit

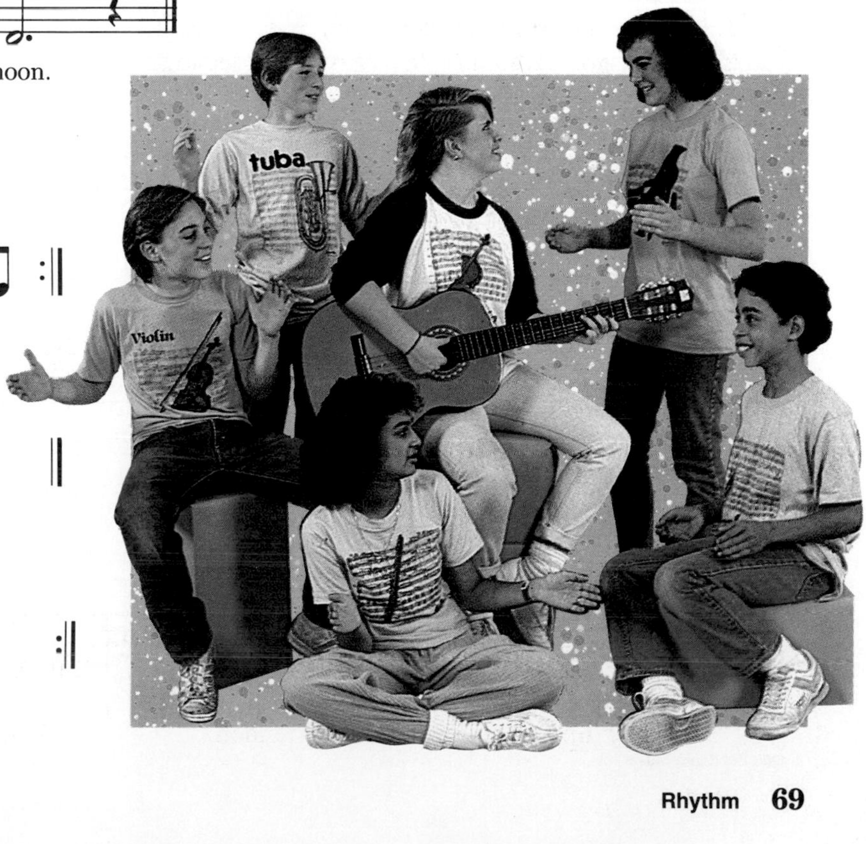
tuba
Violin

# A Rhythmic Song

## Dancing José

Words and Music by Linda Williams

1. I'll tell you a stor-y, the leg-end of Danc-ing Jo - sé. ___
sé was so ter-ri-bly shy and a-fraid he would fall. ___

I'll tell you what hap-pened in San-to Do-min-go that day. ___ A
He danced in the sha-dows up close to the old ci-ty wall. ___ But

danc-ing con-test was held in the square, And ev-'ry-one in the
then he sud-den-ly jumped in the air, And then came danc-ing out

vil-lage was there, All dressed in their best for a danc-ing fi-es-ta,
in-to the square, He whirled and he twirled in his own lit-tle world; He

and there in the crowd was my old friend, Jo - sé. ___ 2. Jo -
was Danc-ing Jo - sé, And the best of them all. ___

**REFRAIN**

3. (In) Santo Domingo they'll always remember his name;
And everyone knows he went on to find fortune and fame.
The dancing contest is held every year;
They wait for Dancing José to appear.
They think of the day he went dancing away,
But he's never come back, and it isn't the same.
*Refrain:*
He danced in a circle all over the square . . .

4. (Now,) I alone know the secret of Dancing José;
For quite by chance I was dancing beside him that day.
When all the dancers began to compete,
José moved back to get out of the street,
And stepped on a cactus, which made him react
As if he'd learned to dance at the Bolshoi ballet!
*Refrain: (begin softly and get louder)*
He danced in a circle all over the square . . .

# Sound and Pitch

Strike a piano key, pluck a guitar string, blow into a clarinet.

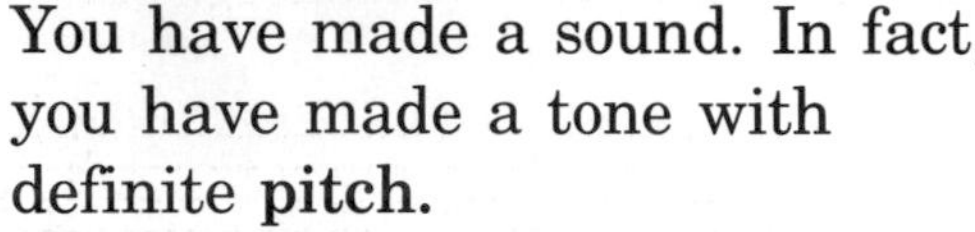

You have made a sound. In fact, you have made a tone with definite **pitch.**

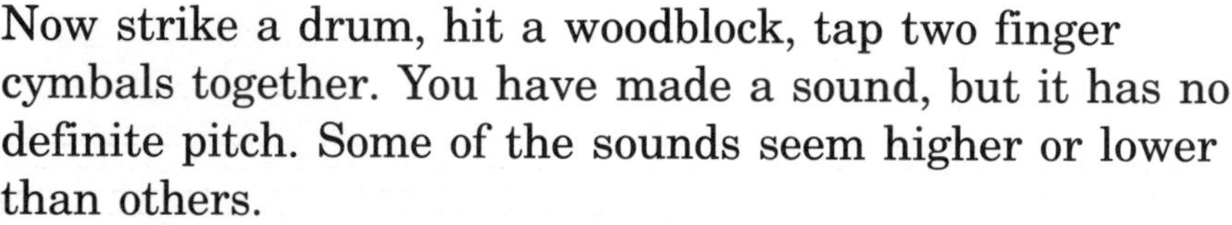

Now strike a drum, hit a woodblock, tap two finger cymbals together. You have made a sound, but it has no definite pitch. Some of the sounds seem higher or lower than others.

Both kinds of sound—pitched and unpitched—can be used to make music.

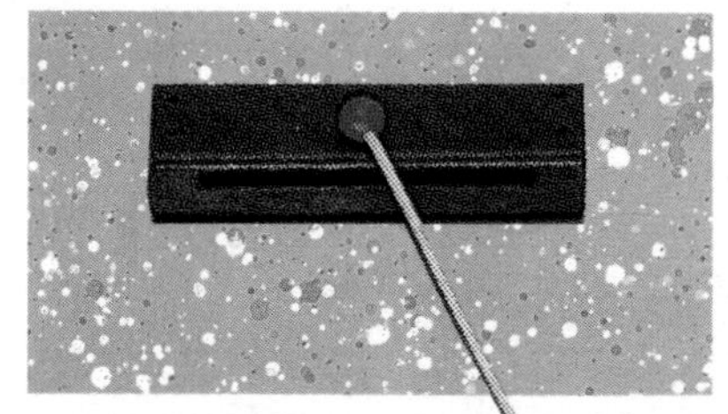

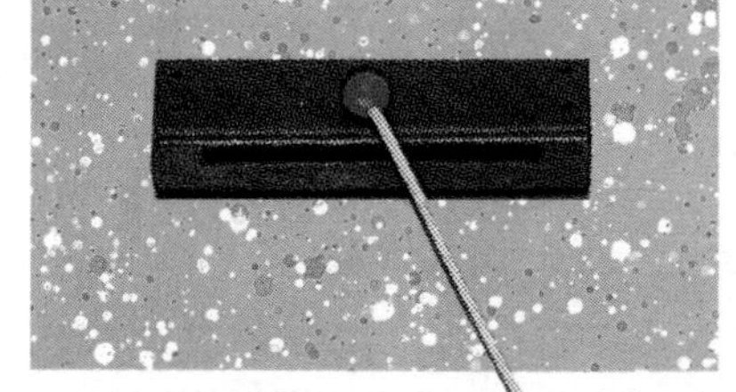

Play this familiar melody with any pitched instrument, and any set of unpitched percussion instruments. You can even invent your own percussion set from objects in your classroom.

# Up and Down, By Steps and Leaps

In this song, all the pitches are next to one another. The melody moves *stepwise* upward and downward.

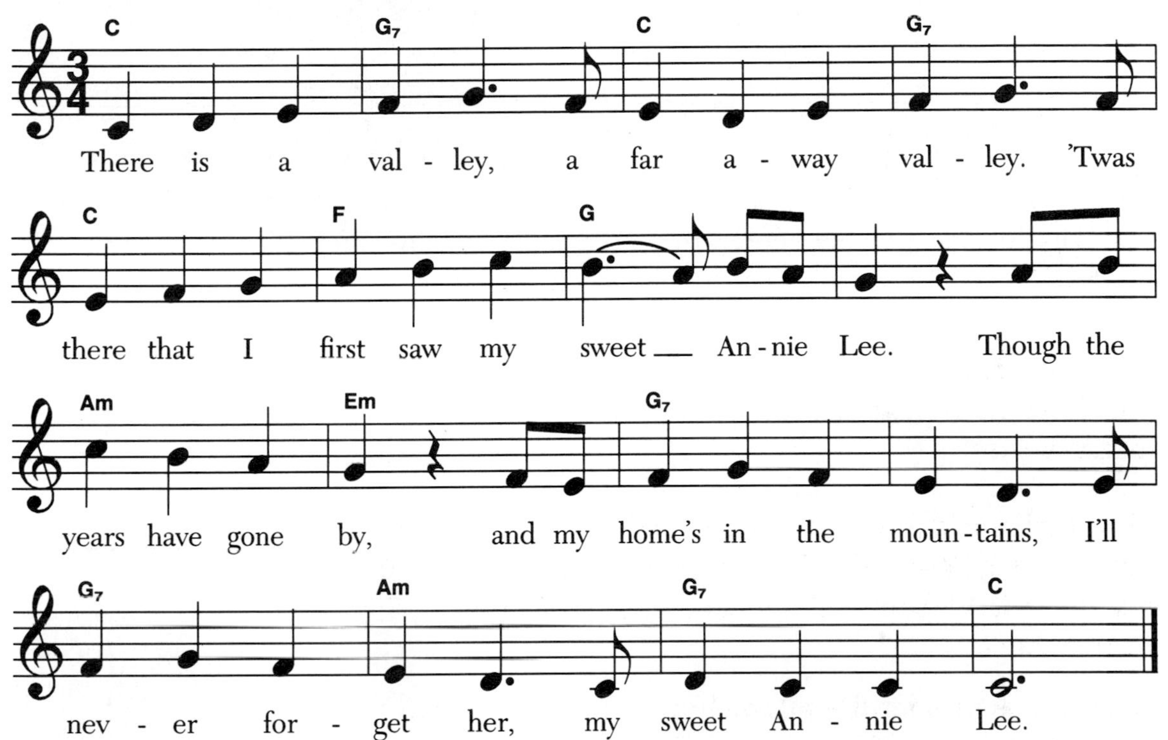


Here is a countermelody that can be sung or played on the bells. Notice that the pitches do not move stepwise. The notes *leap* from pitch to pitch.

Bells, Recorder, Keyboard, or Voices

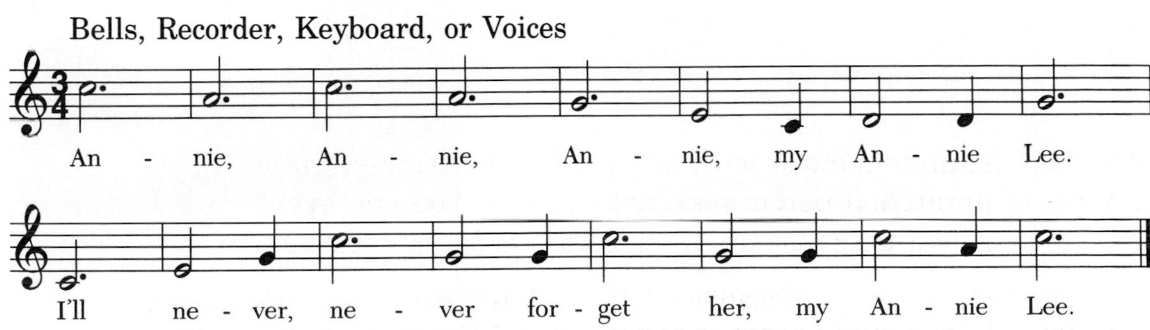


You can play or sing this melody as a descant with "Annie Lee."

# The Tonal Center

## Cadence and Phrase

Here's a **melody**—a **phrase**—without a final note. Even without knowing what it is, you will probably be able to sing the last note correctly.

The rest of the phrase seems to lead you to the last note. This kind of phrase ending is called a **cadence.**

A cadence is like a rest stop. The melody will seem to lead to that point and rest comfortably there.

Often the final note of the piece will be at the tonal center. The note at the tonal center is the *key* note. Every scale is named for the key note.

# A Major Scale

Here is a **scale** with the note *C* as its tonal center.

All of the pitches in the C scale, and in any other scale, move **step**wise. Written, they look as if they are all the same distance apart.

Let's see if this is true. Use a set of resonator bells.

Line all the bells up this way and play them in order. This is called a *chromatic scale.*

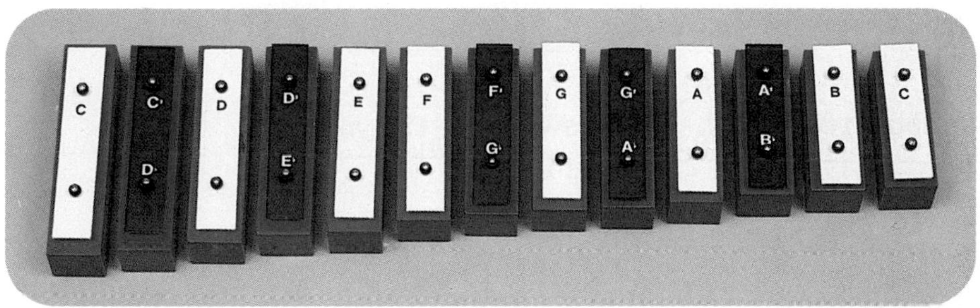


Now remove all the sharps and flats (the black bars).

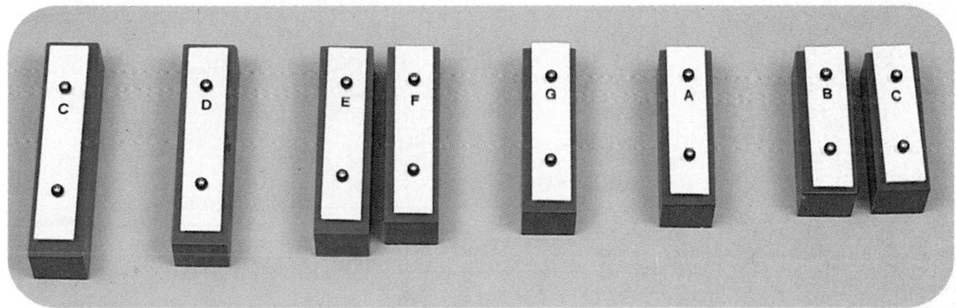


Some bells are closer together than others. The **interval,** or space, between notes 3 and 4, and between notes 7 and 8 is smaller than the other intervals. This pattern—with 3 and 4, and 7 and 8 being closer together—is the pattern of the **major scale.**

"Annie Lee" is a song in a *major* key.

# Minor scales

**Minor scales** and minor keys sound different from major keys. They even seem to be different in mood. This happens because of changes in the way the scale is constructed.

Set up the bells as you did before for the C major scale. Pull out the bells for D♭, E, G♭, A, and B.

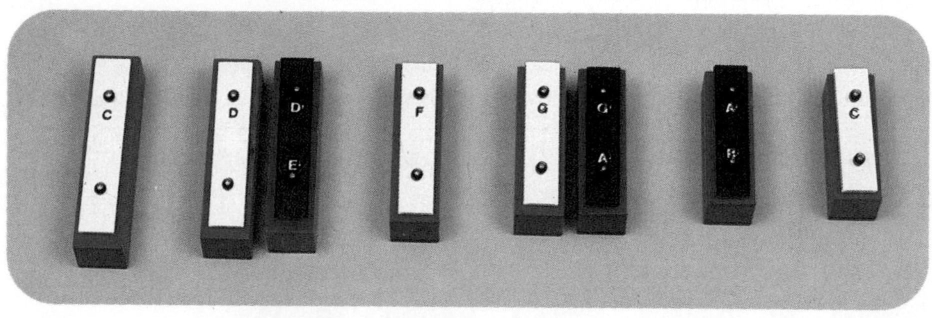

When you play them, you will hear a new scale, the *natural minor scale.* "Dundai" is a song in a minor key.

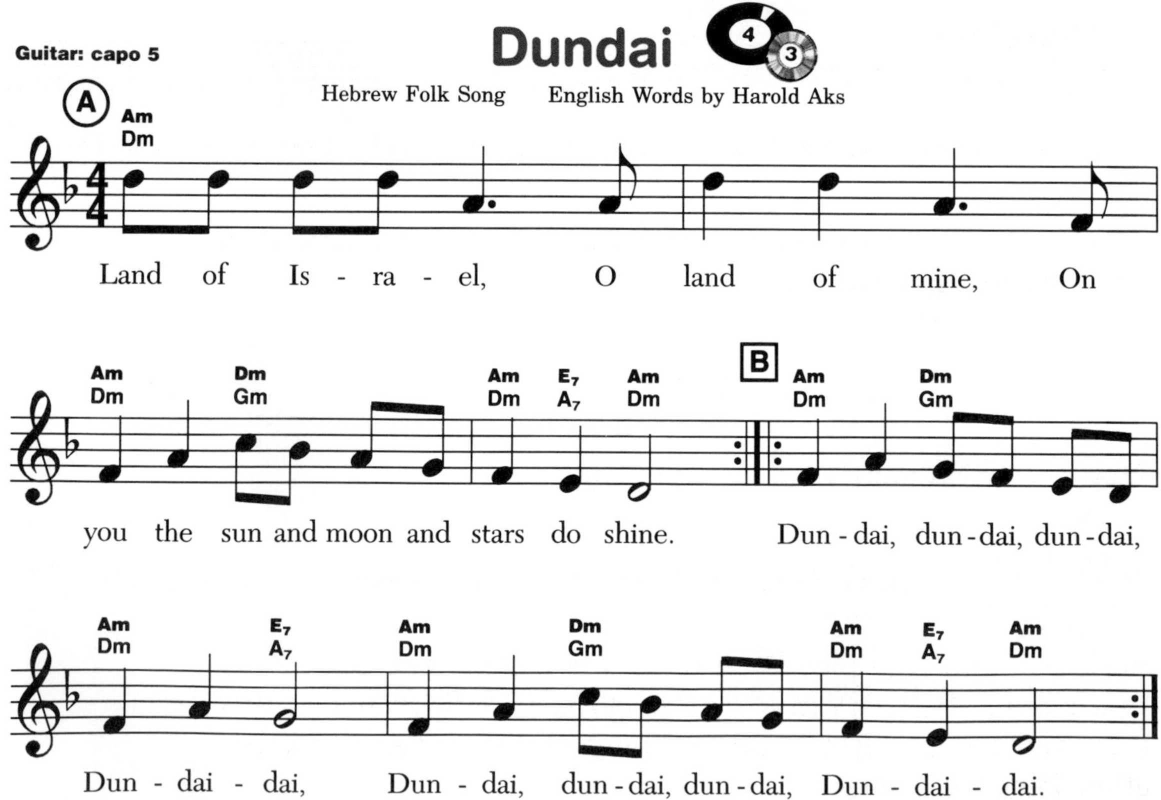

## Hearing the Difference

Listen to this familiar round. It is in a major key.

"Are You Sleeping"

Listen to how different it sounds in a minor key.

Listen to these two musical fragments from the music of Bach. The first one is in a minor key.

*Invention No. 13* .......................... J. S. Bach

The second example is in a major key.

*Brandenburg Concerto No. 3* (excerpt) ... J. S. Bach

Both examples are played on the same instrument, the synthesizer. Both are in a similar style. The difference in how they sound is partly due to one being in a major key and the other in a minor key.

# A Folk Song from Brazil

As you sing this song, listen for the changes in tonality. Does the song end in a major key or in a minor key?

C

D G — $A_7$ $D_7$

A - ran - ha Ta - tan - ha, A - ran - ha Ta - tan - ha,

$A_7$ $D_7$ — D G — $E_7$ $A_7$ — $A_7$ $D_7$

If Tu - tu should come back, he must sure - ly find you sleep - ing.

D G — $A_7$ $D_7$

A - ran - ha Ta - tan - ha, A - ran - ha Ta - tan - ha,

$A_7$ $D_7$ — D G — $A_7$ $D_7$ — D G

All night by your bed, I my watch will be keep - ing.

# PENTATONIC SCALE

Here is a scale that uses a group of notes that are in a different pattern from the major or minor scales. There are five different pitches in this scale.

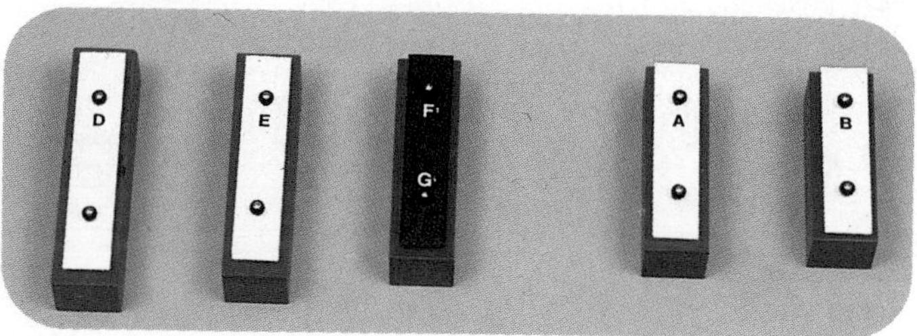


It is called a *pentatonic* scale. Here is a pentatonic song from China.

## A Boat on the Lake *(Tai-hu)*

Folk Song from China    Collected by Shao-Mei Ting

Wind is blow - ing a - cross the __ lake, Qui - et - ly __ the
*Shan ching sho - ei ming iou jing __ jing, hu shin peau _ lai*
shahn cheeng sho - ay meeng yo jeeng jeeng hoo shin payau lahee

rip - ples __ play; We row and __ row, we row and __ row.
*feng i __ jehn, a shyng a __ shyng a, jihn a __ jihn,*
fung ee jehn ah sheeng ah sheeng ah jin ah jin

Few there are who walk by the shore, Where the lake __ re -
*hwang huen shyr hau ren shyng __ shao, baun kong yu - eh ying*
wahng wehn sheer hau rehn sheeng shau baun kawng yoo - eh yeeng

flects the __ moon; We row and __ row, we row and __ row.
*shoei mi - an yau, a shyng a __ shyng a, jihn a __ jihn.*
shoay mee - ahn yau ah sheeng ah sheeng ah jin ah jin

Here are three patterns that can be used as an ostinato for "A Boat on the Lake." Any kind of bells or keyboard that can play the five notes of this pentatonic scale will do. You can also tune glasses of water to these pitches.

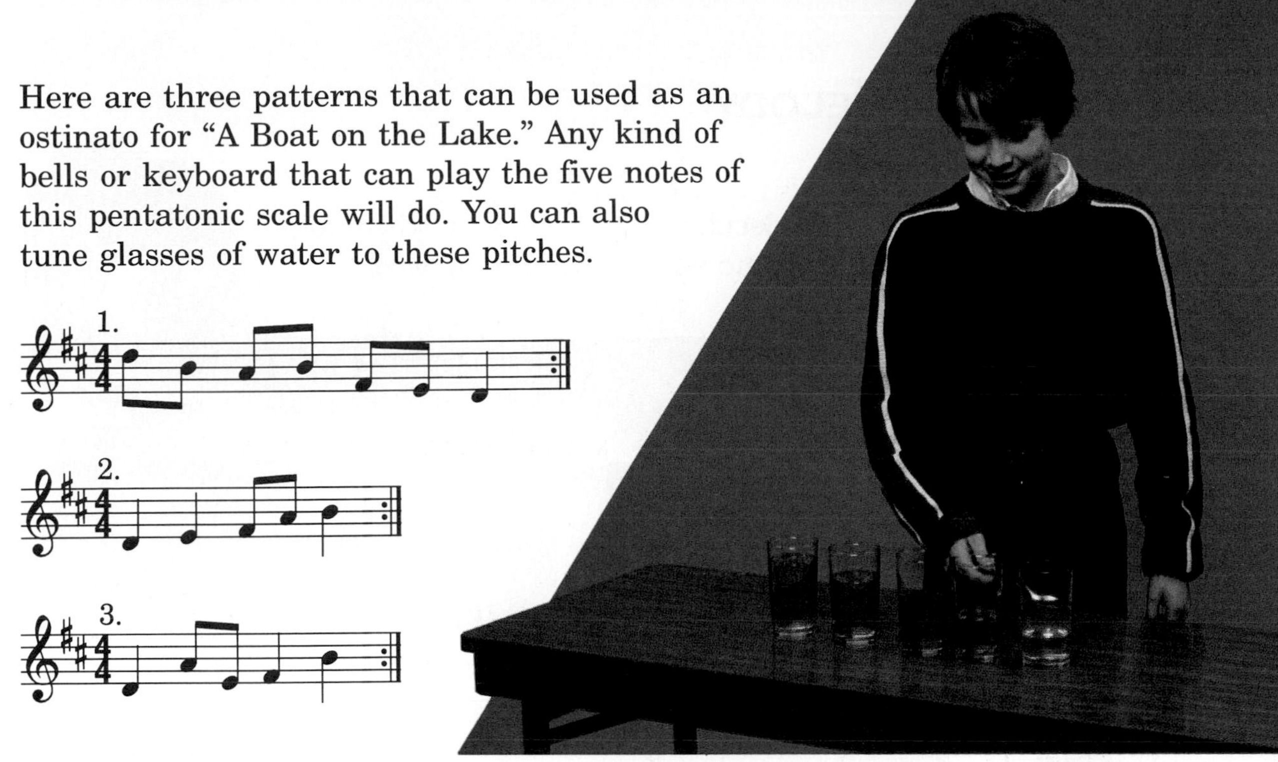


## Out of the Scale

Here is a song that doesn't have a tonal center. It uses only six pitches, from E flat to A flat. Many modern composers like to write in a way that avoids any mode, any tonality, any tonal center.

### A Song with No Key

Words and Music by David Eddleman

# Building a Melody

## Contour

Making a melody means deciding what shape it will take, what the **contour** of the tune will be. It may be very jagged, like a city skyline.

**"Gavotte" from *Classical Symphony* (excerpt) .................................. Prokofiev**

It may move stepwise and be as smooth as rolling hills.

LISTENING LIBRARY

**"Jesu, Joy of Man's Desiring" (excerpt)....... Bach**

## Sequence

If you are aware of contour, it is easier to find a sequence. Compare these two melody patterns.

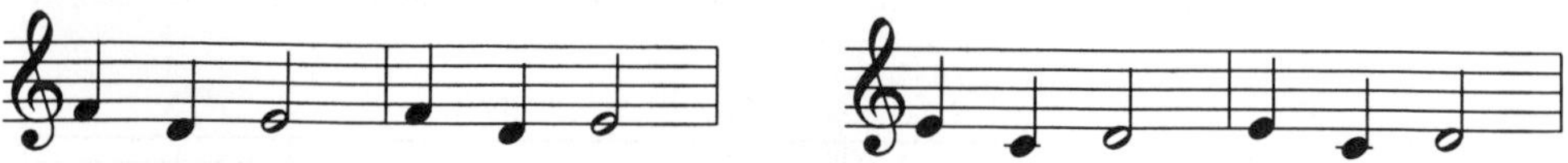

The second pattern starts on a lower pitch but follows the same contour. This repeating of a pattern on a different pitch is called a **sequence.**

# Tea for Two

Words by Irving Caesar    Music by Vincent Youmans

# Repetition and Contrast

Some songs, particularly folk songs, use repeated patterns. Usually, however, there is a section that **contrasts,** making the song more interesting.

Here is a country song that is built on repeated patterns. The middle section contrasts with the rest of the song.

## On the Road Again

Words and Music by Willie Nelson    Arranged by Larry Eisman

Pictured is Willie Nelson. He is considered one of the best songwriters and country singers of our time. His songs are sung by many other country music artists.

# HARMONY

When you sing or play more than one tone at a time, you create **harmony.** Here is one way to create harmony. Start by singing this simple melody.

## Singing in Harmony

Then sing this song in **unison,** with everyone on the same pitches.

# When the Saints Go Marching In

If some students sing the melody on page 86 while the rest sing the song, the result is harmony!

Can you think of more things to add to this song?

# Musical Partnership

Here is a song the whole class can sing.

## My Home's in Montana

American Cowboy Song    Adapted by M. Hoffman

Here is another song of the West you can sing.

## Home on the Range

American Cowboy Song

Now divide the class into two sections and sing these two songs together. You are singing in two-part harmony.

# Canons

Here is a song you can sing together and still make harmony. All you have to do is begin at different times, as on page 91. This kind of imitation is called a *canon*.

## Catch a Falling Star

Words and Music by Paul Vance and Lee Pockriss

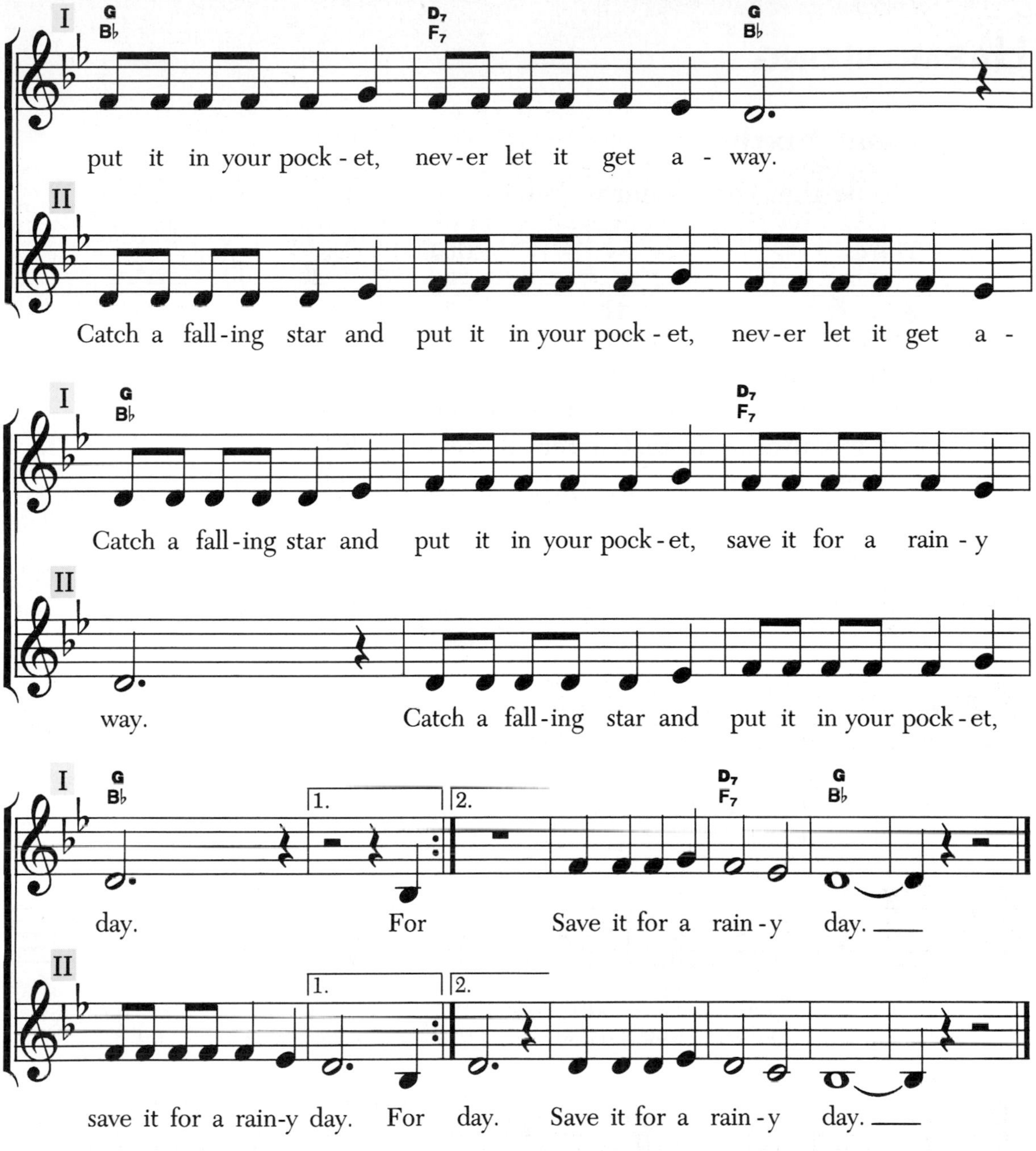

I
G B♭ D7 F7 G B♭

put it in your pock - et, nev - er let it get a - way.

II

Catch a fall - ing star and put it in your pock - et, nev - er let it get a -

I
G B♭ D7 F7

Catch a fall - ing star and put it in your pock - et, save it for a rain - y

II

way. Catch a fall - ing star and put it in your pock - et,

I
G B♭ 1. 2. D7 F7 G B♭

day. For Save it for a rain - y day.

II
1. 2.

save it for a rain-y day. For day. Save it for a rain - y day.

## Round and Round . . .

A **round** is a kind of canon. In a round, you can sing the song any number of times, starting over when you come to the end. Listen to this modern round.

**"A Home on the Rolling Sea" . . . . . . . . . . Eddleman**

# HARMONIZING

## Thirds and Sixths

Here is a song that can be harmonized in *thirds* or in *sixths.*

Thirds:
Sixths:

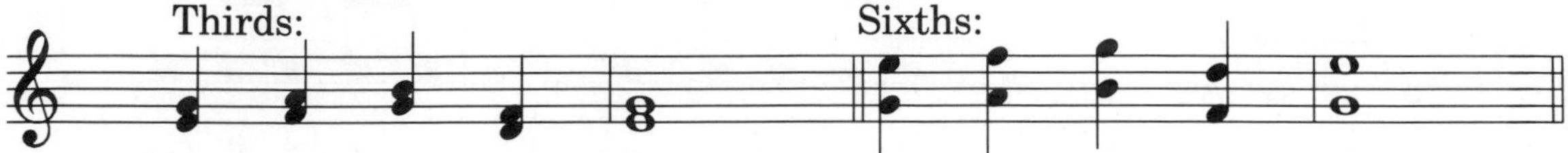

Before you sing this song, listen to the recording. The voices are singing in thirds. The instrumental section is harmonized in sixths, above the melody.

## When the Chestnut Leaves Were Falling

Spanish Folk Song English Words by Luther Wilde

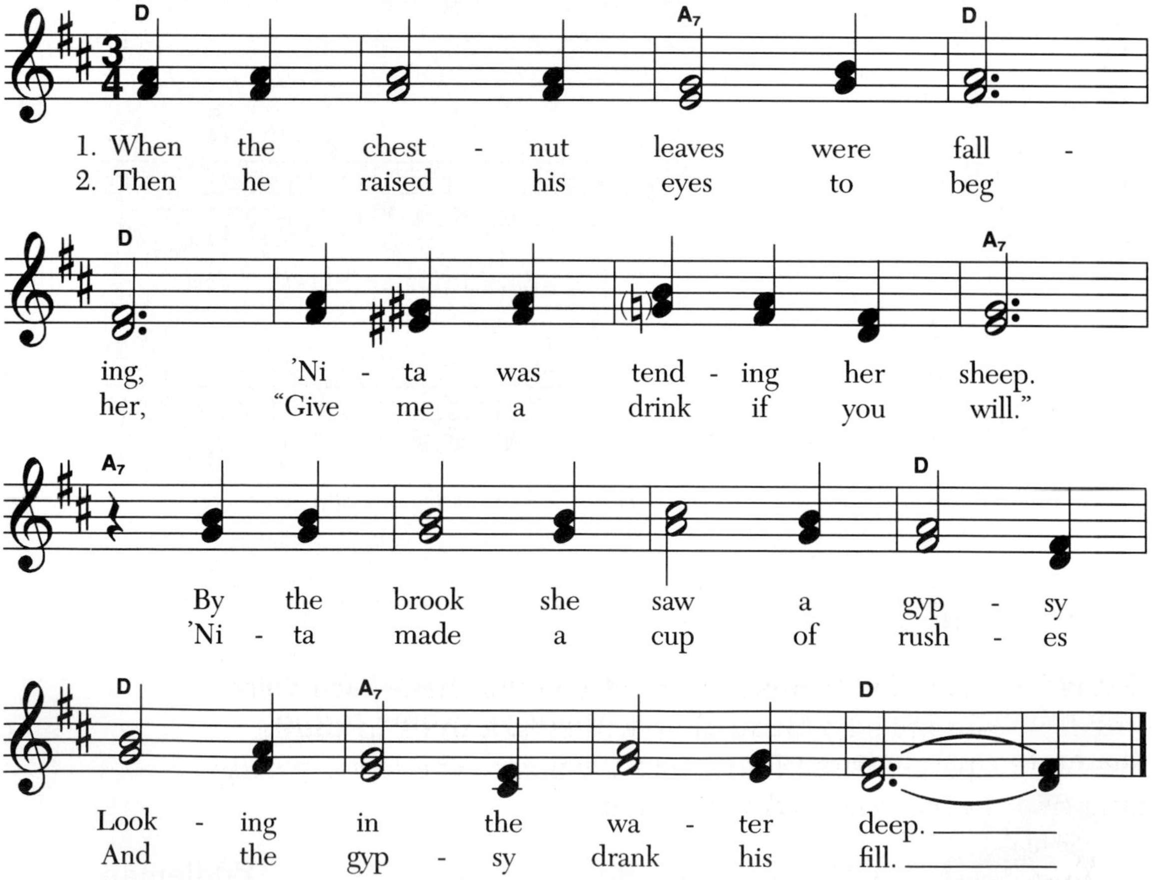

D A7 D
1. When the chest - nut leaves were fall -
2. Then he raised his eyes to beg
D A7
ing, 'Ni - ta was tend - ing her sheep.
her, "Give me a drink if you will."
A7 D
By the brook she saw a gyp - sy
'Ni - ta made a cup of rush - es
D A7 D
Look - ing in the wa - ter deep.
And the gyp - sy drank his fill.

You can see as well as hear the difference. The thirds in the voice parts are closer together than the sixths in the instruments.

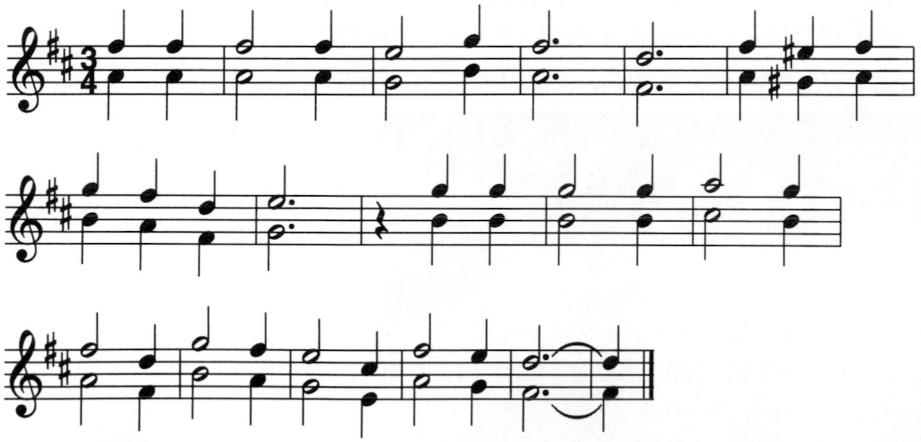

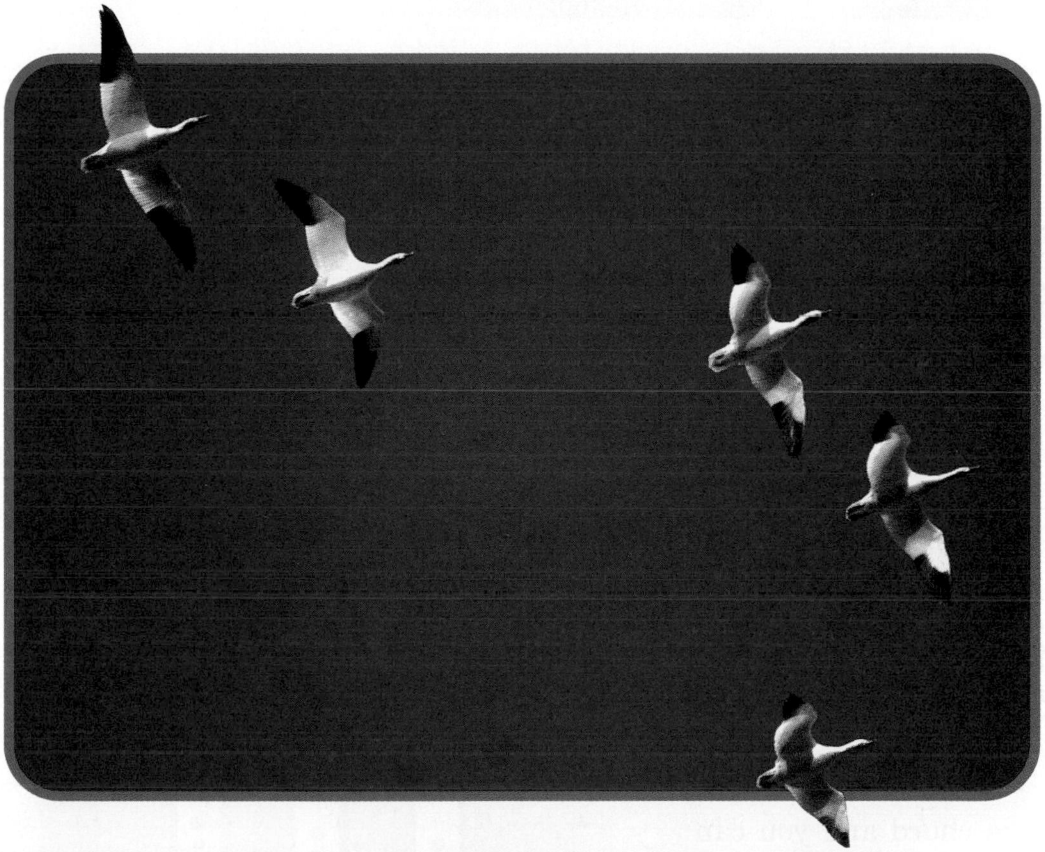

Listen to a song for two voices. First you will hear each voice singing a *solo* melody. Later they will sing a **duet** in thirds. The higher part is sung by an adult woman. The lower part is sung by a twelve-year-old young man.

"Pie Jesu" from *Requiem* ... Andrew Lloyd Webber

# HARMONIZING WITH CHORDS

When two or more pitches sound at the same time, they create a **chord.** When you strike a combination of keys on the piano, or strum several strings at once on the guitar, you are playing a chord.

You can play chords with the resonator bells.

Make a three-note chord to play on the bells.

F

Make another chord, using different bells.

One more chord and you can play an accompaniment for "Catch a Falling Star."

# Chord Progressions

As you harmonize with chords, you will notice that your ear tells you when you need to change from one chord to another. This changing pattern is called the *chord progression.*

Most songs we like to sing have interesting but simple chord progressions. The most commonly used chords are the ones we make on the first, fourth, and fifth notes in the scale.

In the key of D those three chords look like this:

Most of the songs in your book have letter names above the melody.

Using the chords illustrated at the top of the page, add an instrument and harmonize with the chords. Play an accompaniment for the partner songs on pages 88 and 89.

# Form—A Musical Blueprint

No one can build a house just by drawing a picture of it and labeling the sections.

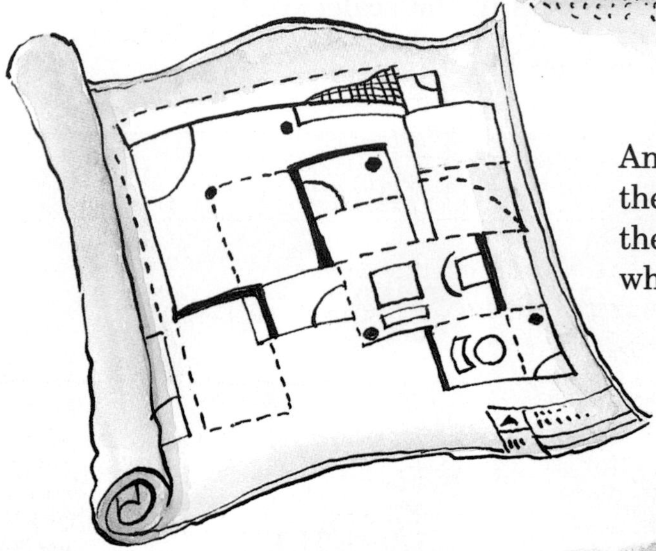

An architect needs a blueprint for the house he is designing so that the builder will know exactly where to put each section.

Without a blueprint, the house could end up like this!

Composers, like architects, have a plan for their compositions. Musical ideas and events cannot be put together in just any way. Try this version of a familiar song.

## Music Taking Shape

A pile of bricks takes shape in the hands of an expert bricklayer. In the same way, musical ideas take shape in the hands of a composer or songwriter.

In music, contrasting sections are extremely important. If a piece of music were the same from beginning to end, we would soon grow tired of it.

Listen to the contrasts in this piece played by Dave Brubeck.

**"Take Five" (excerpt) .................... Desmond**

You have learned to call this form ABA.

"Dundai" on p. 76 also has an A and a B section. However, A does not return after B is heard. The **form** is AB.

# Mix and Match

You can play an ABA percussion piece, using maracas and a guiro.

Here is the A section, played on maracas:

Shake

The B section is played by scraping the guiro.

Scrape

Clap this pattern while two solo players use the A and B patterns to create an ABA percussion piece.

Clap

You can use your ABA percussion pattern to accompany the song on page 99.

# No-Name Bossa Nova

Words and Music by Mary E. Hoffman

Do the No-Name Bos-sa No-va, Do the No-Name Bos-sa No-va.

𝄋 A

We were danc-ing in the sha-dows While a
danc-ing in the sha-dows But we

qui-et Latin gui-tar strummed us a new tune, a
have-n't thought of a name to give to that new tune, the

to Coda

new tune that had no name, Do the No-Name Bos-sa No-va,
new tune that has no name,

Do the No-Name Bos-sa No-va.

B

We swayed to the rhy-thm De-signed for tro-pi-cal nights. This me-lo-dy

D.S. al Coda

haunts us It ech-oes with such de-lights We're still

Coda

Do the No-Name Bos-sa No-va.

# Forming a Rondo

Here are lines from three songs in our book. Sing them in order.

Now mix them up any way you want to. The three musical elements work in almost any order, except that one of them sounds unfinished. Try it this way:

Sing: 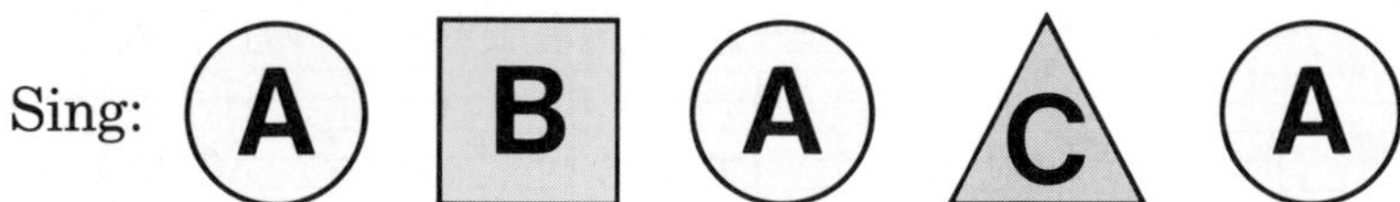


We have turned these bits of songs into a vocal **rondo**.

*Vocal Rondo*

Rondo form his been popular for several centuries. It is a good way to have interesting contrasting sections and still have a familiar idea to return to. Listen to this rondo.

## VARIATIONS

Another kind of form is *Theme and Variations.*

Themes, or musical ideas, can be varied in a number of ways. Composers can be very clever in the way they write variations. Often a composer chooses a familiar tune for a set of variations.

The theme can be played slower or faster, and with changed rhythm patterns. The theme can be turned upside down, or can be decorated with extra notes to make it fancier.

Here is a famous set of variations written by Charles Ives. As you listen to the recording, you will recognize the theme. In fact, you will be able to hear the theme in each variation. However, the personality of the melody has been changed completely in each variation.

*Variations on "America"* (excerpt) ............ Ives

Charles Ives
(1874–1954)

**Meet the Composer**

**American composer Charles Ives lived all his life in New England. He was a prosperous insurance company executive who wrote music in his spare time.**

**His music was very experimental for his time. It was not appreciated by the public until he was quite old and no longer composing. In 1947, when Ives was in his 70s and no longer writing music, he was awarded a Pulitzer Prize for his Third Symphony.**

# Style

Some pieces of music, particularly songs, are timeless. They seem to speak to every age.

Just such a song is "Scarborough Fair." It is an old English folk song with origins that go back many centuries. It has come down to us in several versions. This is one of the most popular.

Folk songs like this one are part of our heritage.

However, musical styles change from age to age. A musician can recognize, through musical clues, the era in which a certain piece of music was written.

## Musical Time Travel

Let us take our song "Scarborough Fair" through a time trip from the Middle Ages to the present day. We will hear it as it might have been used in different time periods.

"Scarborough Fair" Variation 1: Medieval

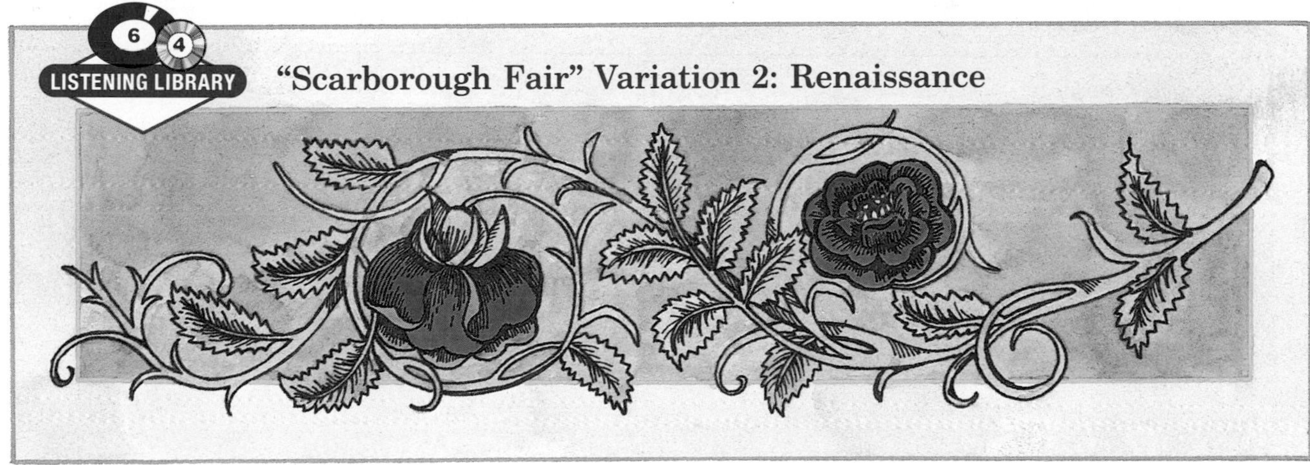


"Scarborough Fair" Variation 2: Renaissance

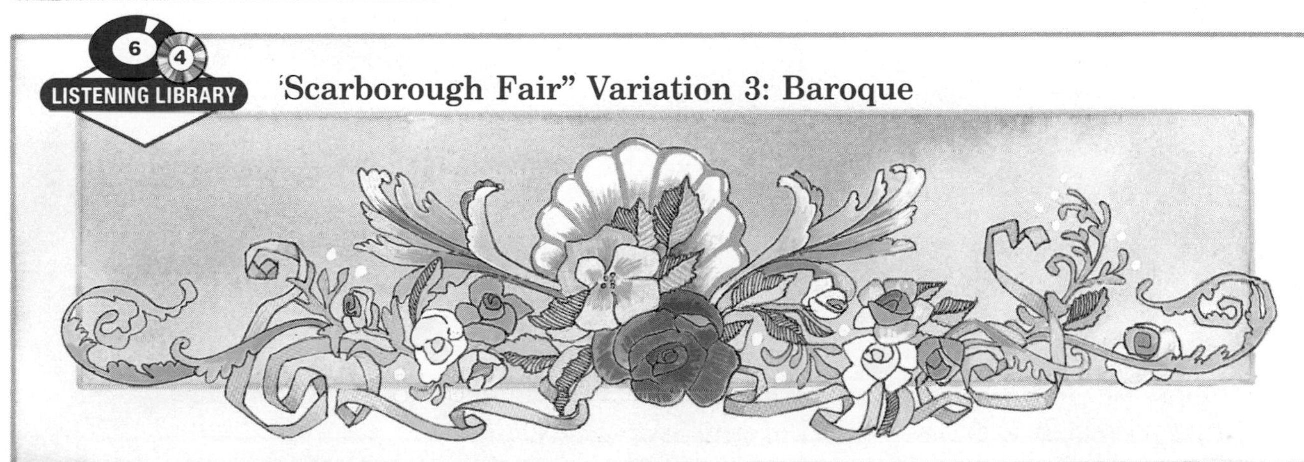


"Scarborough Fair" Variation 3: Baroque

## More Time Travel . . .

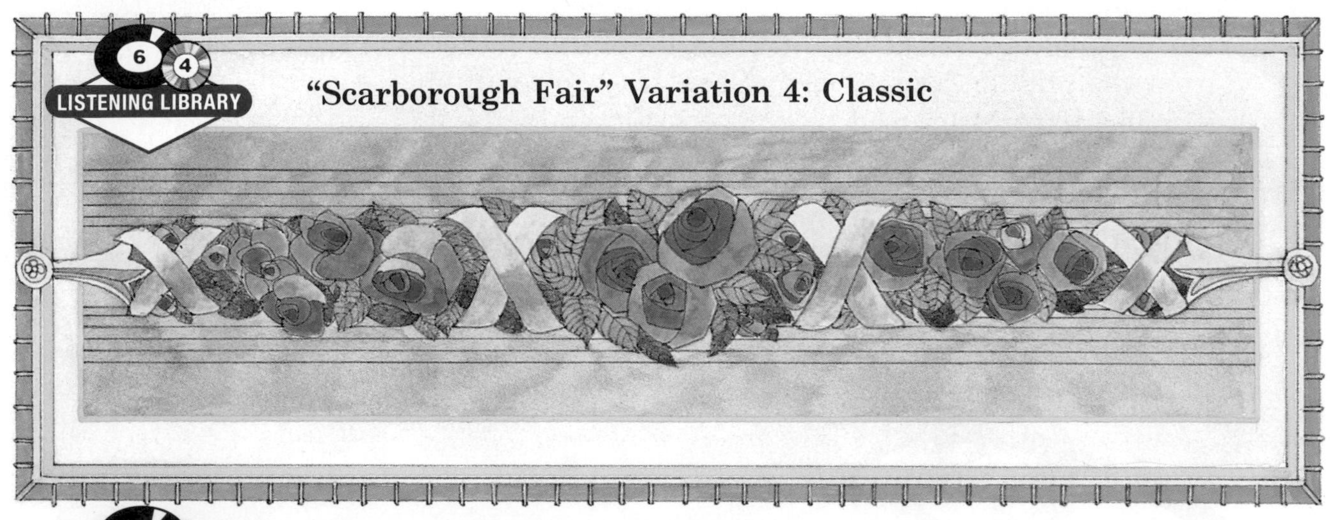


"Scarborough Fair" Variation 4: Classic

"Scarborough Fair" Variation 5: Romantic

"Scarborough Fair" Variation 6: Impressionistic

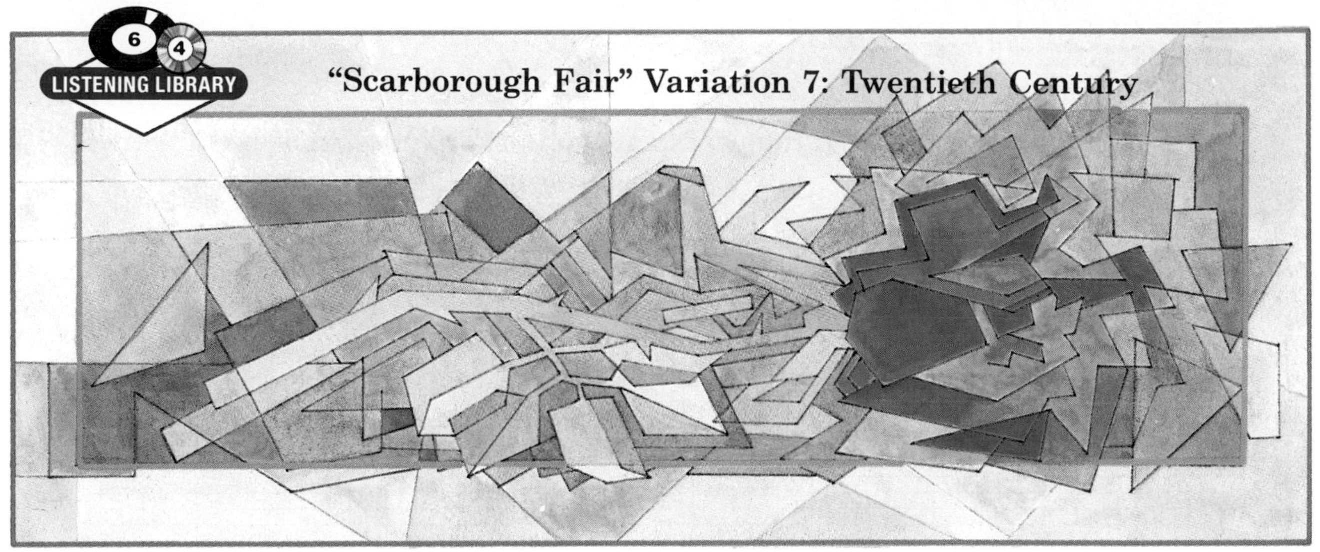


"Scarborough Fair" Variation 7: Twentieth Century

## Call Chart 4

Listen for the musical clues that will tell you the historical period for each of these musical excerpts. You should be able to identify the period by the style of the music.

*Styles Montage:*

1. *Gregorian Chant* ...................... Anonymous
2. *Gigue* .................................. Byrd
3. *Gavotte* ................................ Bach
4. *Sonata in C Major* ....................... Mozart
5. *Piano Concerto No. 2*............... Rachmaninoff
6. "Festivals" from *Nocturnes*............... Debussy
7. "Sacrificial Dance" from *Rite of Spring*. . Stravinsky

# Musical Interaction

Musical *interaction* is like a musical conversation. It can sound like questions and answers, a lively debate, or even a friendly musical argument.

This pattern of musical interaction is known as "call and response."

# A Diagram for Musical Interaction

Sometimes an instrument or voice sounds alone. Listen to this violin piece by Bach.

"Presto" from *Sonata in G Minor for Unaccompanied Violin* (excerpt). . . . . . . . . J. S. Bach

Use the symbol ✧ for one instrument or voice sounding alone.

More often, a number of instruments or voices will perform together. Listen to this string piece by Mozart.

"Minuet" from *Eine Kleine Nachtmusik* (excerpt) . . . . . . . . . . . . . . . . . . . . . . . . . . . . . . . . . . . . . . . . . W. A. Mozart

Use the symbol  for a group of instruments or voices.

In "Long John" the solo voice and the chorus takes turns.

The recording of "Long John" includes an *accompaniment*.

# Another Pattern for Call and Response

In "Long John" the call and response were exactly alike. The chorus simply echoed what they heard in the solo voice.

Often, however, the response will be different. In "Michael, Row the Boat Ashore," the group response of "Hallelujah" is different from the solo call.

## Michael, Row the Boat Ashore

On the recording of "Michael, Row the Boat Ashore," the solo voice and group chorus are accompanied by a solo piano and tambourine.

# A Call and Response for Instruments

Listen to a piece for solo trumpet and string instruments.

*Sonata for Trumpet and Strings,*
**Movement 1. . . . . . . . . . . . . . . . . . . . . . . . . Henry Purcell**

You can hear the musical interaction. The pattern is very similar to one of the call-and-response songs. Which one is it most like?

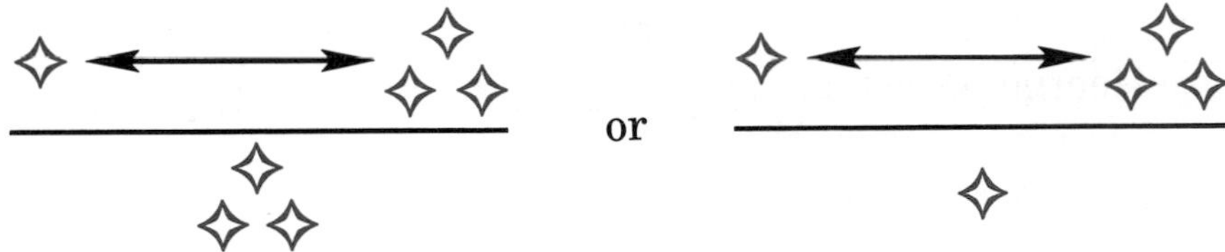


The pattern of this chant is also like one of the call-and-response songs. Which one is it most like?

## Train Chant

Jean Riddle

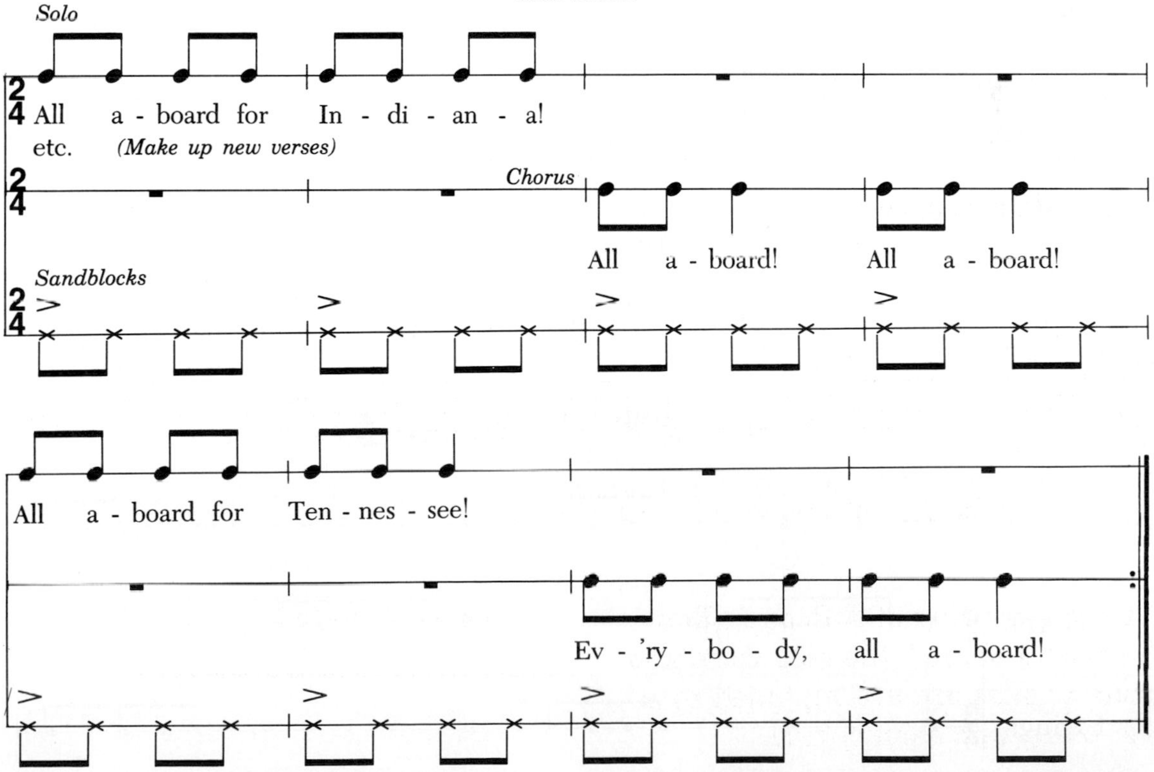

*Solo*

All a - board for In - di - an - a!
etc. *(Make up new verses)*

*Chorus*

All a - board! All a - board!

*Sandblocks*

All a - board for Ten - nes - see!

Ev - 'ry - bo - dy, all a - board!

# Sounds Against Sounds–Antiphonal Music

Composers sometimes use one set of sounds alternating with another set of sounds. This is called **antiphonal** music.

You have probably already guessed that call and response is one kind of antiphonal music. Another kind of antiphonal pattern can be called "group alternating with group."

Listen to this piece by George Frideric Handel. It is an antiphonal piece for instruments, with three sets of instruments trading off. Sometimes one group will sound by itself, and sometimes two will sound at the same time. Once in a while they all play together.

"Allegro" from *Water Music*.......... G. F. Handel

## Following a Score

If you listen to a piece of music while you follow the printed **score,** you can *see* the musical interaction as well as hear it.

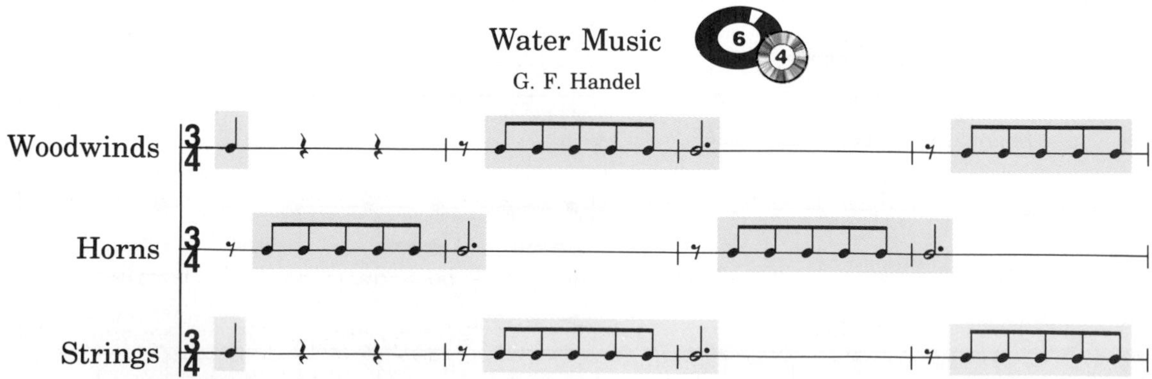

# ANTIPHONAL MUSIC FOR VOICES

"Echo Song" by Orlando di Lasso uses two groups of voices.

The first group sings, followed by the second group singing exactly the same phrase. The two groups overlap and the *antiphonal* effect is like a real echo.

"Echo Song" .................... Orlando di Lasso

Make your own "echo."

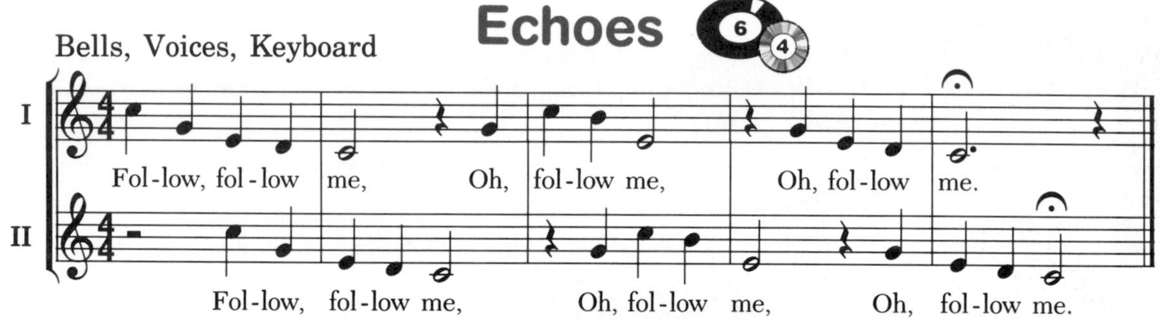

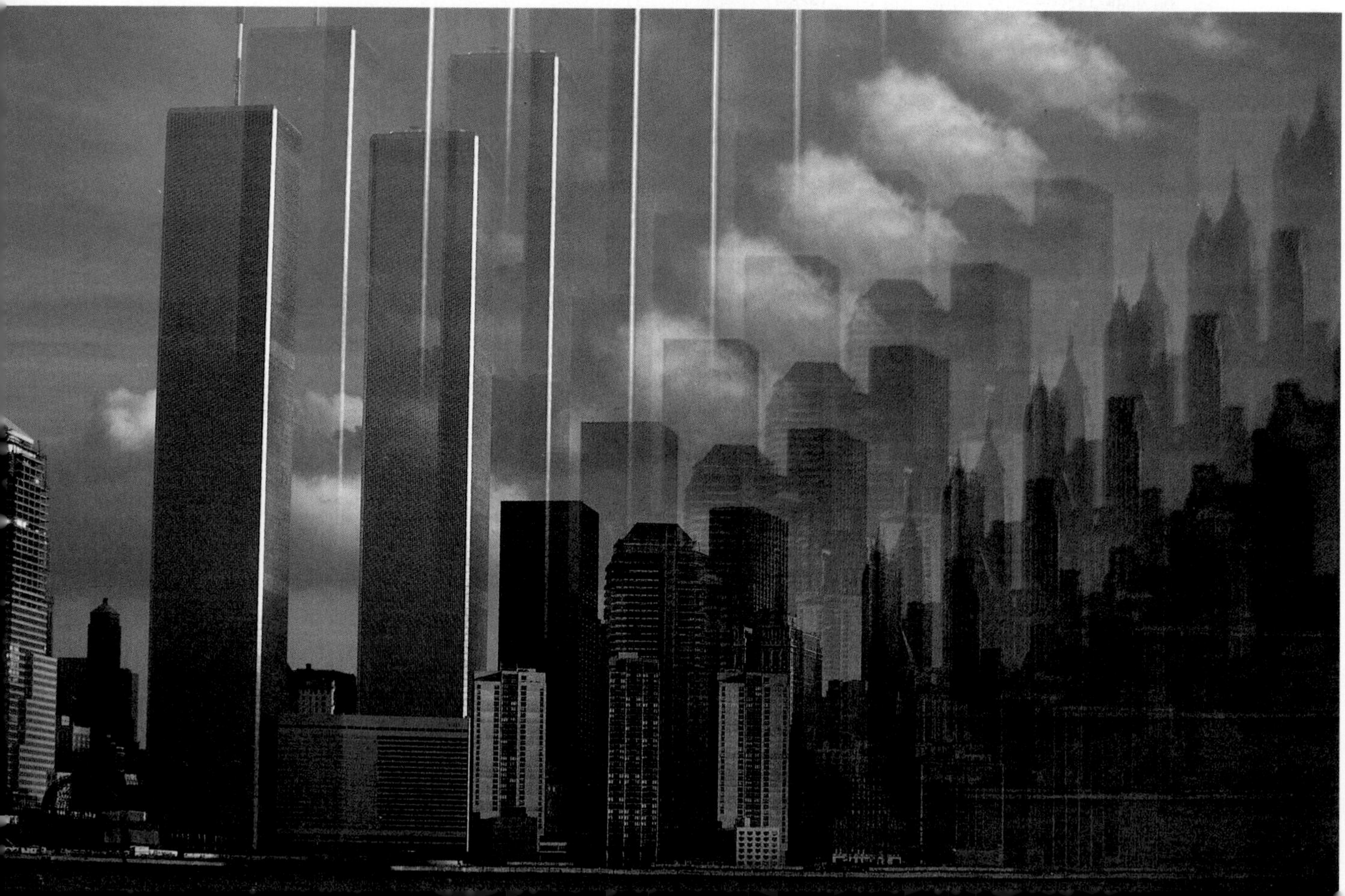

# The Magic of Repeated Patterns

As the elements of a piece of music interact, our ears often notice *repetition* before anything else.

Even works of visual art sometimes use repeated patterns to catch our attention. This kind of pattern is almost like a "visual echo."

Listen to this example and see if you find a resemblance between the music and the pictures on these pages.

AMRAGA *(Morning Raga)*.......... James Roberts

# A Musical S.O.S.

The rock singer and composer Sting often closes his live concerts with this song. Notice how repetition gives a special power to the message of the song.

Sting

## Message in a Bottle

Words and Music by Sting

VERSE

1. Just a cast - a - way __ an is - land lost __ at sea __
2. A __ year __ has passed _ since I wrote my note, _

__ o, __ An - oth - er lone - ly day, _
I should have known __ it right _ from the

No one here _ but me, __ o, __ More
start; On - ly hope _

lone - li - ness _ than an - y - one _ could bear, ______
__ can keep _ me to - geth - er ______

Res - cue me ____ be - fore _ I fall ___ in - to ___ des - pair, _
Love _ can mend ___ your life, _ but love ___ can break _ your heart. _

REFRAIN
o.
I'll send an S. O. S. to the world,
I hope that some-one gets my mes-sage in a bot-
-tle.
Last time to Coda
2
D.C.
3. Walked out this morn-ing,
Don't be-lieve what I saw:
Hun-dred bil-lion bot-tles, washed up on the shore.
3
3
Seems I'm not a-lone in be-ing a-lone.
Hun-dred bil-lion cast-a-ways, look-ing for a home.
D.S. al Coda
Coda
repeat to fade
Send-ing out an S. O. S. I'm

# The Artist's Medium

When artists choose a subject they want to express visually, they must choose the *medium* in which to work.

An artist may choose, for example, oil paint as the best medium for a particular work of art. Another artist may decide to interpret that same subject in stone.

**CONVERSION OF ST. PAUL** ***Niccole Dell Abate***

Niccole Dell Abate, *Conversion of St. Paul*, The Granger Collection

Each artist has chosen the medium that best expresses a particular feeling and response to the subject.

# The Composer's Medium

A composer must choose a *musical medium* to express a musical idea. This is only one of the many decisions a composer must make, but it is a very important one.

In music, the medium is the choice of instruments, voices, or combinations that will be used to make the sounds of music.

Listen to this piece by the French composer Maurice Ravel. The composer made two different choices: he wrote it first for piano, then for orchestra.

"Minuet" from *Le Tombeau de Couperin* ..... Ravel

**1.** Piano solo (excerpt)

**2.** Symphony orchestra (excerpt)

## Meet the Composer

**French composer Maurice Ravel lived most of his life in this century. He wrote many famous piano pieces, but is best known for his orchestral piece, "Bolero."**

**Ravel often wrote a piece for piano, and then rewrote the same piece for orchestra, as he did with the "Minuet."**

**Ravel was considered one of the most skillful orchestrators of his time. His pieces are full of beautiful orchestral "color." His style has often been copied by writers of television and movie music.**

**Ravel admired American Composer George Gershwin so much that he used a jazz style on one of his piano concertos.**

Maurice Ravel
(1875–1937)

# The Artist's Palette

An artist's palette uses colors. The artist chooses the ones that will help express an idea or feeling about the subject of a painting.

Vibrant, warm reds and oranges? Cool, liquid blues and greens? Shimmering yellows and golds?

**ROUEN CATHEDRAL (HARMONY IN BLUE)** ***Claude Monet***

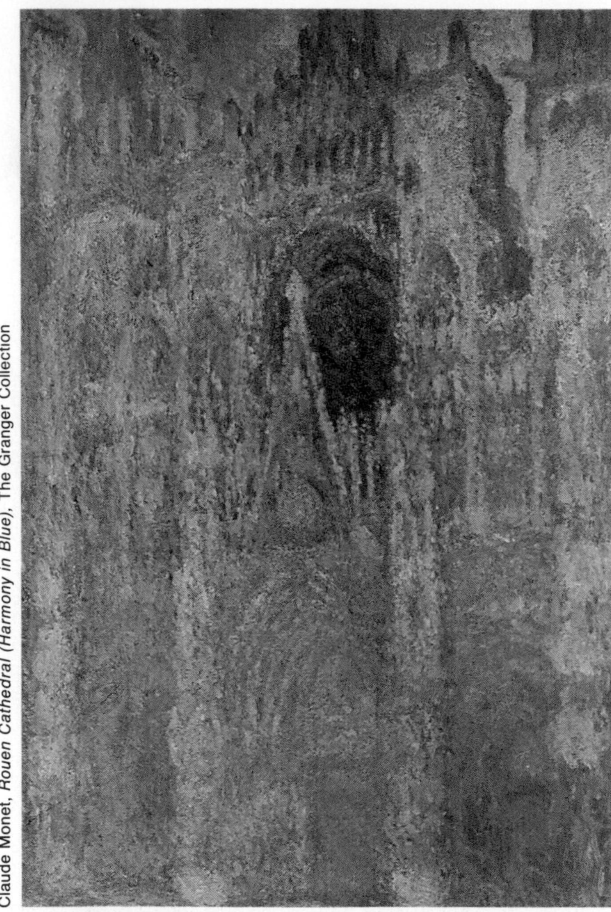

Claude Monet, *Rouen Cathedral (Harmony in Blue)*, The Granger Collection

**ROUEN CATHEDRAL (WEST FACADE—SUNLIGHT)** ***Claude Monet***

Claude Monet, Rouen Cathedral (West Facade-Sunlight), The Granger Collection

The colors in a painting may be quiet and subdued or bright and bold. It all depends on the choices the artist makes in order to express visual ideas.

# The Composer's Palette

The composer's palette is as varied and colorful as the painter's. Composers use **tone color** to express musical ideas.

Listen to these two short musical sketches. Think of them as musical pictures, or as abstract, colorful designs. One is dark and somber and one is bright and cheerful.

**"Bydlo" from *Pictures at an Exhibition* (excerpt) .. .......................................... Mussorgsky**

**Overture from *Candide* (excerpt) ........ Bernstein**

**ANGEL APPEARING TO ST. JOSEPH ASLEEP** ***Georges de la Tour***

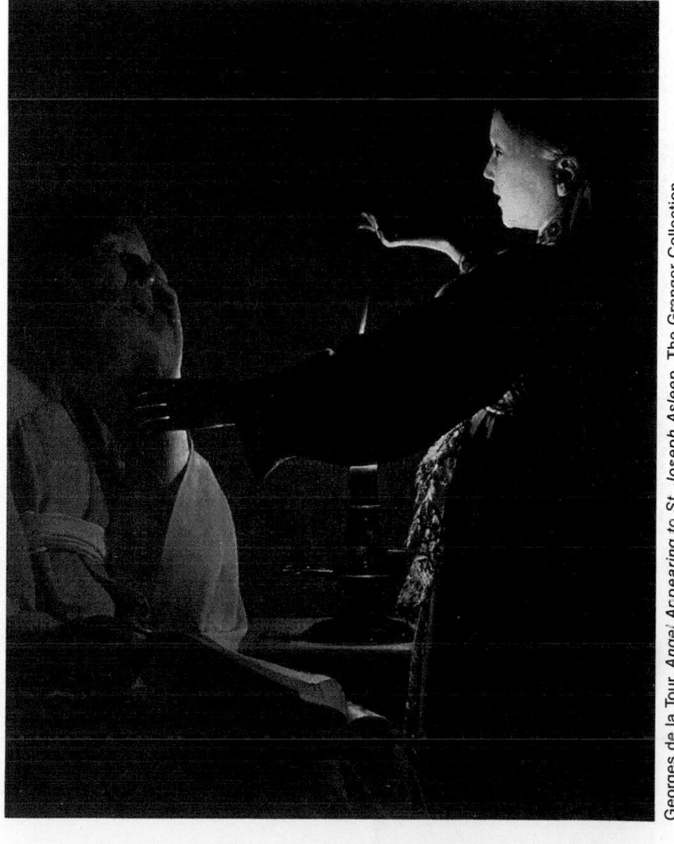

Georges de la Tour, *Angel Appearing to St. Joseph Asleep*, The Granger Collection

A painter may use contrasting colors or may highlight sections of a painting to make the work more interesting.

A composer may do the same thing with sound. Listen to the way a great composer used the bright tone color of the piccolo to add "shine" to the ending of a symphony.

***Symphony No. 5*** **"Finale" (excerpt) ....... Beethoven**

## A Colorful Song for Young Musicians

Here is a song about the tone colors of several instruments.
Each is introduced individually, with a lot of bragging.
Eventually they all become a colorful "orchestra."

# I Am a Great Musician

Traditional Melodic Adaptation and New Words by Linda Williams

1. I am a great mu - si - cian, I prac-tice ev - 'ry day,
And peo - ple come from miles a - round Just to hear me play
2. I am a great mu - si - cian, that's what I hear them say.
They come and set up fold-ing chairs just to hear me play

My trum - pet, my trum - pet, I love to play my trum - pet:
My vi - o - lin, my vi - o - lin, I love to play my vi - o - lin: *To solo 2*

Dee-dle dee-dee-dee, Dee-dle dee-dee-dee, Dee-dle dee-dle dee dee dee-dle dee.

*(Each soloist sings the "instrument" part, and is joined, on the repeat, by all the others who have already been introduced.)

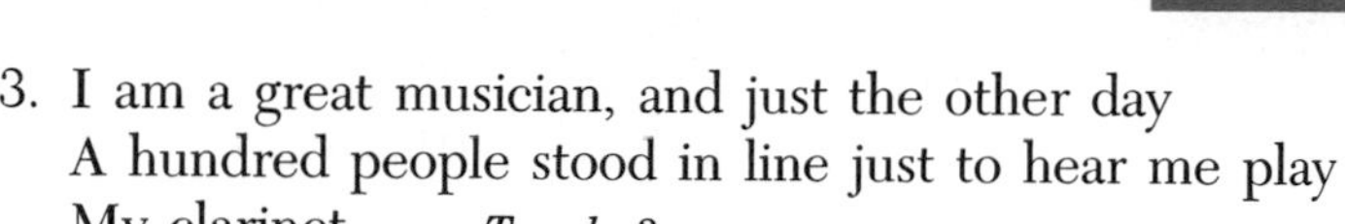

3. I am a great musician, and just the other day
   A hundred people stood in line just to hear me play
   My clarinet . . . *To solo 3*

4. I am a great musician, and people have to pay
   To get a perfect front row seat just to hear me play
   My string bass . . . *To solo 4*

5. I am a great musician, I'm not ashamed to say
   The paper sent reporters out just to hear me play
   My piccolo . . . *To solo 5*

6. (Slower) All:
   We'll all be great musicians, we'll practice every day,
   We hope you'll come from miles around
   Just to hear us play, *(to Coda)*

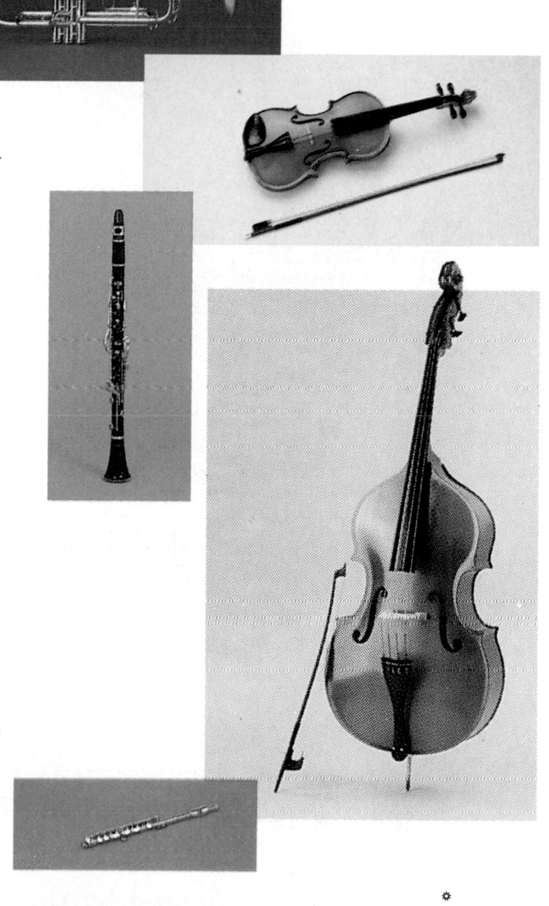

*Each "musician" sings the instrumental line to finish the song.

# The Colors of the Orchestra

## Painting with Sound

A composer paints pictures and designs with musical sound. The particular sound each instrument makes is called *tone color*. Tone color is affected by the materials used to make the instrument.

Tone color is linked to the method of sound production, whether a sound is made by scraping, blowing, striking, or in some other way.

Tone color is affected by the size and shape of the instrument.

Listen to the opening of this piece by Berlioz, and notice the colorful use of the instruments.

*Roman Carnival Overture* (excerpt)......... Berlioz

## Meet the Composer

Hector Berlioz
(1803–1869)

Hector Berlioz was a famous composer when he was still quite young. He had a very colorful personality, and often did things that shocked a lot of people. He was a little like some of our rock stars!

He wrote many famous works, including the *Symphony Fantastique,* which is one of the most popular symphony pieces even today.

Berlioz was very good at choosing and using the colors of the orchestra. He is often spoken of as a musical "colorist." Many of the special effects he created were far ahead of his time.

# Woodwinds

A symphony orchestra contains the instrumental colors a composer needs to paint his musical pictures. The conductor knows which instruments will be playing by looking at a *score*. You can see which instruments the composer has asked for in this piece by looking at the piece of the score printed on the margin of the page.

The woodwind instruments are first in order at the top of the score.

The woodwind instruments with the highest-pitched sounds are the flute and piccolo.

The piccolo is very similar to the flute, but it is smaller and has a higher, more piercing sound.

***Lieutenant Kijé*** **(excerpt: piccolo) . . Prokofiev**

The flute has a high, sweet sound.

***Daphnis and Chloe*** **(excerpt: flute). . . . Ravel**

Next in order on the score are the oboe, then the English horn.

The oboe has an exotic, nasal sound.

***Polovetsian Dance*** **(excerpt: oboe) . . Borodin**

The English horn sound is similar, but darker and deeper.

***Roman Carnival Overture*** **(excerpt: English horn) . . . . . . . . . . . . . . . . . . . . . . . . . . . . . . Berlioz**

The next instrument on the score is the clarinet, followed by the bassoon.

The clarinet has a clear, mellow sound.

*Peter and the Wolf* (excerpt: clarinet) .... Prokofiev

The bassoon is a very low-pitched member of the woodwind family.

*Sorcerer's Apprentice* (excerpt: bassoon) ................................ Dukas

*Woodwind Fantasy on a Thanksgiving Song* ............................................... B. Red

# Brass

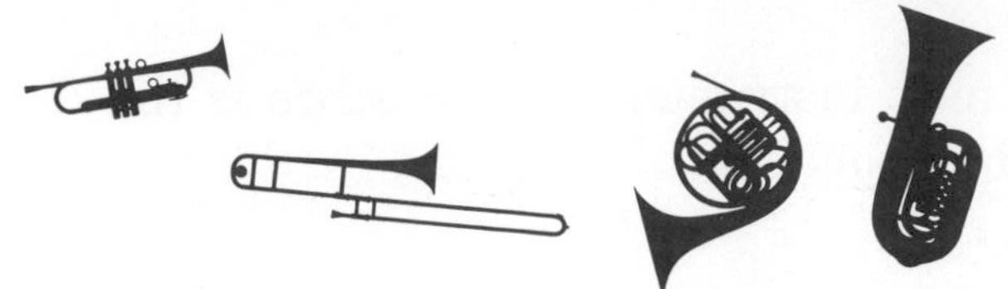

The bright-sounding brass instruments come next.

The mellow sound of the French horns goes well with either the brass instruments or the woodwinds.

*Till Eulenspiegel's Merry Pranks* (excerpt: horn) .............................. Strauss

The trumpet has a number of sounds and styles that it can play. It is very effective in **fanfares** and marches. Listen to this familiar march from an opera.

"Grand March" from *Aida* (excerpt: trumpets) ........................................ Verdi

## JOSHUA'S CAPTURE OF JERICHO *Jean Fouquet*

Jean Fouquet, *Joshua's Capture of Jericho*, The Granger Collection

Brass instruments have coiled tubing. Otherwise they would take up too much space. An ancient kind of trumpet with straight tubing is sometimes used for special occasions. It is used to make an announcement or to introduce someone very important.

# The Low Brass

The trombone is the only instrument that changes pitch with the use of a *slide*.

**"Pilgrim's Chorus" from *Tannhäuser* (excerpt: trombones)................. Wagner**

The tuba has a low sound.

**Pictures at an Exhibition "Bydlo" (excerpt) ........................ Mussorgsky**

# THE BRASS CHOIR

Listen to the sound of the brass instruments playing together as a brass **choir** in the accompaniment for this song.

Brass instruments have loud, assertive voices. However, they can also play softly and can sound very lyrical when the music calls for it.

# PERCUSSION

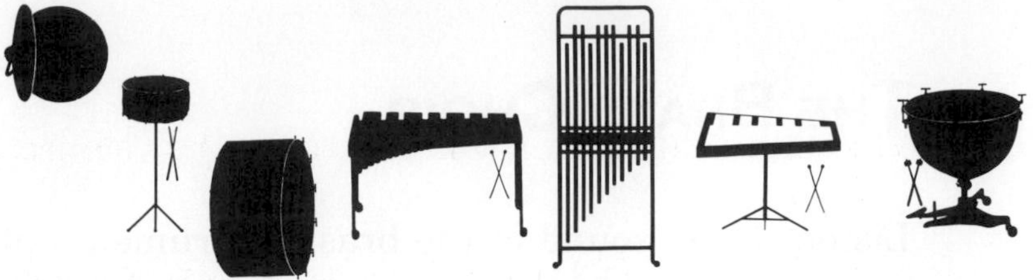

The percussion section adds excitement and color to the sound of the orchestra. Percussion instruments are most often used to emphasize the rhythm of a piece of music.

*Symphony No. 9* **(excerpt: percussion) . . . . . . . . . . . . . . . . . . . . . . . . . . . . . . . . . . . . . . . . . Beethoven**

However, percussion sounds are sometimes used to create special effects, sometimes without playing any beat at all.

*Sundance* **(excerpt: percussion) . . . . . Williams**

Percussion instruments are generally divided into two groups: those that play definite pitches, and those that play sounds with no definite pitch.

The snare drum and bass drum are instruments of indefinite pitch. They usually play strong rhythm patterns. The cymbals add splashes of sound.

*Battery* **(excerpt: snare drum, bass drum, cymbals) . . . . . . . . . . . . . . . . . . . . . . Williams**

Percussion instruments of definite pitch are called *mallet instruments*. The xylophone, orchestra bells, marimba, and chimes are all mallet instruments, and can play melodies.

Listen to the sound of the xylophone. The composer wanted to use an instrument that could sound like "old bones."

**"Fossils" from** ***Carnival of the Animals*** **(excerpt: xylophone) . . . . . . . Saint-Säens**

The chimes are often used to sound like church bells or clocks.

"Great Gate at Kiev" from *Pictures at an Exhibition* (excerpt: chimes)........... Mussorgsky

The orchestra bells, marimba, and other mallet instruments are often used to reinforce a melody line played by another instrument. Although they can be used to play tunes, they are often used to create interesting colors or textures.

The timpani, sometimes called kettledrums, can play definite pitches. Listen for the timpani in this short excerpt.

"Sherzo" from *Symphony No. 9* (excerpt: timpani)................................ Beethoven

## Strings

The orchestral string instruments are the violin, viola, cello, and string bass. The string section forms the main body of any symphony orchestra.

The violin is the highest sounding orchestral string instrument, followed by the viola, cello, and string bass. There are some notes that are the same on the violin, viola, and cello.

Listen to the way the strings sound when they are all playing on the same pitches.

**"Jupiter" from *The Planets* (excerpt: string section)................................Holst**

Violins have a wide **range** and can play very high.

***Young Person's Guide to the Orchestra*** **(excerpt: violins)....................Britten**

The viola is a larger version of the violin. Its sound is dark and mellow.

**Concerto No. 2 (excerpt: violas) ..... Rachmaninoff**

The low-voiced cello has a rich, mellow sound.

***Symphony No. 5* (excerpt: cellos)...... Tchaikovsky**

The string bass has a very deep voice.

***Lieutenant Kijé Suite* (excerpt: string bass)............................ Prokofiev**

String instruments make a singing sound when playing together. The recording of this song is accompanied by a string group.

## Alleluia

Music by W. A. Mozart    Adapted by Joseph Fisch

*When each voice reaches this measure, the next voice begins line one. Each voice sings the canon twice through, then stops. This way the canon ends with a single voice.

# Putting It All Together

These young musicians are playing in a regional youth symphony. Many of them will go on to careers in music. They play the same instruments and the same music as an adult symphony orchestra.

*Roman Carnival Overture* (excerpt: full orchestra) ........................................ Berlioz

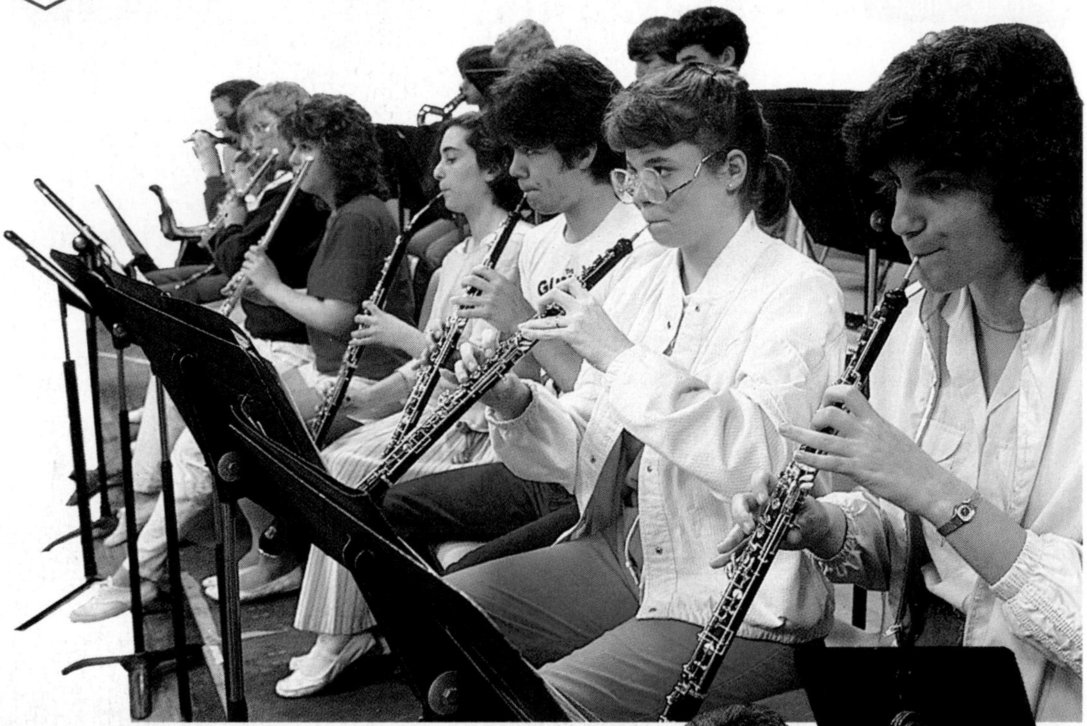

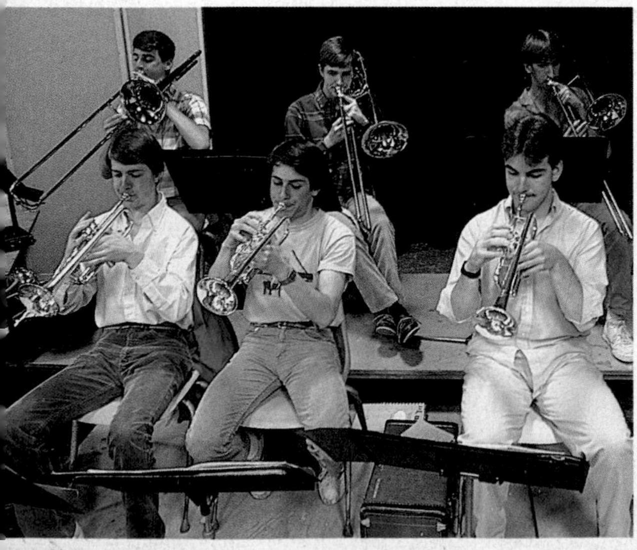

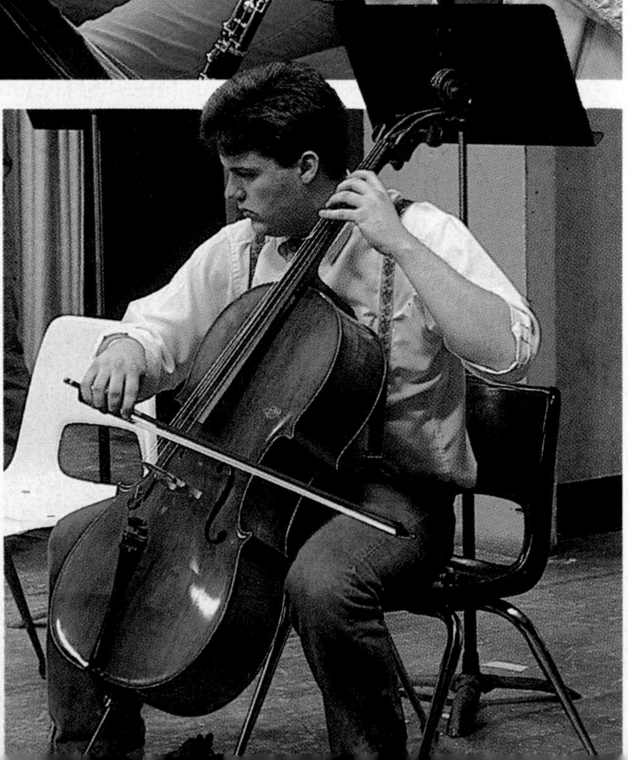

*Norwalk Youth Symphony (Connecticut)*
*Conducted by Gisele Ben-Dor*

# Careers in Music

## Making a Career as a Violin Soloist

A performer whose ability and dexterity are far above the usual level is sometimes called a *virtuoso*.

Listen to part of a virtuoso piece played by a young violinist named Gil Shaham. You will be able to tell that he is a performer of great skill. He is also able to perform very expressively. The ability to create a mood and to express emotion in music is just as important as technical skill.

*Carmen Fantasy* (excerpt). . . . . . . . . . . . . . . Bizet/Sarasate

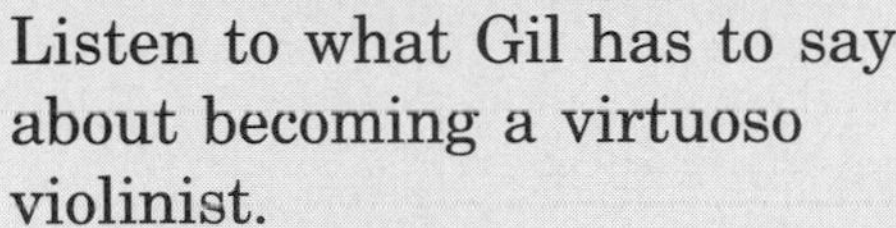

Listen to what Gil has to say about becoming a virtuoso violinist.

Interview with Gil Shaham

# Here Comes the Band

What is a **band**? How is it different from an orchestra? Where might you hear a band? Where did bands originate?

The music a band plays can be sweet and mellow, but it is often very loud, exciting, and rhythmic. Here is a band song to sing. It describes the excitement of watching a marching band at a Saint Patrick's Day celebration.

## MacNamara's Band

Words by John J. Stanford    Music by Shamus O'Connor

Usually the term *band* means a group of musicians who play wind and percussion instruments—from a few up to hundreds—including brasses, woodwinds, and various members of the percussion family.

## An Ancient Tradition

Bands have existed for thousands of years. There were bands even before there was a system for writing down music. References to bands are found in the Bible. Probably these bands consisted of trumpets and drums used for military ceremonies and for signals during battle.

During the Middle Ages and Renaissance in Europe, each town had a band. These town bands probably played for community events as well as for military parades. Gradually, over the years, the number of players in a band increased.

## Ceremonies and Celebrations

Through the ages, the sounds of wind and percussion instruments have signaled important events and ceremonies. *Fanfares*—bright-sounding trumpet calls—have been played to introduce important people or proclamations.

"Overture" to *La Peri* (excerpt) ............ Dukas

Band music is still played on special occasions in military or political settings. One of the most exciting things about a parade is the sound of a marching band.

Even in concert, a band can make a stirring, exciting sound rarely found in other kinds of music. One of the most famous American band composers was John Philip Sousa. His marches have become concert and parade favorites all over the world.

*Semper Fidelis* ............................ Sousa

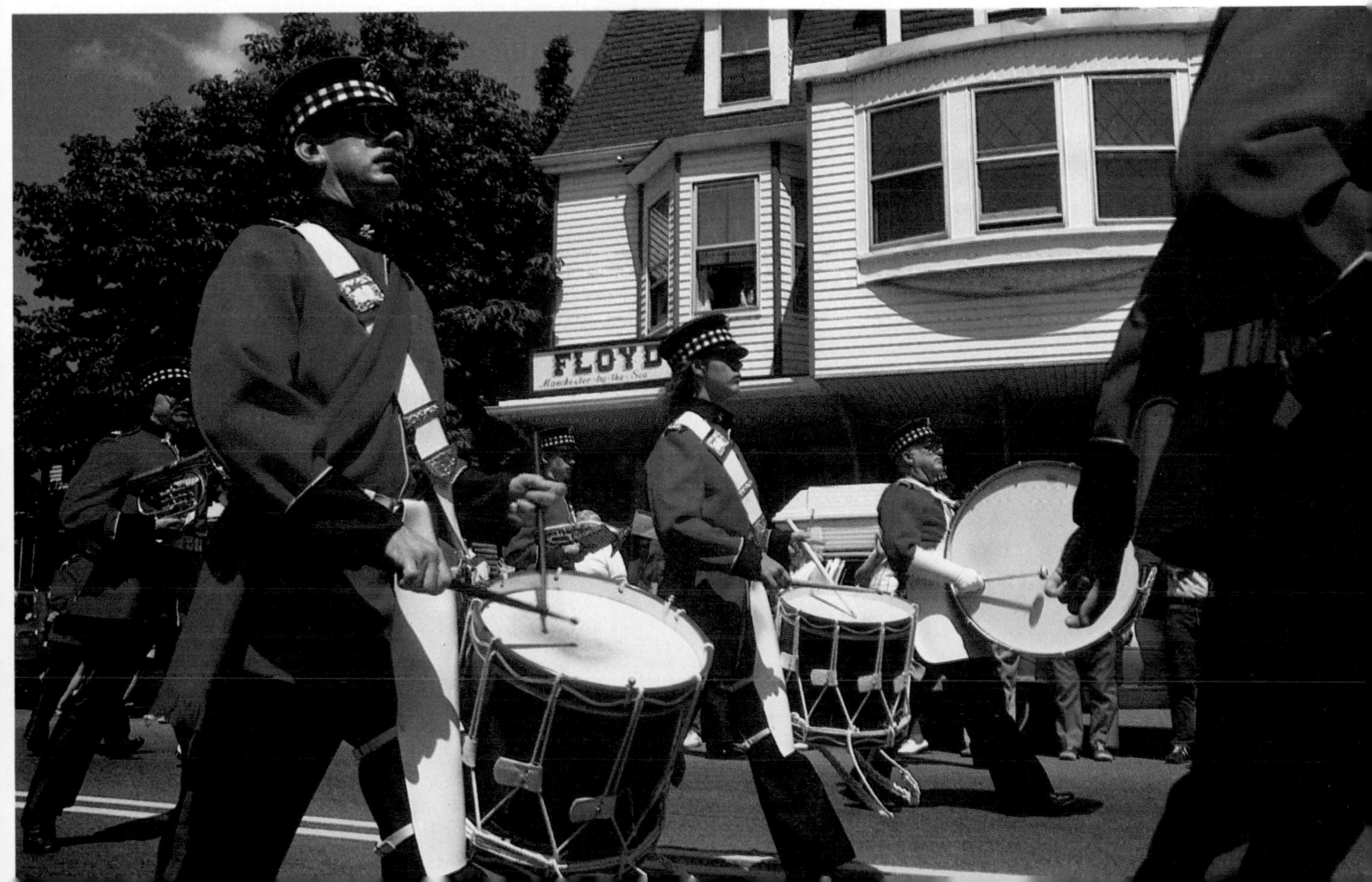

# Band Music for Dancing

Bands have always been ideal for playing dance music. Wind and percussion instruments can play loudly and rhythmically. The band music can be heard over the noise of people laughing and talking as they slide, jump, and stamp around a dance floor.

American dance bands have taken many forms over the years, but they have always been popular.

## A Song for Waltzing

Here is a song that was very popular in 1895. The melody is in $\frac{3}{4}$ time, so the dance that Casey and his "strawberry blonde" were doing was the *waltz*.

# School Bands in America

Think of a school subject that can begin in grade school and continue through high school and even college, one where you might sit down, or stand, or march. You might even wear a uniform.

That subject would be band. If your school has a band, it is part of a strong American tradition.

D
F
drum to a spry step! Then the trum - pets sing,
step! The trum - pets sing, The tu - bas
D
F
D7
F7
G
B♭
The tu - bas ring, there is - n't an - y - thing like the
ring, And ev - 'ry pic - co - lo's a trill;
G
B♭
F DIM7
G♯ DIM7
D
F
trill of a pic - co - lo! Oh, hear them play,
Oh, hear them play, This hol - i -
B7
D7
Em
Gm
A7
C7
D
F
This ho - li - day; Get that band sound thrill!
day; Come get that band sound thrill!

# Hear the Band

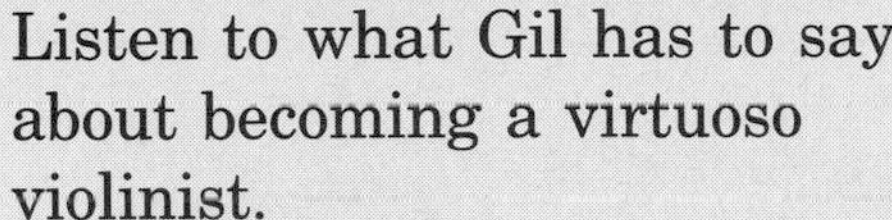

Listen to what Gil has to say about becoming a virtuoso violinist.

Interview with Gil Shaham

# Here Comes the Band

What is a **band**? How is it different from an orchestra? Where might you hear a band? Where did bands originate?

The music a band plays can be sweet and mellow, but it is often very loud, exciting, and rhythmic. Here is a band song to sing. It describes the excitement of watching a marching band at a Saint Patrick's Day celebration.

## MacNamara's Band

Words by John J. Stanford Music by Shamus O'Connor

A kind of band often found in schools is the *concert band*. Band members often form other kinds of ensembles. They may put on uniforms and become a *marching band* for parades and sports events. They may form a *stage band,* using instruments from the Swing era bands of the 1930s and 40s. A stage band might perform jazz and rock pieces, or arrangements from the swing era, like this popular piece from the 1940s.

"A String of Pearls" .......................... Gray

## A Famous Band Composer

Many famous composers have written pieces for concert band. Here is a concert band piece to listen to. You will probably recognize one of the themes.

"Fantasia on Dargason" from *Suite for Band, No. 2* .......................... Gustav Holst

### Meet the Composer

Gustav Holst
(1875–1935)

**Gustav Holst was an English composer whose music was often inspired by oriental subjects or English folklore. His best-known work, a piece for orchestra called *The Planets,* is based on the eight planets of the solar system that were known in his time.**

**Holst was a very important teacher of music. He might have written more, but his health was poor and working at composing was often very difficult for him.**

**Holst's two band suites are among the best and most important works for concert band.**

# What Do You Hear? 3

*Rhythm Patterns*

**You will hear ten melodies. The rhythm pattern of each example is repeated several times. Each number is followed by two written rhythm patterns. Circle the rhythm pattern you hear.**

1.

2.

3.

4.

5.

6.

7.

8.

9.

10.

# TEST 3

Here are eight examples of *tied* notes. After each tied-note example you will find two choices of notes that equal the time value of the tied notes. Circle the correct note. The first example has been done for you.

1. 𝅗𝅥‿♩ = 𝅝 𝅗𝅥.
2. ♩‿♩ = 𝅗𝅥 𝅗𝅥.
3. ♩‿♪ = ♩. 𝅗𝅥
4. ♩‿𝅗𝅥 = 𝅗𝅥. 𝅝
5. ♪‿♪ = ♩. ♩
6. ♪‿♩ = ♩. 𝅗𝅥
7. 𝅗𝅥‿𝅗𝅥 = 𝅗𝅥. 𝅝
8. ♪‿𝅘𝅥𝅯 = ♩ ♪.

# What Do You Hear? 4

*Major and Minor Tonalities*

**You will hear ten instrumental examples. They are accompaniments for songs in your book. Some are in *major* keys and some in *minor.* Circle the tonality you hear in each example, major or minor.**

| | | |
|---|---|---|
| **1.** | MAJOR | MINOR |
| **2.** | MAJOR | MINOR |
| **3.** | MAJOR | MINOR |
| **4.** | MAJOR | MINOR |
| **5.** | MAJOR | MINOR |
| **6.** | MAJOR | MINOR |
| **7.** | MAJOR | MINOR |
| **8.** | MAJOR | MINOR |
| **9.** | MAJOR | MINOR |
| **10.** | MAJOR | MINOR |

# Test 4

Here are ten melodies. Each has a very different melodic *contour* or shape. Some of the melodies move mostly *by step.* Some move mostly *by leap.* Look at each one. Write S in the space if the melody moves mostly by **step.** Write L if the melody moves mostly by **leap.**

1. S
2. L

3. ________
4. ________

5. ________
6. ________

7. ________
8. ________

9. ________
10. ________

# What Do You Hear? 5

*Harmony Patterns*

You will hear six songs from your book. Each is sung in *harmony*. After each number, write the letter that tells how the harmony is made.

| | |
|---|---|
| 1. ________ | A. Harmony in thirds |
| 2. ________ | B. Melody with countermelody |
| 3. ________ | C. Partner songs |
| 4. ________ | D. Canon |
| 5. ________ | E. Melody with ostinato |
| 6. ________ | F. Melody with chords |

# What Do You Hear? 6

*Form*

**You will hear seven musical examples. Each example will be in one of three forms: Some will have only one musical idea, and will use it in variations. Some will have two musical ideas and alternate them in an A B A form. Some will have two ideas, but will appear in an A B form.**

**After each example, circle the correct form.**

| | | | |
|---|---|---|---|
| **1.** | Variations | A B A | A B |
| **2.** | Variations | A B A | A B |
| **3.** | Variations | A B A | A B |
| **4.** | Variations | A B A | A B |
| **5.** | Variations | A B A | A B |
| **6.** | Variations | A B A | A B |
| **7.** | Variations | A B A | A B |

# What Do You Hear? 7

*Musical Interaction*

**You will hear seven musical examples. You will listen for the *musical interaction*. Use the diagrams to indicate which kind of musical interaction you hear.**

**= solo alternating with group**

**= group alternating with group**

**Circle the correct diagram for each example.**

**1.**

**2.**

**3.**

**4.**

**5.**

**6.**

**7.**

# WHAT DO YOU HEAR? 8

*Tone Color*

You will hear eight short musical examples. Listen for the tone colors in order to identify the instruments you hear. Circle the correct instrument or combination of instruments for each number. The first example has been done for you.

| | | |
|---|---|---|
| 1. | Concert band | Full orchestra |
| 2. | Trumpet and strings | Oboe and orchestra |
| 3. | Brass instruments | Woodwind instruments |
| 4. | Solo violin | Solo clarinet |
| 5. | Brass instruments | Woodwind instruments |
| 6. | Piano and orchestra | Percussion ensemble |
| 7. | Drums and cymbals | Xylophone and strings |
| 8. | Trumpet and orchestra | String ensemble |

# SECTION III

# MAKING MUSIC

# Using Your Voice

## Take a Big Breath

Before you can speak or sing, you first have to breathe. The breath you take is very important when you are singing.

If you breathe correctly, you can expand your lungs to hold a greater volume of air. This will make it easier to sing. You can sing longer without taking a breath, and you will have more air to help you control your singing.

When you are quietly breathing, the air is released through your mouth or nose with very little sound. When you want to sing or speak, you let the air vibrate a set of vocal cords, or folds deep in your throat. This is the way the sound is created.

The higher you want to sing or speak, the faster the cords must vibrate. You are so used to the way you change the pitch of your voices that you do not have to think about how you do it. It simply seems to happen.

However, you can control the sound, the pitch and loudness, even the tone quality of your voice. And you use your breath to control all of these changes.

## Making Musical Phrases

Sing this song, taking a breath only at the end of each phrase line. Notice that some phrases are longer than others. You will need more breath for these longer phrases.

### Bye-Bye, Blues

Words and Music by Fred Hamm, Dave Bennett, Bert Lown, and Chauncey Gray

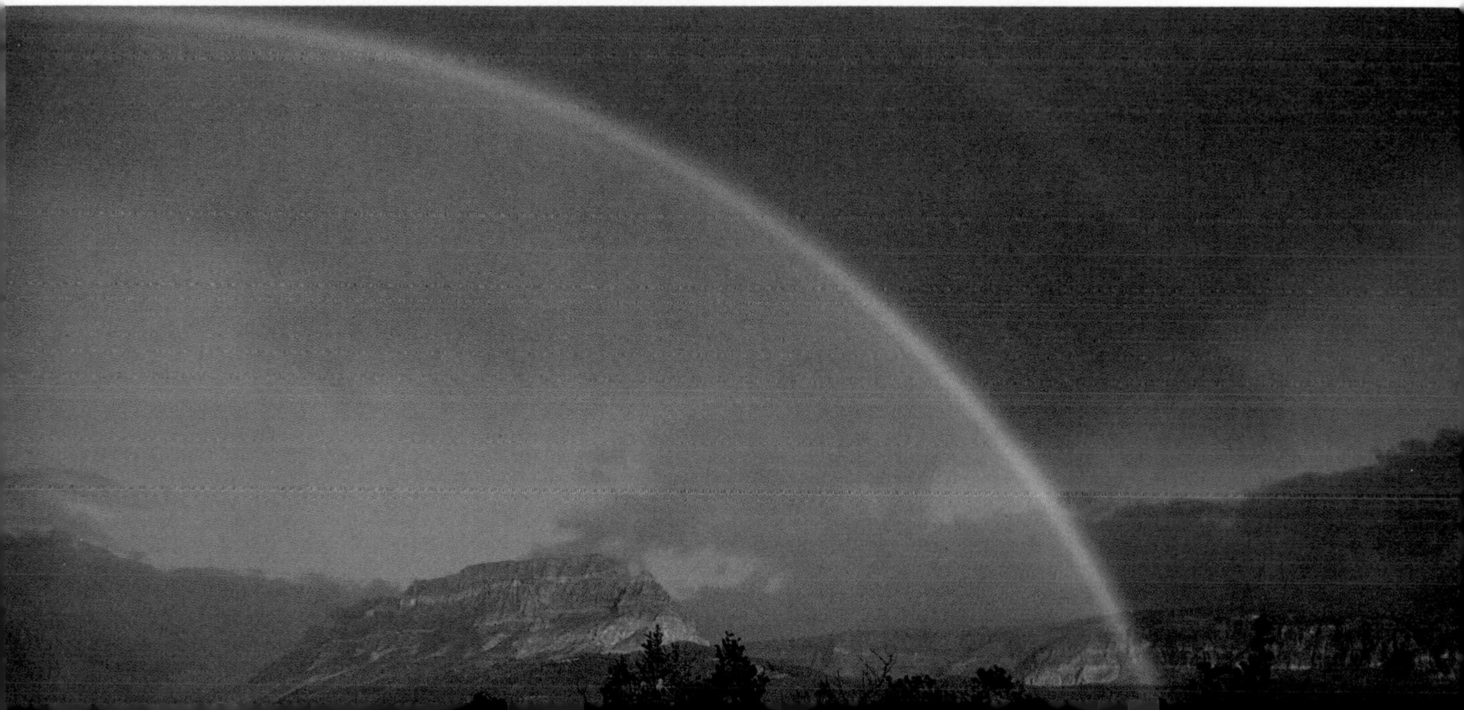

## Sing It—Clearly!

Here is a song that tells a story. There are three verses with a refrain in between each verse and at the end. As you and your classmates sing the song, imagine that you are singing the story to an audience. Pronounce the words clearly and as nearly together as you can, so a listener can follow the story.

As you perform "Dona Dona," you will find the **accelerando** section at the end will be the most difficult part of this song. *Accelerando* means "getting faster and faster," and you will have to listen carefully to one another to stay together.

This song is in the style of an Israeli folk-dance.

# Dona Dona

Words and Music by Sholom Secunda English Words by Arthur Kevess and Teddi Schwartz

*Moderately*

**Guitar: capo 5**

1. On a wag - on bound for mar - ket there's a calf with a mourn-ful eye,
2. "Stop com - plain - ing," said the far - mer, "Who told you a ___ calf to be,
3. Calves are eas - i - ly bound and slaught-ered, nev-er know-ing the rea - son why,

High a - bove him there's a swal - low wing-ing swift - ly ___ through the sky.
Why don't you ‗ have wings to fly ‗ with, like the swal-low so proud and free?"
But who - ev - er trea-sures free-dom, like the swal-low has learned to fly,

How the winds are laugh - ing, They laugh with all their might.

Laugh and laugh the whole day through, and half the sum - mer's night.

Accelerando
E7 A7
Am Dm
G7 C7
C F
Do-na, do-na, do - na, do - na, Do-na, do-na, do - na, _ don,
E7 A7
Am Dm
1. & 2.
E7 A7
Am Dm
Do-na, do-na, do - na, do - na, Do-na, do-na, do - na, don.
3.
Am Dm
E7 A7
Am Dm
Do - na, do - na, do - na, don.

# Warming Up

If you go early to a sports event, you'll probably see players going through exercises that get their muscles ready for the game. Without these warm-up exercises, they will not play as well and they risk injuring muscles that are not prepared.

Musicians warm up their voices or instruments before beginning to make music. Here are some warm-up exercises.

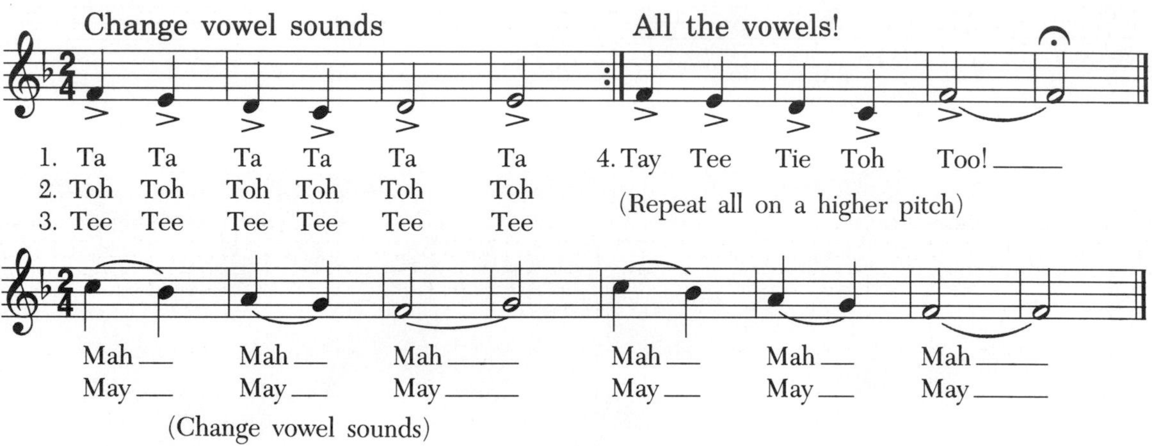


Now that your voice is warmed up, here is a song to sing.

## Charlottetown

Guitar: capo 3

Folk Song from Southern United States Countermelody by Mary Hoffman

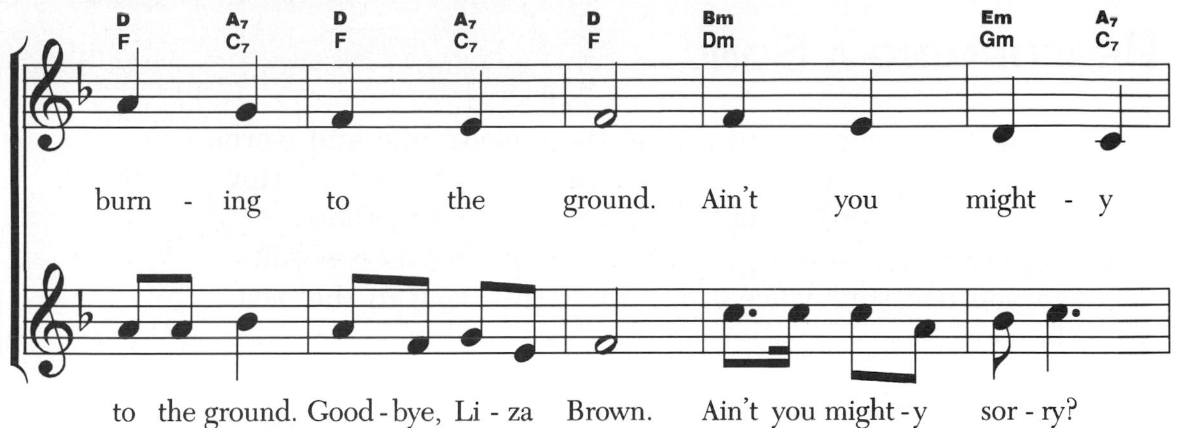


Bm Dm A7 C7 Bm Dm Em Gm A7 C7 Bm Dm A7 C7 D F

sor - ry? Ain't you sor - ry, Li - za Brown?

Good-bye, good-bye. Ain't you might-y sor-ry? Good-bye, Li-za Brown.

## Singing With Style

Different songs need different voices. The tone quality a singer chooses for a song can completely change the style. How will you decide on the tone quality and style for a song?

Look at this list of descriptive words. Then look at the list of songs. Which words best describe the vocal style for each song?

| | |
|---|---|
| brassy, soft, loud, | I Got Rhythm, p. 49 |
| flowing, accented, jerky, | On the Road Again, p. 84 |
| rhythmic, legato, staccato, | Waters Ripple and Flow, p. 16 |
| crisp diction, smooth diction | Mister Touchdown, U.S.A., p. 63 |

## Performing a Song

How should this song be sung? Use the melody line and words to decide how to use your voice. Where will you breathe? How do you think the words should be pronounced? Are there places where you would sing louder? Softer? In other words, how can you use your voice to interpret this song in the best possible way?

2. I've got joy like a fountain . . .

3. I've got love like the ocean . . .

# Call Chart 5

*Singing Styles*

1.

Dolly Parton

Singing well means singing a song in the style best suited to it. You can almost hear the style of singing when you look at these pictures of singers in performance.

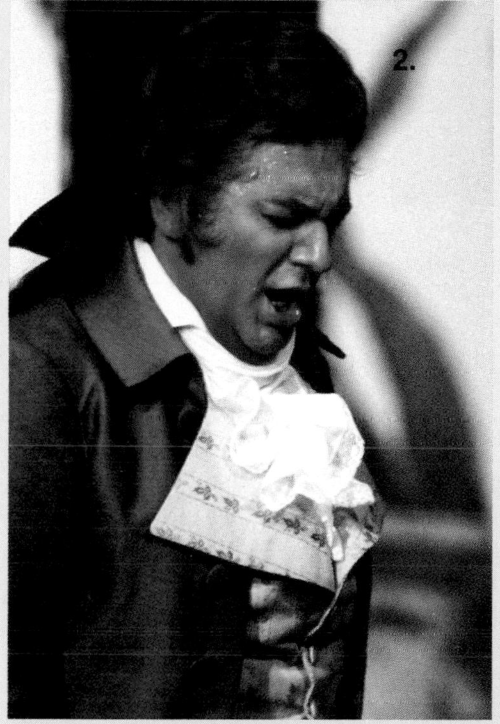

2.

Placido Domingo

3.

The Bangles

4.

A church choir

# Stage Movement

## Sharing Music with an Audience

"I'll send an S. O. S. to the world."

Performing music in front of an audience means sharing the music with people who are watching and listening.

"I'll send an S. O. S. to the world."

Always know what you want to be doing with a song. Decide how you will stand or move or interpret the song. These performers seem to have found themselves on stage by accident.

## Songs With Movement

Some songs work well with movement. If you are singing in a group, it is very effective if you make movements together.

"I've got rhy - thm"

Other songs are more easygoing. The movements you make should reflect a smoother, more relaxed rhythm. But you can still move together.

"Mi - chael, row the boat ashore . . . ."

## Making a Movement

Try making movements on important words or beats in the music. However, you should always make the movements natural and appropriate to the song. Crazy actions on the stage can be a lot of fun for both the performers and the audience, but even comical antics should be planned and well-rehearsed.

"My string bass, my string bass, I LOVE to play my string bass."

You can "underline" important words in a song with movements. Sometimes just bringing out a single word can be very effective.

"I've got STAR - light . . . ."

# Mixed Movement

Sometimes everyone on the stage can be doing something different, and it can be fun to watch. Even this visible confusion should be well planned, however.

"Well, it's a good day for singin' a song . . . ."

## Coordinated Movement

Movement that is coordinated, where everyone moves at the same time, is one of the best ways to make an audience pay attention.

"It's a good day from morn - in' till night."

# A Song You Can Perform

F7 G Em | 1. Am7 D7 G

In a world of mu - sic, That's where we be - long.

2. Am7 D7 G C B7 Em F7

That's where we be - long. I can bring you there, I can sing you there;

F7 G Em Am7 D7 G

In a world of mu - sic, That's where we be - long.

## Making Contact

If you want an audience to pay attention to you, you must pay attention to them. Remember, for an audience, the most important part of your face is your eyes!

"And an - y key will o - pen an - y door . . . ."

# Singing Concert Style

Whether you perform a song with motion and dancing, or just by standing still and singing, there is one thing to remember.

An audience is looking at you when you perform. You can have a pleasant face even when you are singing.

Always look at the conductor. Show the feelings of the music on your face.

## Sheep May Safely Graze

Music by J. S. Bach English Words by Linda Williams

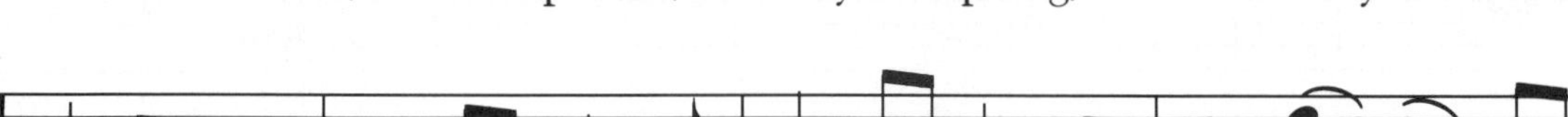

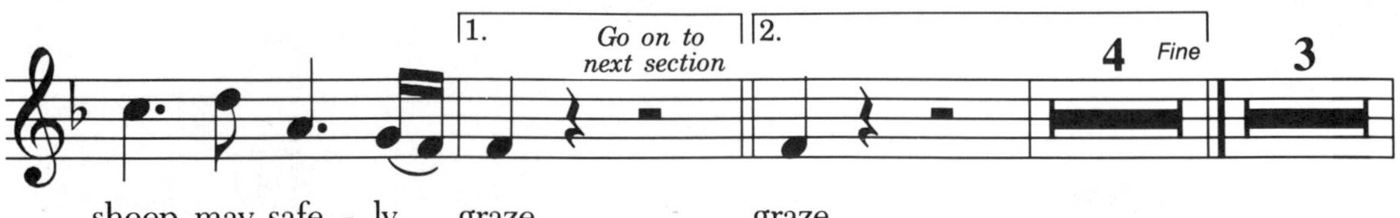

face to shine ___ up - on us, __ when the __ storm - y wind ___ and
rain de - scend, ___ Be our _ shep - herd and friend. ___ No ___ harm _
poco rit.
D.S. al Fine
___ shall come to us with _ thee watch-ing o - ver _ us, _ till _ jour-ney's _ end.

# The Pirates of Penzance

Sir William Gilbert and Sir Arthur Sullivan were English writers of a number of very famous **operettas.** Although they lived around 1900, during the time of Britain's Queen Victoria, their musical plays still delight audiences around the world. Gilbert wrote the words and Sullivan composed the music.

One of the most famous of all Gilbert and Sullivan musical plays is *The Pirates of Penzance.* You can learn some of the songs from this operatta. Listen to the **overture.** It will set the mood of the story.

**Overture to *Pirates of Penzance***
**.................................Gilbert and Sullivan**

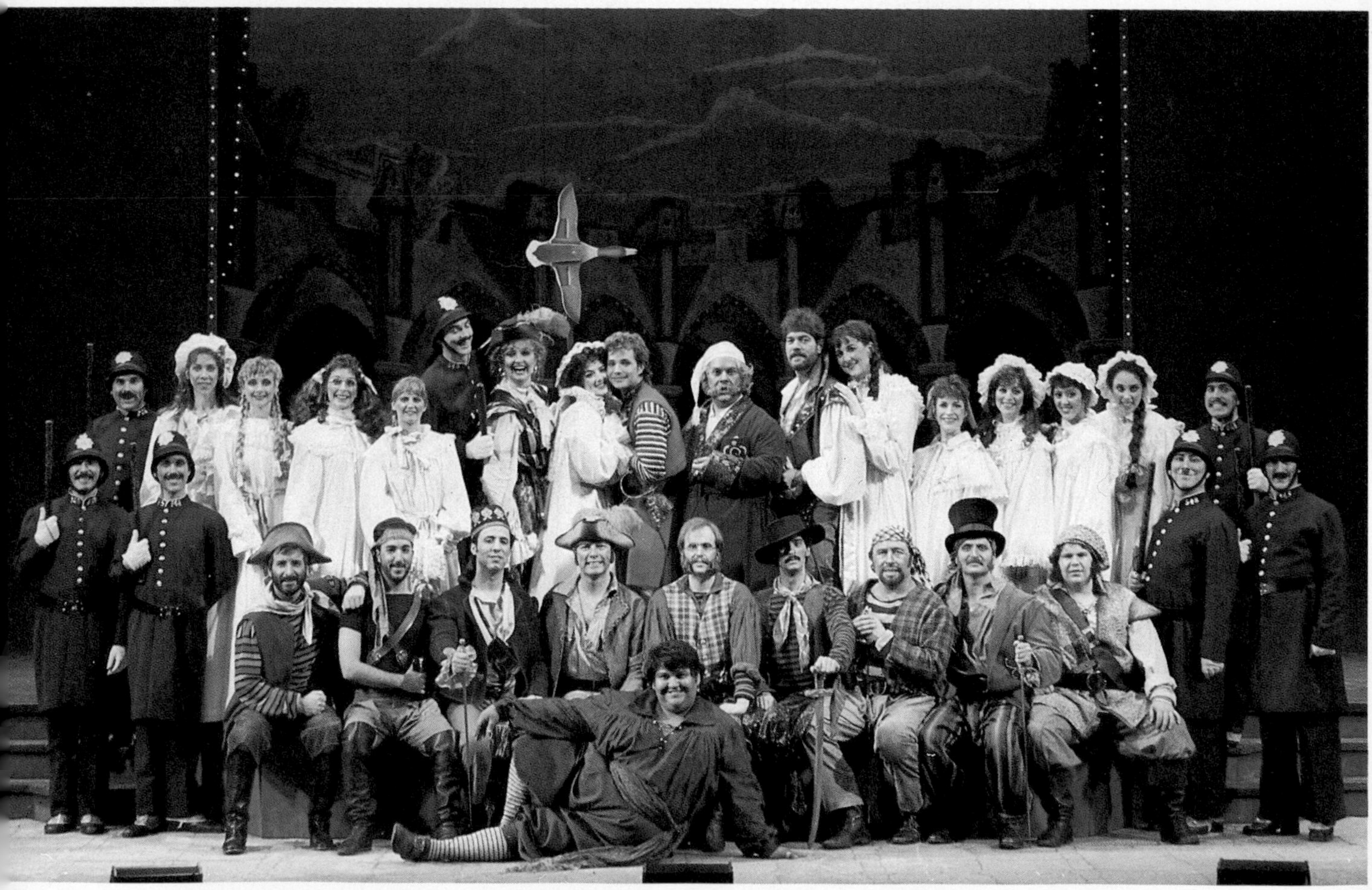

## The Story

A young man, Frederic, is an accidental pirate. When he was a lad, his nurse was told to apprentice him to a *pilot.* She misunderstood and made him a *pirate* instead. As he is an honorable young man, he will be true to his pirate comrades for the duration of his apprenticeship.

In fact, Frederic is a "slave of duty." He has vowed that on the day he reaches his twenty-first birthday, he will destroy the pirate band, and leave that life behind him.

Frederic's nurse, Ruth, who has been with him all these years, wants to leave the pirate ship and marry her young charge. However, Frederic meets and fall in love with Mabel, one of the daughters of the Major General.

This famous patter song introduces the Major General to the audience. By the end of the song, you know exactly the kind of person he is!

**"A Modern Major General". . . . Gilbert and Sullivan**

## A Musical Introduction

The pirate band is led by a fierce—yet humorous and understanding—buccaneer, a Pirate King. However, he is not nearly so terrible as he describes himself in this song.

# I Am a Pirate King

Words by W. S. Gilbert Music by Sir Arthur Sullivan

pi - rates all ___ are well - to - do, But I'll be true to the
wants to call ___ his crown his own, Must man - age some - how
song I sing, And live _ and die a Pi - rate King.
to get through More dir - ty work than ever I do.
For ___ I
Chorus
Solo
am a Pi - rate King (You are! Hur-rah for the Pi - rate King) _ And it
is, it is a glo - rious thing _ To be a Pi - rate King! ___ For I
Chorus
Solo
am a Pi - rate King (You are! Hur-rah for our Pi - rate King!) _ And it
Chorus
is, it is a glo - rious thing _ To be a Pi - rate King! (It is! Hur-
All
rah for our Pi - rate King) Hur-rah for our Pi - rate King! ___

# Sisters and Sweethearts

Unaware that the pirates are plotting their capture, the carefree sisters wander on the beach. When they notice that Mabel and Frederic are having a romantic conversation, they tactfully sing about the weather.

## How Beautifully Blue the Sky

from *The Pirates of Penzance*

Words by W. S. Gilbert Music by Sir Arthur Sullivan

*Mabel and Frederick (second time only)*

ev - er mai - den wake from dream of

*Chorus of Girls*

How beau-ti-ful-ly blue the sky, The glass is ris-ing ver-y high, Con -

home - ly du - ty, To

tin - ue fine I hope it may, And yet it rained but yes-ter-day. To -

*to* 𝄌

find her day - light break with such ex -

*second time to* 𝄌

mor-row it may rain a - gain, (I hear the coun - try wants some rain) Yet

peo - ple say, I know not why, That we shall have a

warm Ju - ly. To - mor-row it may pour a - gain, (I hear the coun-try

wants some rain) Yet peo-ple say, I know not why, That we shall have a

Mabel and Frederic
Did
ceed - ing beau - ty!
warm Ju - ly. How
peo-ple say, I know not why, That we shall have a

Ah, yes!
warm Ju - ly, Yet peo-ple say, I know not why, That we shall have a

Ah, yes, Ah, yes!
warm Ju - ly, a warm Ju - ly.

# The Plot Thickens

The story is further complicated when Frederic discovers that he was born on Feb. 29 in leap year and has had only five birthdays. Now his sense of duty forbids him to leave the pirate band.

The pirates capture the girls and their father. But the clever Major General tells the pirates that he is a poor orphan. Out of sympathy, since the pirates are all orphans themselves, they let him go.

A band of policemen come to save the day. This song tells about the joy of battle. But like the pirates, they are not nearly as brave as they like to think they are!

## Ta-Ran-Ta-Ra

Words by W. S. Gilbert Music by Sir Arthur Sullivan

find the wis - est thing
Is to
Ta-ran - ta - ra, ta-ran - ta - ra!
slap our chests and sing Ta-ran - ta - ra!
For when
Ta-ran - ta - ra!
threat-en'd with e-meutes
And your
Ta-ran - ta - ra, ta-ran - ta - ra!
heart is in your boots,
There is
Ta-ran - ta - ra!
Solo
no - thing brings it round, Like the trum-pet's mar - tial sound, Like the

Solo and Chorus of Policemen
trum - pet's mar - tial sound. Ta - ran - ta - ra, ta -
ran - ta - ra, ta - ran - ta - ra, ta - ran - ta - ra, ta - ran - ta - ra, ta - ran - ta -
Chorus of Girls
Go, ye he - roes, go to im - mor - ta - li - ty! Go, ye
ra, ta - ran - ta - ra, ta - ran - ta - ra, ta - ran - ta - ra, ta - ran - ta -
he - roes, go to im - mor - ta - li - ty! Tho' ye
ra! Ta - ran - ta -
die in com - bat go - ry, Ye shall live in song and sto - ry; Go to
ra, ta - ran - ta - ra, ta - ran - ta - ra!
im - mor - ta - li - ty!

## A Happy Ending

The Pirate King and Mabel inform Frederic that he has actually celebrated only *five birthdays*—because he was born on Feb. 29 in a leap year! His indentures (contracts to work) run until his twenty-first *birthday*. He will be a pirate for a long, long time!

The pirates defeat the police in a battle, but the police insist that the pirates yield "in the name of the Queen." They do.

Ruth explains that the pirates are actually "noblemen who have gone wrong." They are pardoned.

The Major General and his daughters are safe and sound. The pirates and police are happy. Best of all, Mabel and Frederic are together at last, and they are sure to live happily ever after.

# Dance to the Music

Throughout the ages, dancing has had a strong impact on the music of the time.

**THE JOLLY FLATBOATMEN** *George Caleb Bingham*

George Caleb Bingham, *The Jolly Flatboatmen,* Private Collection, on loan to the National Gallery of Art, Washington, D.C.

Primitive peoples danced to chanting, clapping, and the sound of drums and other instruments.

Dancing was important to the Greeks, and dance training was required as part of the standard education of the young people.

## Dance—The Royal Treatment

In the Renaissance and Baroque courts, the noble lords and ladies loved to dance.

A stately dance called the *minuet* was introduced in the French court around 1670. Like other court dances, the minuet was based on a country dance, transformed by its regal setting. This familiar minuet by Bach is still popular in our own time.

**Minuet in G Major....................J. S. Bach**

## The Waltz King

Early in the 1800s in Austria, a man named Johann Strauss became famous for his waltzes.

Johann Strauss's son, who had the same name, carried on the family tradition. He became even more renowned than his father. He wrote so many famous waltzes that he was called The Waltz King. Listen to this famous waltz by the younger Strauss.

**"The Blue Danube" (excerpt)...Johann Strauss Jr.**

## Country Dancing

The waltz had existed for a long time. It had been danced in the villages of Germany and Austria for longer than anyone could remember. The country version of this three-quarter-time dance was rough and vigorous.

The *Scherzo* movement of a symphony by Gustav Mahler is in the style of these country dances.

**"Scherzo" from *Symphony No. 1* (excerpt)...Mahler**

# A New Song in the Old Tradition

Square dancing originated in America's early days.

The energy and high spirits of the traditional square dance can be heard in this song, which was written for a movie in 1947.

## Country Style

Words and Music by Johnny Burke and James Van Heusen

1 Dance and share a lov - in' cup with dif - f'rent part - ners for a - while,

2 Dance with dif - f'rent part - ners for a - while,

*Clap:* D.S.

1 But for hitch - in' up with, Make mine coun - try style.

*Clap:* D.S.

2 But for hitch - in' up with, Make mine coun - try style.

*last time* *Shout:*

1 Make mine coun - try style. ______ All right!

*last time* *Shout:*

2 Make mine coun - try style. ______ All right!

# Social Dancing in America

Most of the aristocrats in colonial America loved social dancing. Adults took lessons from "dancing masters," and they insisted that their children learn dancing as part of their general education.

Thomas Jefferson made a schedule for his daughter to practice dancing every other day from ten until one. John Quincy Adams wrote that he often danced from seven in the evening until four in the morning!

*Allemande* ................................ Bach

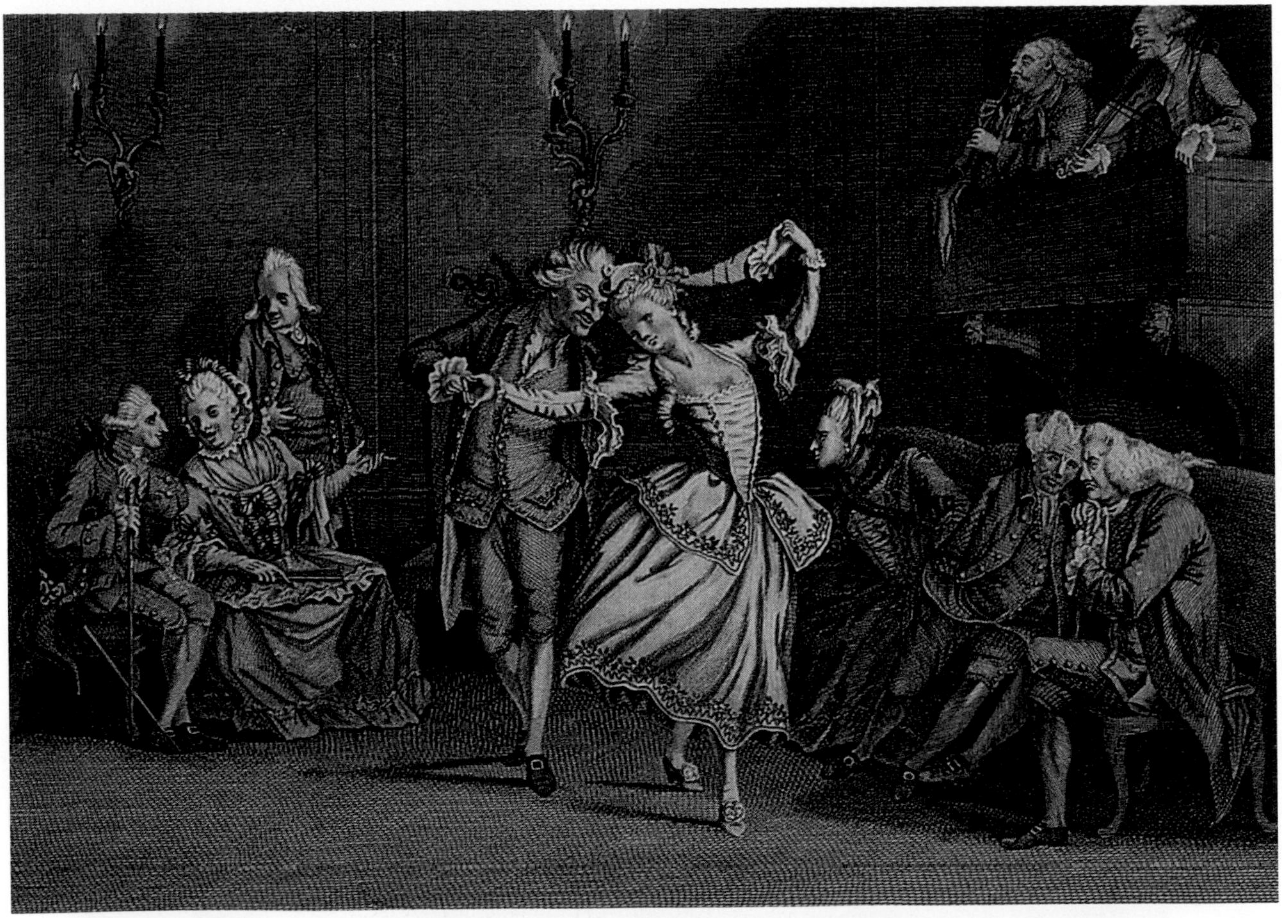

*The Allemande Dance*, New York Public Library, Dance Collection, New York

## A Polka from Our Century

There were numerous society balls during the 1800s. Many of the dances were performed in lines or sets. But the most popular dances were the waltz and the polka, which continue to be danced today.

Here is a famous polka from the 1940s.

# A Circle Dance

America has a rich cultural heritage, much of it borrowed from other countries. Our country has adopted the spirit, traditions, and dance patterns of a multitude of immigrants.

This song goes with a popular circle dance from Israel called the *Horah*.

The world heritage of Jewish song, poetry, and instrumental music reaches back into the writings of the Old Testament. Even the earth seems to dance to this joyous music.

O sing unto the Lord a new song. . . .
Make a joyful noise unto the Lord,
  all the earth:
Make a loud noise, and rejoice, and sing praise.

Sing unto the Lord with the harp;
With the harp, and the voice of a psalm.

With trumpets and sound of cornet
  make a joyful noise. . . .

Let the sea roar, and the fullness thereof;
The world, and they that dwell therein.

Let the floods clap their hands;
Let the hills be joyful together. . . .

*—from Psalm 98*

# A Dance Style Made in America

Just as the music of black Americans was the seed for our truly American music, so it is with the dance. Even during the days of slavery, black people began to develop songs and dances that were distinctly theirs. This style was so powerful and exciting that it has had a worldwide and lasting effect on all music and dance as we know it.

Traditional African steps and body movements, combined with European set dances, evolved into something completely new. The popular dance style we call "tap" was invented by black artists.

**John Bubbles**

Some famous black dancers from the early 1900s were John Bubbles, Peg-Leg Bates—who could do almost any dance step in spite of his disability—and Bill Robinson. Bill "Bojangles" Robinson has often been called the greatest tap dancer of all time.

Peg-Leg Bates

Bill Robinson

# Dancing on Sand

The "soft shoe" was a dance style similar to tap. The dancer sprinkled sand on the sidewalk or the stage, and made scraping sounds by dancing on the sanded surface.

## Soft Shoe Song

Words and Music by Roy Jordan and Sid Bass

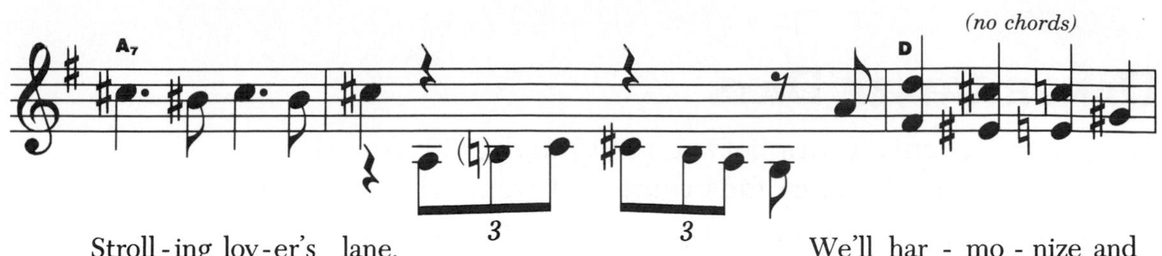


Stroll-ing lov-er's lane, We'll har - mo - nize and

*(Just like we're play-ing a scene)*

A7 D7 Coda G E7

doo-dle-dee doo-dle-dee-doo. Give me that else will do; Mis - ter

Lead - er, play the song and dance I love to do: the old *(I'm talk-in' a-bout the old)*

soft *(I'm talk-in' a-bout the soft)* shoe. Soft shoe!

# Dance Craze Days

During the twenty years between 1910 and 1930, Americans were dance crazy! Dance fads came and went with real 20th century speed.

There were *dance songs,* songs that gave instructions for steps and movements in the lyrics. There were dance *marathons.* Couples danced continuously until exhaustion forced them to stop. Sometimes they danced for several days. The last couple on their feet usually won a big price.

The greatest dance craze of all was the Charleston. It became the dance sensation of the country when the chorus line of an all-black Broadway show, *Running' Wild,* danced to "Charleston."

# Charleston

10 7

Words and Music by Cecil Mack and Jimmy Johnson

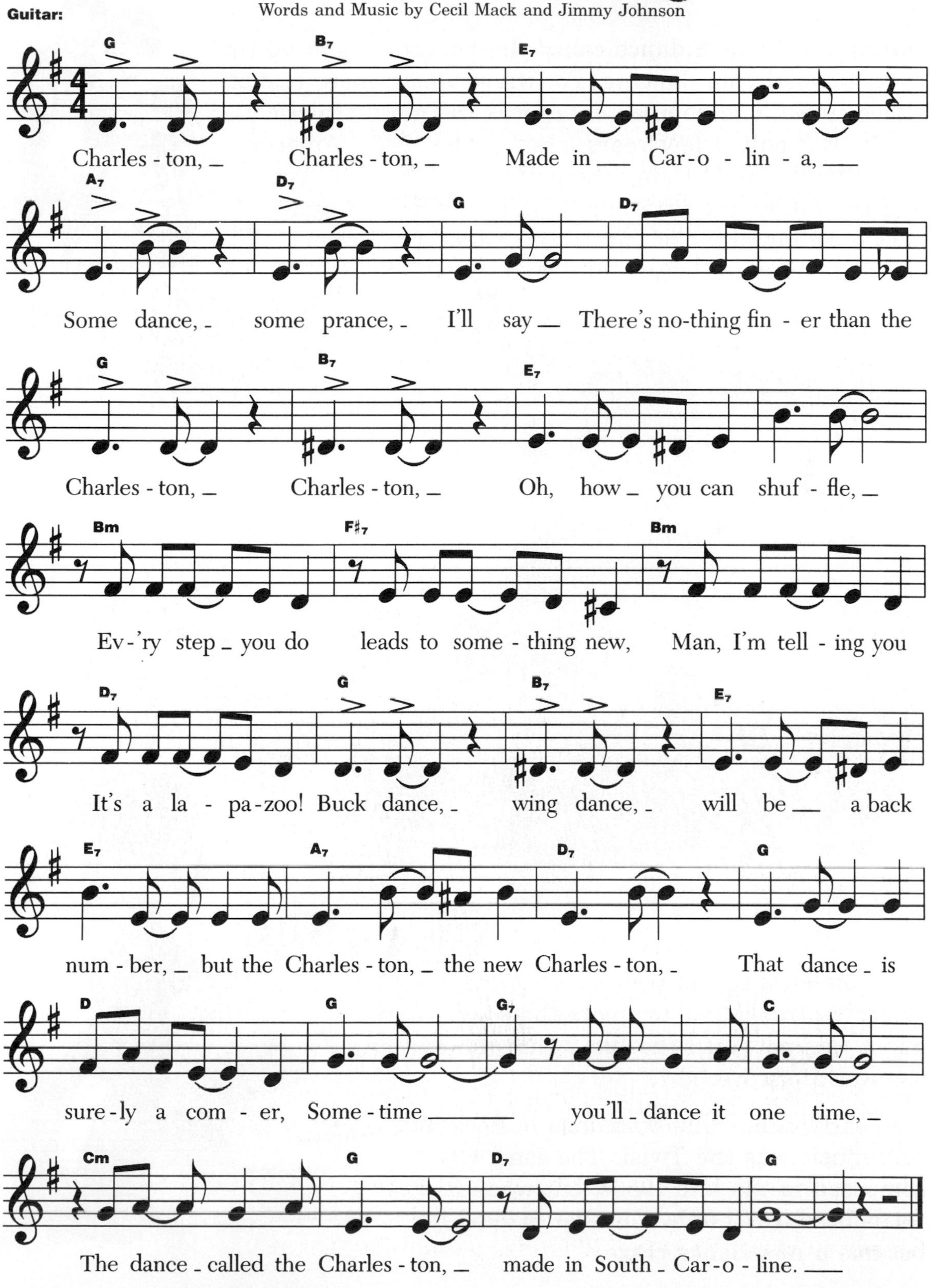
Guitar:
G B7 E7
Charles - ton, _ Charles - ton, _ Made in ___ Car - o - lin - a, ___
A7 D7 G D7
Some dance, _ some prance, _ I'll say ___ There's no-thing fin - er than the
G B7 E7
Charles - ton, _ Charles - ton, _ Oh, how _ you can shuf - fle, _
Bm F♯7 Bm
Ev-'ry step _ you do leads to some - thing new, Man, I'm tell - ing you
D7 G B7 E7
It's a la - pa-zoo! Buck dance, _ wing dance, _ will be ___ a back
E7 A7 D7 G
num - ber, _ but the Charles - ton, _ the new Charles - ton, _ That dance _ is
D G G7 C
sure - ly a com - er, Some - time ________ you'll _ dance it one time, _
Cm G D7 G
The dance _ called the Charles - ton, _ made in South _ Car - o - line. ___

# Dancing Gets a New Twist

During the 1930s a dance called the Fox Trot replaced the waltz for ballroom dancing. For the younger, more casual dance crowd, one popular dance was the more athletic Lindy. But only a few years later, in the 1940s, America began to jitterbug! Using the patterns of the Fox Trot and the Lindy, the jitterbug dancers improvised and developed hundreds of variations. These were often spectacular turns, jumps, lifts, and spins.

Then came Rock and Roll!
Black musicians had been playing and recording this music for more than fifty years, but it was not until the 1950s that the rest of the world discovered it.

One early dance that was done to Rock and Roll music was the Twist. The song was composed in the late 1950s, but when it was introduced by Chubby Checker in 1960 it became a new dance craze.

***Chubby Checker***

# The Twist

Words and Music by Frank Ballard

# Song and Dance—American Musical Theater

America has given birth to a special kind of popular musical theater. It grew out of the European opera and operetta.

In 1943 came the landmark musical, *Oklahoma!* The songs were in the popular style but were used to develop the characters and set the scenes.

Listen to a recording of the final scene from *Oklahoma.*

*Oklahoma* (Finale) ..... **Rodgers and Hammerstein**

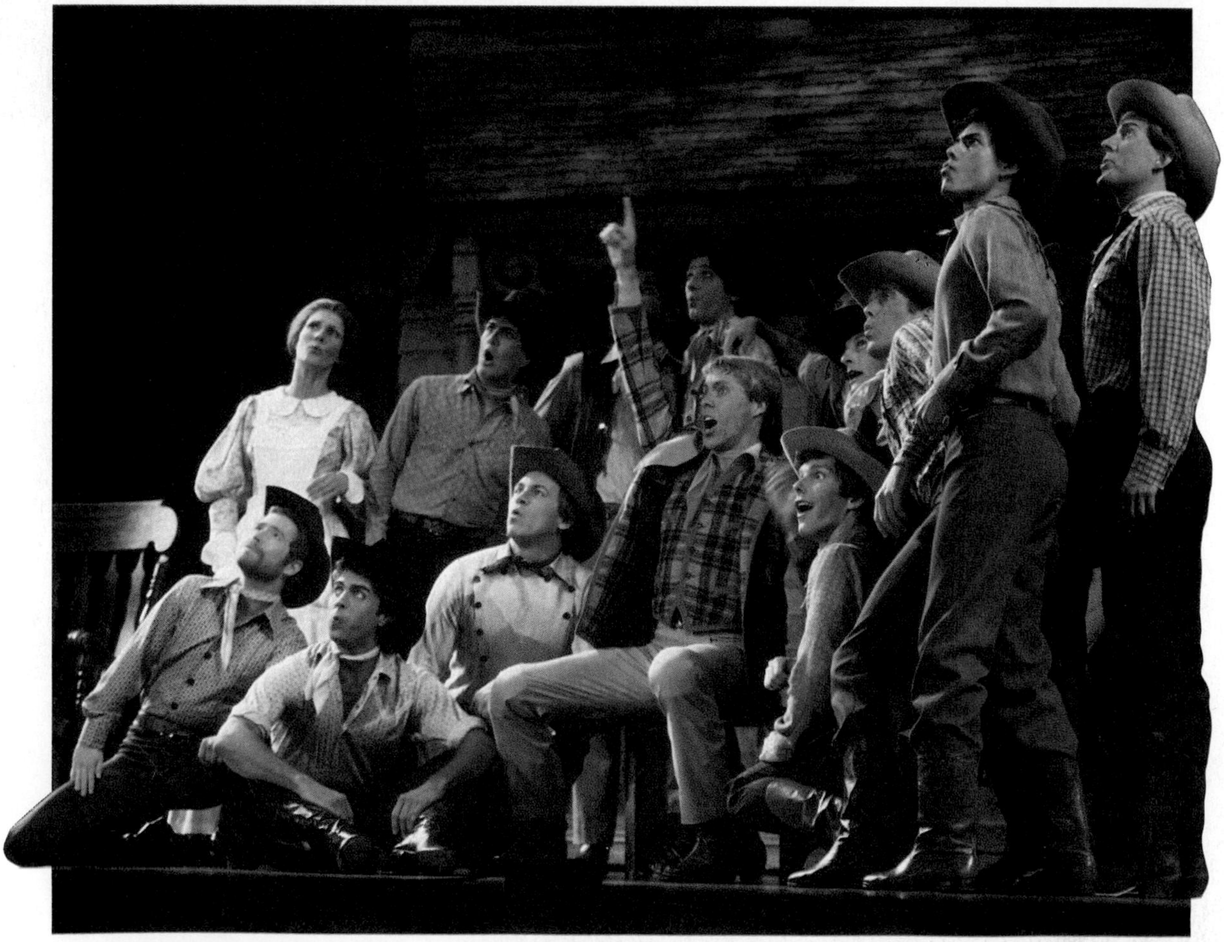

***Oklahoma***

*The Wiz*

American musical shows have gained enormous popularity worldwide.

*Godspell*

*Cats*

They are even performed in other languages.

# Test 5

Here are some songs that might be performed, either in the classroom or in public. Each song is useful in a different way. Read the descriptions, and then decide which song fits the description. Put the letter in the blank space.

A. Bye-Bye, Blues
B. Dona Dona
C. I Am a Pirate King
D. Sheep May Safely Graze
E. In a World of Music
F. I Got Rhythm
G. I Am a Great Musician

1. ________ A song that tells a story. It must be sung clearly and carefully, especially as it speeds up at the end.

2. ________ A song from a musical play. It has both solo and chorus parts, and introduces a colorful character.

3. ________ A song with long notes. It should be carefully sung in order to make smooth phrases.

4. ________ A comical song with several solos. It can be sung with stage movement to describe various instruments.

5. ________ A lively song by George Gershwin. It can be performed with rhythmic stage movements on important words.

6. ________ A beautiful concert-style song. It should be sung simply and as beautifully as possible.

7. ________ A song about making music. With or without movements it is a good song to share with an audience.

# Test 6

Here are three categories, A, B, and C. Each has words that describe a singing and performing style.

| A | B | C |
|---|---|---|
| Jazzy | Humorous | Lyrical |
| Accented | Dance-like | Calm |
| Cheerful | Lively | Smooth lines |
| Rhythmic | Full of motion | Quiet mood |

Here is a list of songs from your book. Choose the category that fits each song *best.* Put the letter of that category (A, B, or C) in the space next to the song title.

__________ The Twist

__________ Peace Like a River

__________ Ta-Ran-Ta-Ra

__________ In a World of Music

__________ Sheep May Safely Graze

__________ Dona Dona

__________ Country Style

__________ I Got Rhythm

__________ I Am a Great Musician

__________ Bonnie Doon

PRESENTING
I LIKE MUSIC
A THEME MUSICAL
By
CARMINO RAVOSA

I Like Music
10
7
Words and Music by Carmino Ravosa
Guitar:
G C D7 G
1. Solo
2. Chorus
3. Chorus
I like mu - sic, __ An-y kind of mu - sic! __
Am7 D7 G Am7 D7 G C
I like mu-sic, yes, I do. __ I like mu - sic, __
3rd time to Coda
D7 G Am7 D7
An-y kind of mu - sic! __ I like mu-sic, yes, I do. __
G C D7
__ Mu-sic can make _ me feel __ hap - py, __
G C
Mu-sic can make _ me sad. __ Mu-sic can make _ me sing __
D7 Am7 D7
__ and __ dance, _ Mu - sic can make _ me glad __
Am7 D7 rit. . . . G
that I like mu - sic, yes, I do. __

Student: I am music. I make the world weep, laugh, wonder, and worship.

Student: Music is one of our great material needs. We need food, clothing, shelter—and we need music!

Student: Singing makes the heartache easier, lifts the spirits, makes the work go faster.

Student: Singing makes us feel good. Even when we are sad, a song can make us feel better.

Speaker: People don't sing because they're happy . . . .

All: They're happy because they sing!

## People Don't Sing Because They're Happy

Words and Music by Carmino Ravosa

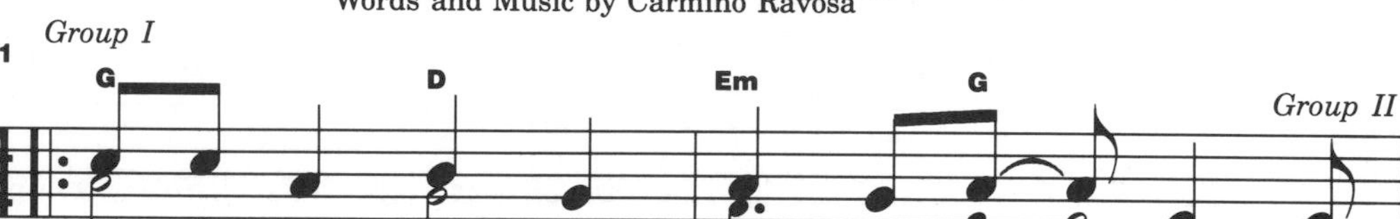


{ Peo - ple don't sing be - cause they're hap - py, they're
*You'll be hap - py ___*

hap-py be-cause they sing; Peo-ple don't sing be -
*when you sing, You know that you'll be*

cause they're hap - py, they're hap-py be-cause they sing!
*hap - py ___ when you sing!*

Full Chorus
B7
Em
Mak - ing mu - sic is sure to make you hap - py,
Em
A7
D7
Mak - ing mu - sic is sure to make you smile.
G
D
Em
G
Peo - ple don't sing be - cause they're hap - py, they're
C
G
Am7
D7
G
D
hap - py be - cause they sing; Peo - ple don't sing be -
Em
G
C
D7
G
cause they're hap - py, they're hap - py, be - cause they sing! Sing!

Student: We know music is good for us. Aldous Huxley said, "After silence, that which comes nearer to the inexpressible is music."

Student: Someone else once said, "Music is another planet."

Student: Goethe said, "A man should hear a little music, read a little poetry, and see a fine picture every day of his life."

Student: You can read a poem or look at a fine picture, but music is different. It isn't there unless somebody *makes* it. You have to sing it, play it, or dance it. You've got to really get into the music, pass the melody into the beat. (Begins snapping fingers)

Student: The beat! (picks up finger snaps) Do you know what rhythm is?

All: No, what?

Student: If you have to ask . . . . you haven't got it!

## You've Got to Get Into the Music

Words and Music by Carmino Ravosa

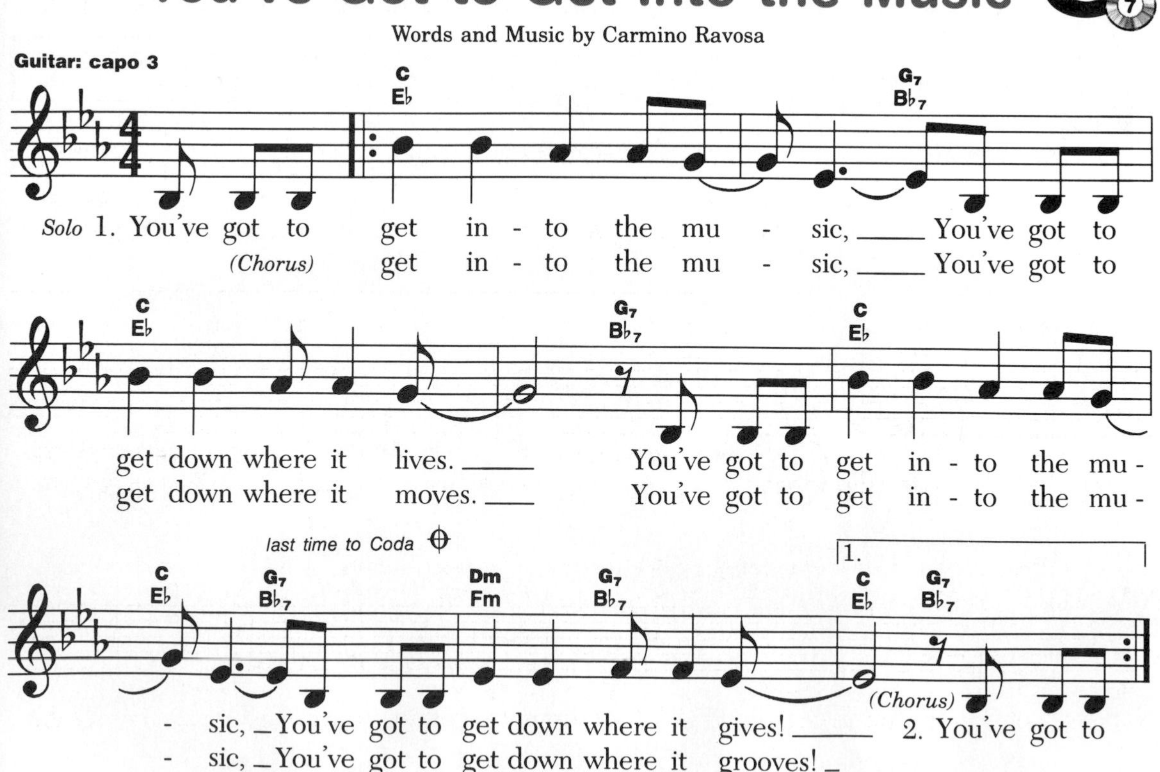

2.
C Eb Am Cm
(Solo)
— You've got to get to where the bass is play - in',
(Chorus 2nd time)
Am Cm D7 F7
get down to the beat; — You've got to get to where the
D7 F7 G7 Bb7
drum - mer's drum - min', - till it hits your feet! — You've got to
Solo 1st time
Chorus 2nd time
C Eb G7 Bb7 C Eb
get in - to the mu - sic, — You've got to get in - to that part. —
C Eb G7 Bb7 C Eb G7 Bb7
— You've got to get in - to the mu - .sic, — You've got to
1. 2.
Dm Fm G7 Bb7 C Eb C Eb G7 Bb7
(Chorus) (All)
get in - to the heart. — You've got to — You've got to
Dm Fm G7 Bb7 C Eb G7 Bb7 Dm Fm G7 Bb7 C Eb
get in - to the heart, — You've got to get in - to the heart. — Yeah!

Student: Now, wait a minute! The beat and the rhythm are important, but it is the melody that is most difficult to write. Haydn said, "The invention of a fine melody is a work of genius."

Student: Do you know, there are no books to tell you how to write a melody, or even what a good melody *is*. But you know one when you hear it.

Student: A famous composer once said, "If a man would know me, let him find me in my music."

Student: Heinrich Heine said, "Where words leave off, music begins."

Student: Words and music—rhythm and melody—Do you know what's missing?

All: Harmony!

Student: Right! Now, put it all together . . . and let's make music.

## Let's Make Music

Words and Music by Carmino Ravosa

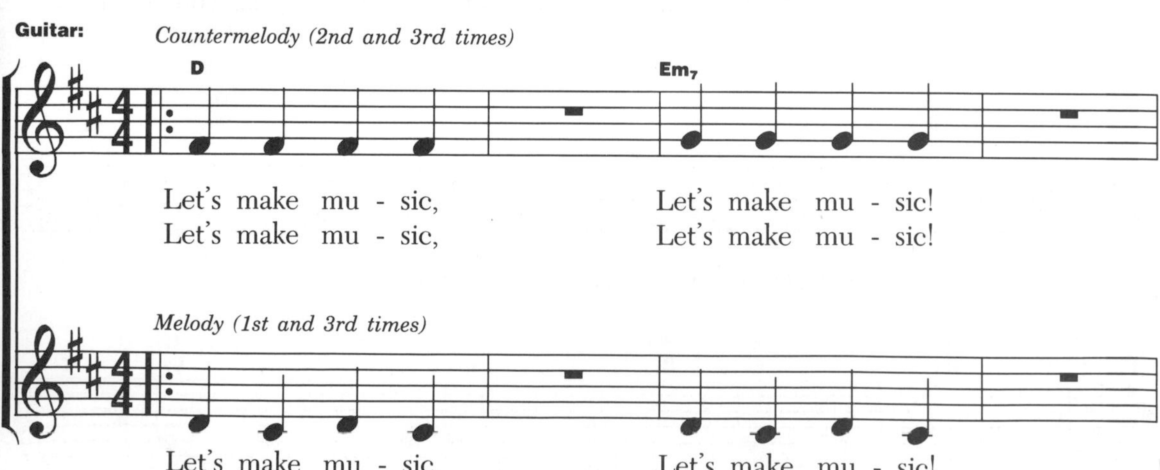

1.
D
G
A7
Let's make mu - sic, You and me.
Let's make love - ly Har - mo -
1.
Let's make mu - sic, You and me.
Let's make love - ly Har - mo -
2.
G
D
D7
ny. Come and sing a - long with
2.
ny. Let's not let this mel - o - dy get a - way from
E7
D
Em7
A7
D
(Em7 A7) D.C.
me; Let's make mu - sic, you and me!
D.C.
you and me; Let's make mu - sic, you and me!

Student: "Music is the shorthand of emotion." That's what Tolstoy said.

Student: Some say music is love in search of a word. Others say music is love itself.

Student: Everyone has a different opinion. But this we know. Music is in a continual state of *becoming.* Each person brings something different to a piece of music. Each person gets something different out of it.

Student: If there's music in us, we should express it. Oliver Wendell Holmes said, "Alas for those who never sing, but die with their music in them."

Student: If there's music in you, let it out!

# If There's Music in You

Guitar: capo 3

Words and Music by Carmino Ravosa

C
F
B♭
now don't you hide. Put all your doubts _ and fears a - side, You'll
1.
D.S.
(Chorus)
2.
D7
G7
G7
nev - er know _ un - less you've tried. If there's tried. ___
E
F♯m7
If there's mu - sic in ___ you let it out
B7
E
Let it sing or dance _ or let it shout. If there's
E
ril.
F♯m7
B7
E
mu - sic in ___ you let it out, let it out, let it out.

Student: I shot an arrow into the air,
It fell to earth, I know not where.

All: For so swiftly it flew the sight
Could not follow in its flight.

Student: I breathed a song into the air,
It fell to earth, I know not where.

All: For who has sight so keen and strong,
That it can follow the flight of song.

Student: Long, long afterward, in an oak,
I found the arrow, still unbroke.

All: And the song, from beginning to end,
I found again . . . .

Student: In the heart of a friend.

## I Am Music

Words and Music by Carmino Rav

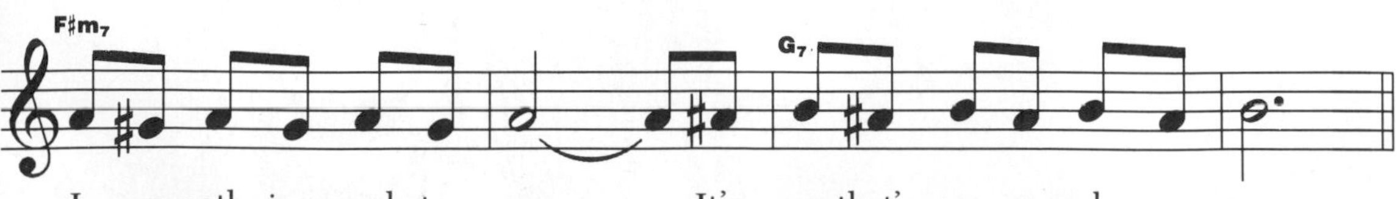

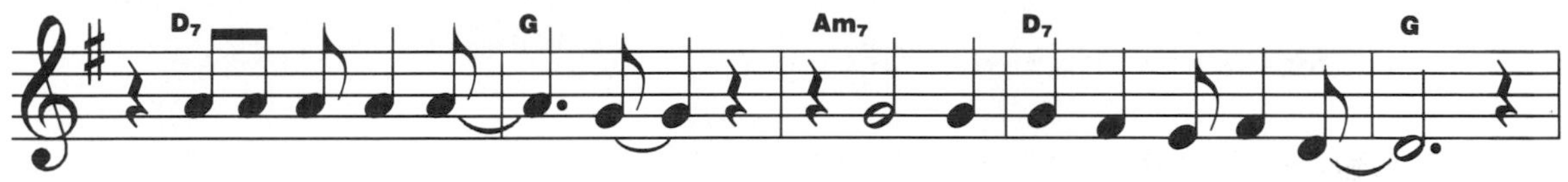


*Turn to "I Like Music," page 205, and finish the song:*

I like music, any kind of music,
I like music, yes I do!

Music can make me feel happy,
Music can make me sad.
Music can make me sing and dance,
Music can make me glad that

I like music, any kind of music,
I like music, yes I do.
I like music, any kind of music,
I like music, yes I do!

Jan 1 2 3 4 5 6
7 8 9 10 11 12 13 14 15
16 17 18 19 20 21 22 23 24
25 26 27 28 29 30 31
Jul 1 2 3 4 5 6
7 8 9 10 11 12 13 14 15
16 17 18 19 20 21 22 23 24
25 26 27 28 29 30 31
Feb 1 2 3 4 5 6
7 8 9 10 11 12 13 14 15
16 17 18 19 20 21 22 23 24
25 26 27 28
Aug 1 2 3 4 5 6
7 8 9 10 11 12 13 14 15
16 17 18 19 20 21 22 23 24
25 26 27 28 29 30 31
Mar 1 2 3 4 5 6
7 8 9 13 14 15
16 17 18 20 22 23 24
25 26 27 30 31
Sep 1 2 3 4 5 6
7 8 9 10 11 12 13 14 15
16 17 18 19 20 21 22 23 24
25 26 27 28 29 30
Apr 1 2 3 4 5 6
7 8 9 10 11 12 13 14 15
16 17 18 19 20 21 22 23 24
25 26 27 28 29 30
Oct 1 2 3 4 5 6
7 8 9 10 11 12 13 14 15
16 17 18 19 20 21 22 23 24
25 26 27 28 29 30 31
May 1 2 3 4 5 6
7 8 9 10 11 12 13 14 15
16 17 18 19 20 21 22 23 24
25 26 27 28 29 30
Nov 1 2 3 4 5 6
7 8 9 10 11 12 13 14 15
16 17 18 19 20 21 22 23 24
25 26 27 28 29 30
Jun 1 2 3 4 5 6
7 8 9 10 11 12 13 14 15
16 17 18 19 20 21 22 23 24
25 26 27 28 29 30
Dec 1 2 3 4 5 6
7 8 9 10 11 12 13 14 15
16 17 18 19 20 21 22 23 24
25 26 27 28 29 30 31

## SECTION IV

# SING AND CELEBRATE

## YOUNG CITIZENS OF THE WORLD

"I Am But a Small Voice" is a song to sing anytime, but you might want to save it for a special occasion!

## Barter

Life has loveliness to sell,
  All beautiful and splendid things,
Blue waves whitened on a cliff,
  Soaring fire that sways and sings,
And children's faces looking up
Holding wonder like a cup.

Life has loveliness to sell,
  Music like a curve of gold,
Scent of pine trees in the rain,
  Eyes that love you, arms that hold,
And for your spirit's still delight,
Holy thoughts that star the night.

Spend all you have for loveliness,
  Buy it and never count the cost;
For one white singing hour of peace
  Count many a year of strife well lost,
And for a breath of ecstasy
Give all you have been, or could be.

*Sara Teasdale*

# Our National Anthem

Our national anthem is an expression of victory over enemies of freedom.

Words by Francis Scott Key  Music by John Stafford Smith

1. Oh, __ say! can you see, by the dawn's ear - ly light, What so
2. On the shore, dim - ly seen through the mists of the deep, Where the
3. Oh, __ thus be it ever when __ free men shall stand Be -

proud - ly we hailed at the twi - light's last gleam - ing, Whose broad
foe's haugh - ty host in dread si - lence re - pos - es, What is
tween their loved homes and the war's des - o - la - tion! Blest with

stripes and bright stars, through the per - il - ous fight, O'er the
that which the breeze, o'er the tow - er - ing steep, As it
vic - t'ry and peace, may the heav'n - res - cued land Praise the

ram - parts we watched were so gal - lant - ly stream - ing? And the
fit - ful - ly blows, half con - ceals, half dis - clos - es? Now it
Pow'r that hath made and pre - served us a na - tion! Then __

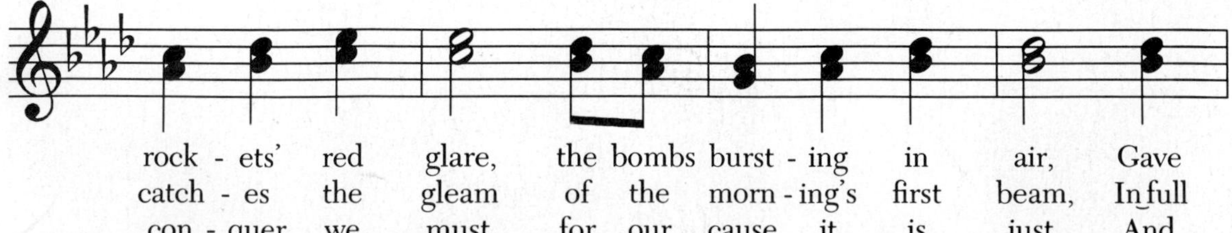

rock - ets' red glare, the bombs burst - ing in air, Gave
catch - es the gleam of the morn - ing's first beam, In full
con - quer we must, for our cause it is just, And

proof through the night that our flag was still there. Oh,
glo - ry re - flected now shines on the stream; 'Tis the
this be our motto: "In God is our trust!" And the
say, does that Star-Span-gled Ban - ner yet wave O'er the
Star-Span - gled Ban - ner, oh, long may it wave O'er the
Star-Span - gled Ban - ner in tri - umph shall wave O'er the
land of the free and the home of the brave?
land of the free and the home of the brave!
land of the free and the home of the brave!

# From Sea to Shining Sea

## America, the Beautiful

Words by Katharine Lee Bates     Music by Samuel A. Ward

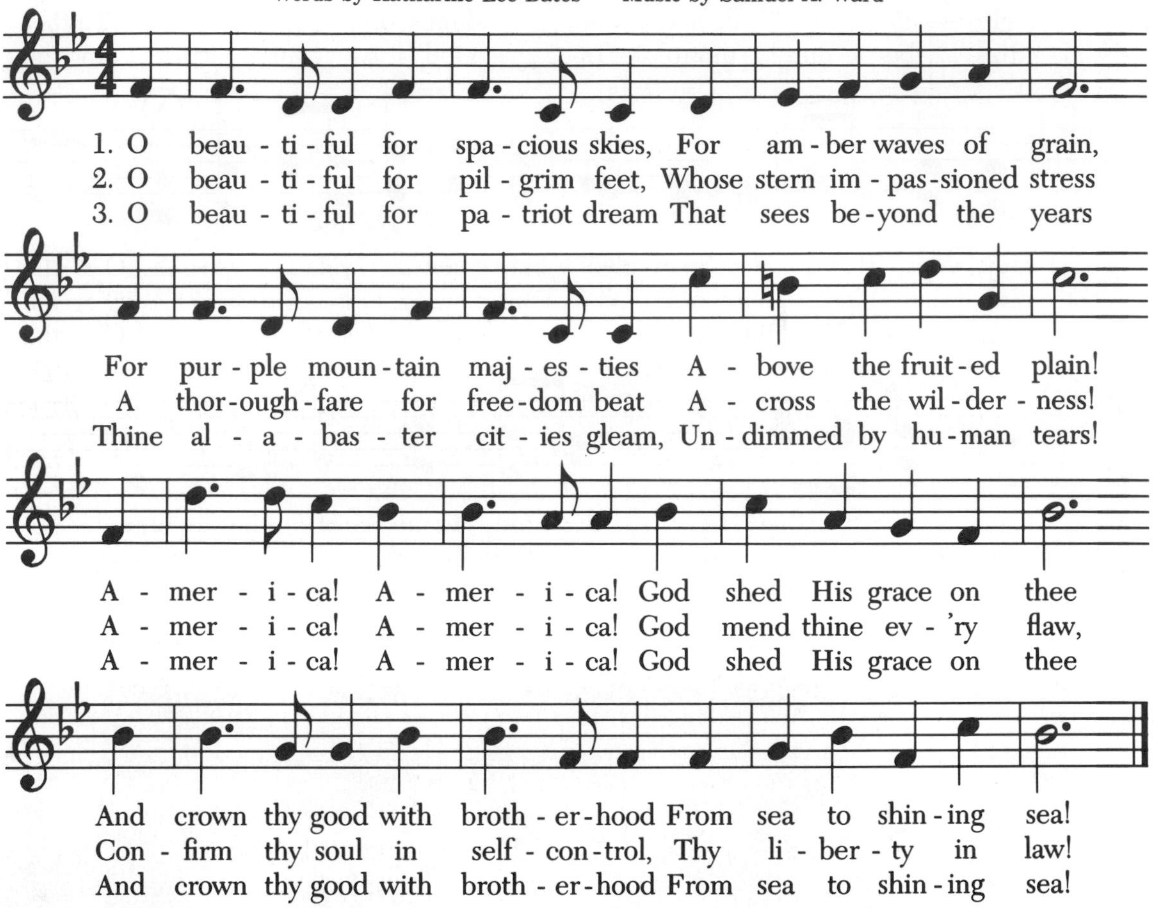

1. O beau - ti - ful for spa - cious skies, For am - ber waves of grain,
2. O beau - ti - ful for pil - grim feet, Whose stern im - pas - sioned stress
3. O beau - ti - ful for pa - triot dream That sees be - yond the years

For pur - ple moun - tain maj - es - ties A - bove the fruit - ed plain!
A thor - ough - fare for free - dom beat A - cross the wil - der - ness!
Thine al - a - bas - ter cit - ies gleam, Un - dimmed by hu - man tears!

A - mer - i - ca! A - mer - i - ca! God shed His grace on thee
A - mer - i - ca! A - mer - i - ca! God mend thine ev - 'ry flaw,
A - mer - i - ca! A - mer - i - ca! God shed His grace on thee

And crown thy good with broth - er - hood From sea to shin - ing sea!
Con - firm thy soul in self - con - trol, Thy li - ber - ty in law!
And crown thy good with broth - er - hood From sea to shin - ing sea!

# Let Freedom Ring

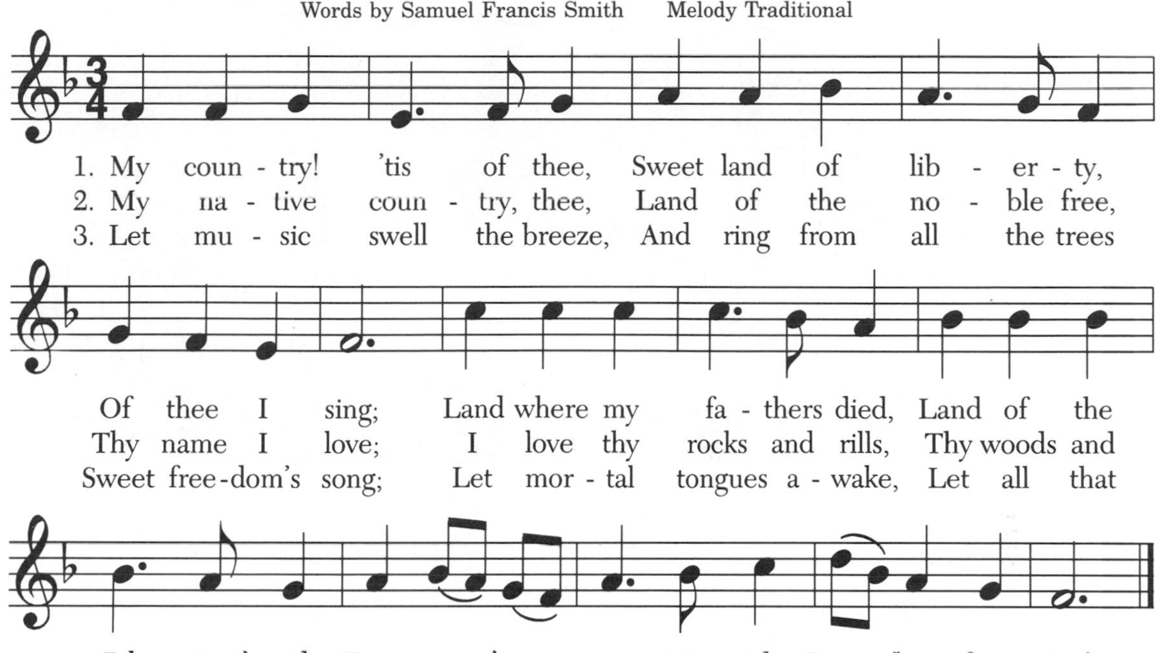


4. Our father's God, to Thee, Author of liberty,  
To Thee we sing;  
Long may our land be bright with Freedom's holy light  
Protect us by Thy might, Great God, our King!

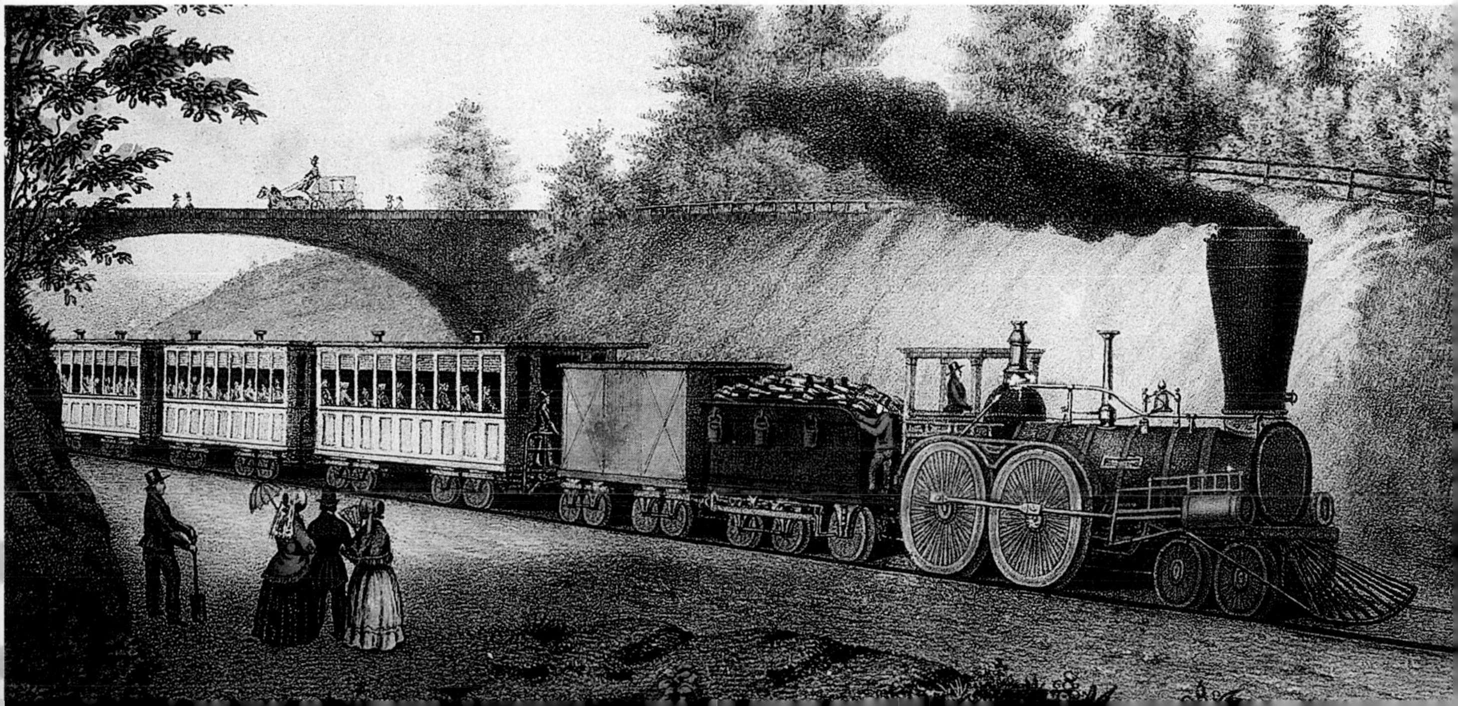

# AUTUMN COLORS

Here is a Halloween song that tells about the warm colors and the cold chill of the autumn season.

Words and Music by Jean Riddle

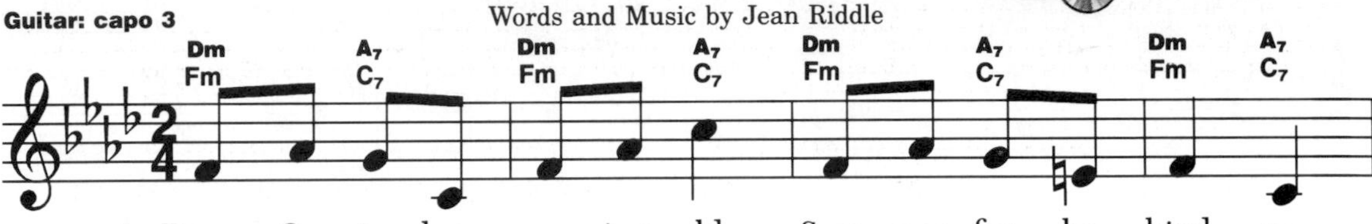


1. Brown Oc - to - ber grow - ing old, Sum - mer far be - hind us;
2. Hands and toes be - gin to freeze, Chil - ly winds are sigh - ing;
3. Prowl - ing in the dark of night When the ghosts are wak - ing;

All the leaves are red and gold Hal - low - een will find us
Some - one cries, he thinks he sees Owls and witch - es fly - ing
Quiv - er - ing with cold and fright, Shiv - er - ing and shak - ing,

Walk - ing in the au - tumn cold; May - be we'll see it soon:
Out a - cross the au - tumn trees; May - be we'll see it soon:
How we need your sil - ver light! May - be we'll see it soon:

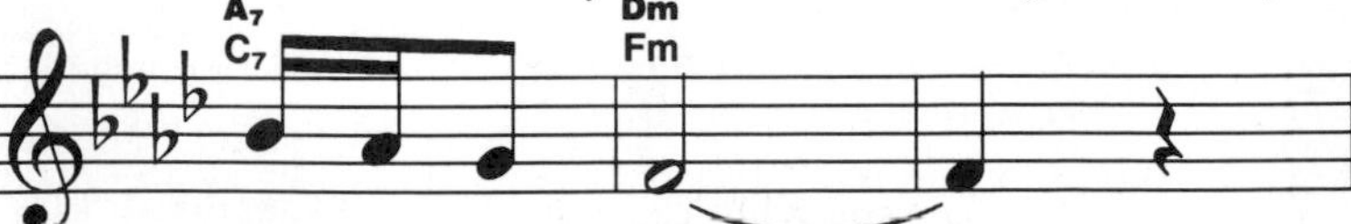


Hal - low - een moon. ______
Hal - low - een moon. ______
Hal - low - een moon. ______

# Harvest Time

Harvest time in the fall is traditionally a time of feasting and celebrating in many countries. In America, we mark the passing of the growing season with the feast of Thanksgiving.

# FESTIVAL OF LIGHTS

The celebration of Chanukah, the Jewish Festival of Lights, takes place on late fall dates that vary from year to year.

**Guitar: capo 5**

Jewish Folk Song    English Words by Judith Eisenstein

Am / Dm

O Cha - nu - kah, O Cha - nu - kah, come light the me - no - rah.
Let's __ have a par - ty, we'll all dance the ho - rah.

Am / Dm — E7 / A7 — Am / Dm

Gath - er round the ta - ble, we'll give you a treat,

Am / Dm — E7 / A7 — Am / Dm

Shin - ing tops to play with and pan - cakes to eat;

Am / Dm — Dm / Gm — Am / Dm

And while we are play - ing, The can - dles are burn - ing __ low,

Am / Dm — Dm / Gm — Am / Dm — Dm / Gm

One for each night, they __ shed a sweet light to re -

1. Am / Dm — E7 / A7 — Am / Dm

mind us of days long a - go,

2. Am / Dm — E7 / A7 — Am / Dm

mind us of days long a - go.

From *Gateways To Jewish Song* collected and translated by Judith Eisenstein. Used by permission.

## Lighting the Menorah

A favorite part of the holiday is the lighting of the candles of the menorah, one candle on each of the eight nights of Chanukah.

# Around About Chanukah

Words and Music by David Eddleman

Accompany this round with a rhythm pattern on the tambourine.

Bells, Recorder, Keyboard

# A Song for Snowy Weather

Some parts of our country never see snow. But this is a favorite winter song even where the sun shines all year.

Play this countermelody with "Winter Wonderland":

Let us walk in the white snow
  In a soundless space;
With footsteps quiet and slow
  At a tranquil pace
    Under veils of white lace.

We shall walk in velvet shoes:
    Wherever we go
Silence will fall like dews
    On white silencc bclow.
    We shall walk in the snow.

*from "Velvet Shoes"*
*by Elinor Wylie*

# A Holiday Tradition

## We Wish You a Merry Christmas

English Carol

1. We wish you a mer-ry Christ-mas, We wish you a mer-ry Christ-mas,
2. Now bring us some fig-gy pud-ding, Now bring us some fig-gy pud-ding,

We wish you a mer-ry Christ-mas, And a hap-py New Year!
Now bring us some fig-gy pud-ding, And bring it out here.

3. We won't go until we get some . . .
So bring some out here.

4. We wish you a merry Christmas . . .
And a happy New Year!

Bells or Keyboard

Descant

# A Beloved Carol

# A French Carol

## Bring a Torch, Jeannette, Isabella

17th Cent. French Carol Arranged by Linda Williams

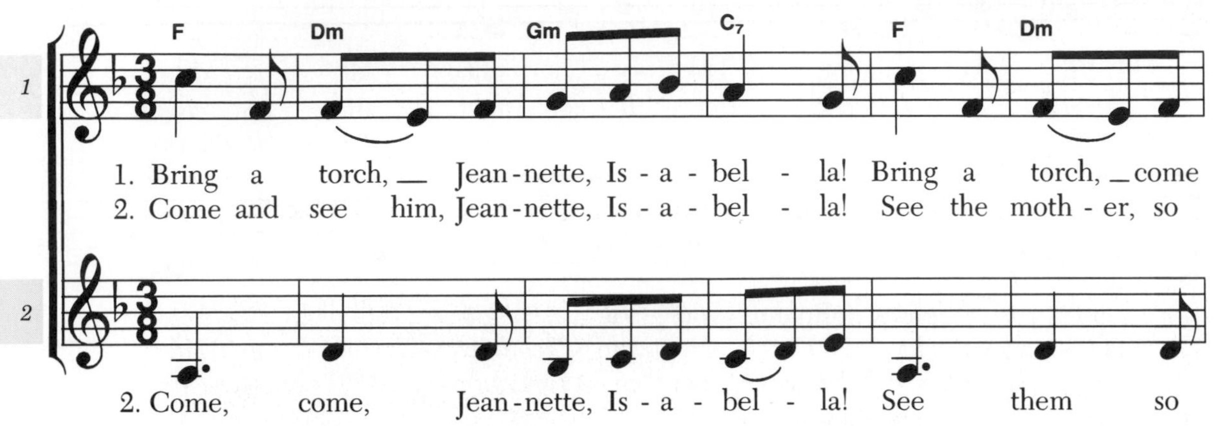

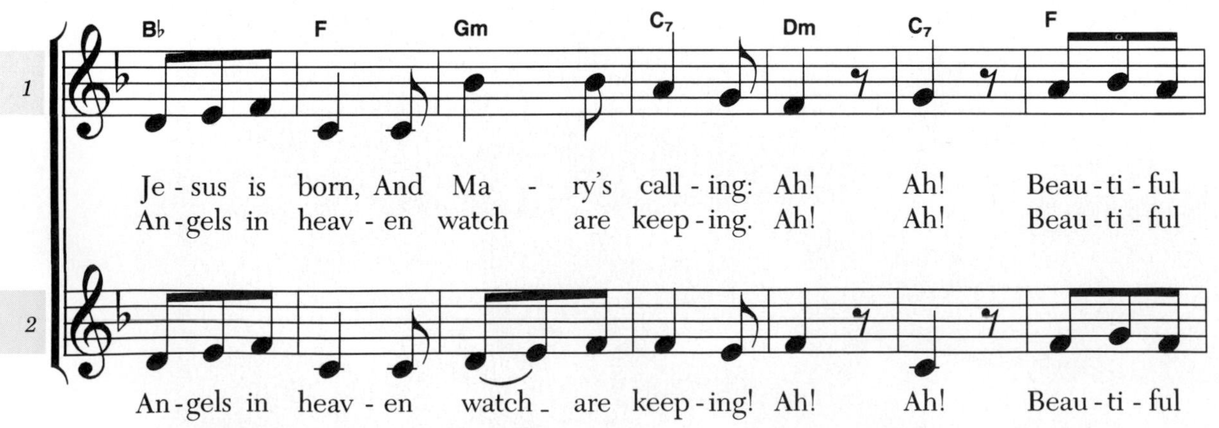

This traditional carol from France is a favorite in many countries of the world. The lower voices sing a harmony part that is like another melody.

# From England

This English carol has a second part that is like a separate melody.

2. They looked up and saw a star Shining in the East beyond them afar,
And to the earth it gave great light, And so it continued both day and night.
*Refrain*

## A Chilly Round

The sound of a cold winter wind blows through this round. The repeated "wind and snow" sounds as chilly as this old etching looks.

### Wind and Snow

Words and Music by Joseph Fisch

I

Win - ter, win - ter, ice on the win - dow, Wind and snow, cold and blow - ing

II

wind and snow. Can - dles glow - ing, light - ing a win - ter hol - i - day.

III

Come out of the wind and snow, By the warm fire ___ come and stay.

# CHRISTMAS BELLS

This carol has a countermelody for the *higher* voices.

## Ding-Dong Merrily on High

French Carol English Words by G. R. Woodward Arranged by Linda Williams

*Countermelody*

G D7 G C D7

3. Ding-dong mer-ri-ly, in heav'n the

*Melody*

1.,3. Ding-dong! mer-ri-ly on high in heav'n the bells are
2. Pray you, du-ti-ful-ly prime your mat-in chime, ye

G D7 G

bells__ are__ ring-ing. Ding-dong ver-i-ly, on

ring - ing. Ding-dong! ver-i-ly the sky is
ring - ers. May you beau-ti-ful-ly rime your

C D7 G

high the an - gel__ sing-ing. Glo - ri -

riv'n with an-gel sing - ing. Glo - - -
eve-time song, ye sing - ers.

**ANGEL PLAYING VIOLIN** ***Melozzo da Forli***

Melozzo da Forli, *Angel Playing Violin*, Vatican, Art Resource, New York

**ANGEL PLAYING THE LUTE** ***Melozzo da Forli***

Melozzo da Forli, *Angelo che suona il liuto*, Rome. Scala/Art Resource

# Green Leaves for Christmas

This beautiful carol has been a favorite for many centuries.

## The Holly and the Ivy

12 8

Traditional English Carol    Arranged by Mary Hoffman

Guitar: capo 3

C Eb

1. The holly and the ivy, when they are both full

G7 Bb7 C Eb G7 Bb7 C Eb G7 Bb7

grown, of all the trees that are in the wood, the holly bears the

C Eb

crown; The rising of the sun, and the running of the

G7 Bb7 C Eb G7 Bb7 C Eb G7 Bb7

deer; The playing of the merry pipes, sweet singing in the

C Eb C Eb

choir. 2. The holly bears a blossom, as white as lily

holly bears a berry, as red as any

II (Tacet verse 2, sing verse 3)

choir. 2. (Tacet)

holly bears a berry, as red as any

C
E♭
F
A♭
C
E♭
G7
B♭7
flow'r, And Mar - y bore a ba - by boy, and laid him in a
blood, And Mar - y bore a ba - by boy, to do poor sin - ners
blood, And Mar - y bore a ba - by boy to do poor sin - ners
C
E♭
p
(Second time f)
bow'r.
good.
The ris - ing of the sun, and the run - ning of the
(Second time only)
good. The ris - ing of the sun, and the run - ning of the
G7
B♭7
C
E♭
G7
B♭7
1.
C
E♭
G7
B♭7
deer; the play - ing of the mer - ry pipes, sweet sing - ing in the
1.
deer; the play - ing of the mer - ry pipes, sweet
C
E♭
2. G7
B♭7
C
E♭
choir. 3. The
sing - ing in the choir.
2.
3. The
sing - ing in the choir.

# A New Song for the Holidays

A young student in an Illinois grade school wrote a poem about the holiday season. Her music teacher like the poem so much that she set it to music.

## Sounds of Christmas

Music by D. L. Brubaker    Based on a poem by Jenny Delaney

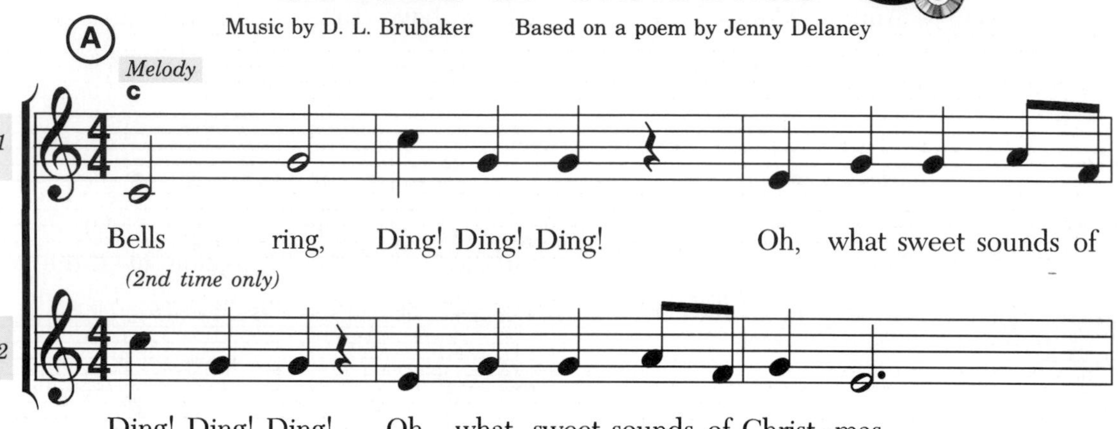


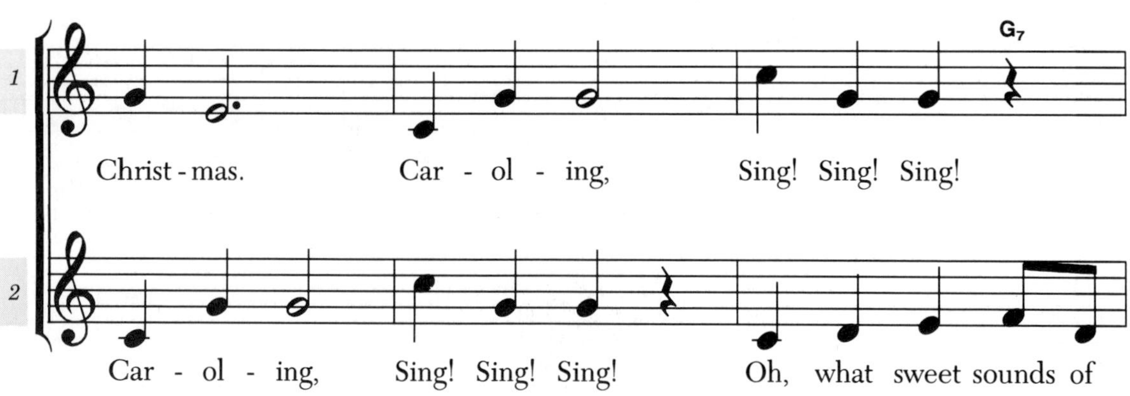


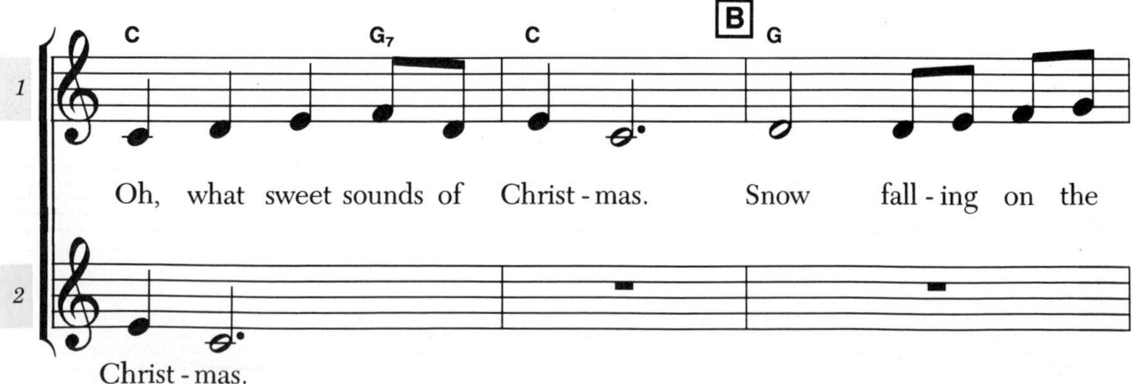

C
F
G7
1
trees, Ping! Ping! Chil - dren play - ing in the snow.
2
Snow fall - ing on the trees, Ping! Ping! Chil - dren play - ing in the
C
1
Hear the laugh - ter the sea - son brings. Hear the sweet sounds of
2
snow. Hear the laugh - ter the sea - son brings.
C
G7
C
1
Christ - mas. Oh, what sweet sounds of Christ-mas.
2
Hear the sweet sounds of Christ-mas. Oh, what sweet sounds of
C
1.
3
1
3
(2nd time starts here)
2
Christ - mas. Bells ring,
2.
C
G7
C
1
Oh, what sweet sounds of Christ - mas.
2
Oh, what sweet sounds of Christ - mas.

# A Very Old Carol

"Gabriel's Message" is an ancient Basque carol that is still often sung in England. Although it mentions Christmas, it is actually a carol for a Christian holy day that comes in the early springtime.

After you learn the song, you may want to add some simple percussion parts. The small hand drum, finger cymbals, and tambourine are typical of medieval and renaissance music.

## Gabriel's Message

Basque Carol   Words by Sabine Baring-Gould

## Percussion Parts

These parts may be used one at a time with different verses of the song, or all at once. You may want to design your own routine.

Small Hand Drum (softly)

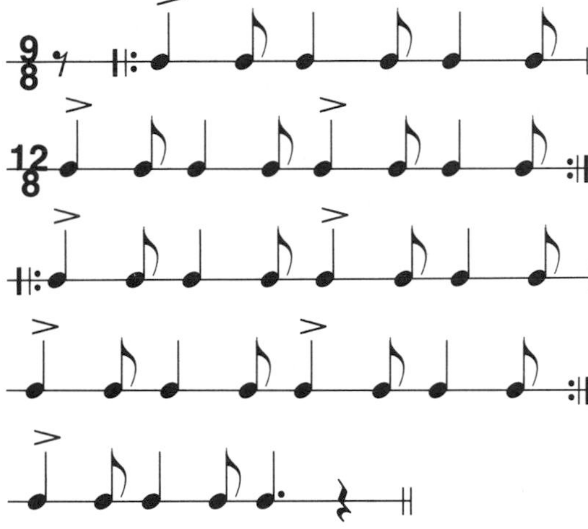

Finger Cymbals (♩⌒: "let ring")

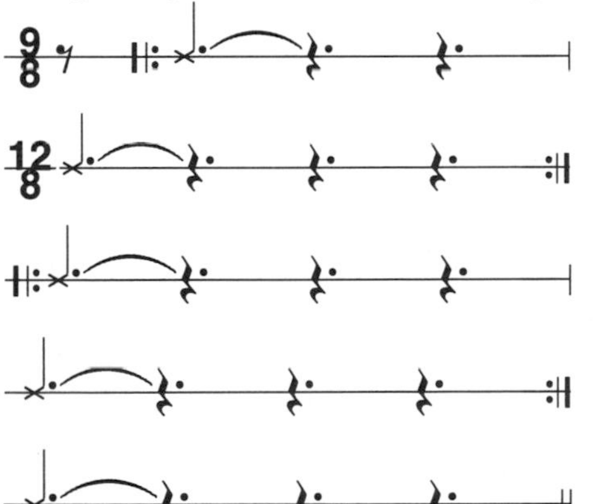

Tambourine (very soft)

Play on every beat throughout, except on the last beat of the song.

# Be My Valentine

This old song can be decorated with a little countermelody. Play it on the bells, keyboard, or any other melody instrument.

Voice, Bells, Recorder, Keyboard
Love that mel - o - dy,
Oh, those mem - o - ries,
How we'd play a - round,
Yes, we could sing!
They were dear - er then,
It was too bad that we part - ed.
A tear,
oh, hear,
Love that heart of my heart.
(don't sing high F)

## A Song About Love

As you sing this song, you will see that the words are about a special kind of love.

**ANGEL MUSICIAN** *Rosso Fiorentino*

# A Change of Seasons

This beautiful Spanish-American song describes the coming of spring. Sing *"La primavera"* ("Springtime") in both Spanish and English.

Many Spanish songs use "Ay" the way "Oh" is used in English.

## Springtime

*(La primavera)*

**Guitar: capo 3**

Spanish Folk Song from California — English Words by Linda Williams

C / E♭

At last comes the spring, the sea - son so ___ full of
*Ya vie - ne la pri - ma - ve - ra, sem - bran - do*
yah vyeh - neh lah pree - mah - veh - rah sehm - brahn - doh

$G_7$ / $B♭_7$ — C / E♭

flow - ers, so ___ full of flow - ers, ay, ay! And now ev - 'ry
*flo - res, sem - bran - do flo - res, ay, ay! Y ya los cam -*
floh - rehs sehm - brahn - doh floh - rehs ahee ahee ee yah lohs kahm -

C / E♭ — $G_7$ / $B♭_7$

field is paint - ed so ___ man - y col - ors, so ___ man - y
*pos se‿es - mal - tan de ___ mil co - lo - res, de ___ mil co -*
pohs sai‿ehs - mahl - tahn deh meel koh - loh - rehs deh meel koh -

C / E♭ — F / A♭ — G / B♭ — C / E♭

col - ors. ___ Song - birds are sing - ing, ___
*lo - res. ___ Can - tan las a - ves, ___*
loh - rehs kahn - tahn lahs ah - vehs

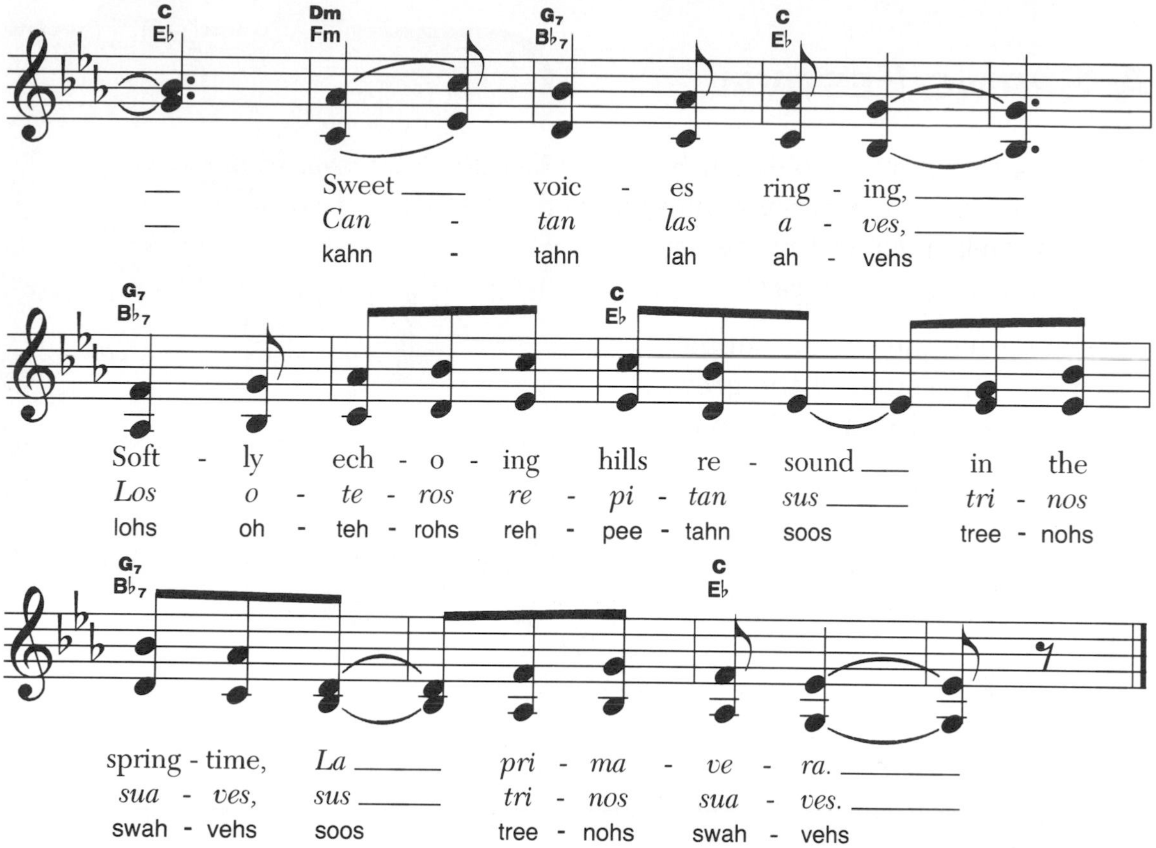

C Dm G7 C
E♭ Fm B♭7 E♭

— Sweet ___ voic - es ring - ing, ___

— *Can - tan las a - ves,* ___

kahn - tahn lah ah - vehs

G7 C
B♭7 E♭

Soft - ly ech - o - ing hills re - sound ___ in the

*Los o - te - ros re - pi - tan sus ___ tri - nos*

lohs oh - teh - rohs reh - pee - tahn soos tree - nohs

G7 C
B♭7 E♭

spring - time, *La* ___ *pri - ma - ve - ra.* ___

*sua - ves, sus* ___ *tri - nos sua - ves.* ___

swah - vehs soos tree - nohs swah - vehs

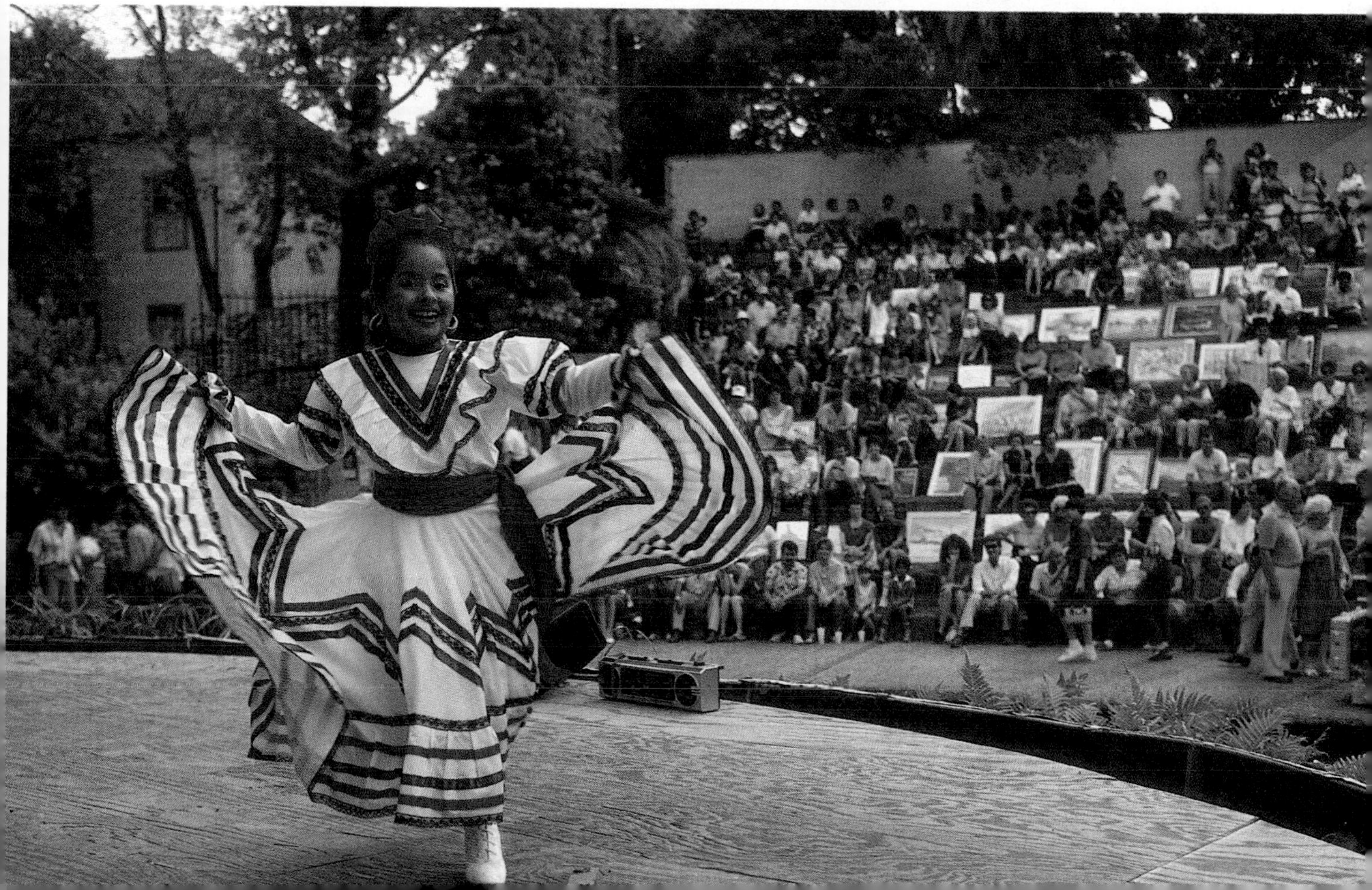

## A Spring Festival

Purim is a traditional Jewish holiday that comes in springtime. Children dress in costumes and make as much noise as they possibly can!

This song for the Purim holiday describes the sound of the *greger,* a hand-held spinning noisemaker that goes "rash, rash, rash."

## Purim Day

Traditional Melody Hebrew Verse by L. Kipnis English Words by Dav ben Shmuel

# A Popular Spring Song

## April Showers

Words by B. G. DeSylva  Music by Louis Silvers

## SECTION V

# READING MUSIC

LINEAR MODE SYMPHONY NO. 1
*Marcus Uzilevsky*

# A Pentatonic Song

Can you tell if this song is in major or in minor?

## Leatherwing Bat

Traditional

1. "Hi," said the lit - tle lea-ther-wing bat, "I'll tell you the rea - son that,

The rea - son that I fly by night Is be-cause I lost my heart's de-light."

**REFRAIN**

How - dy, dow - dy did-dle - o - day, How - dy, dow - dy did-dle - o - day,

How - dy, dow - dy did-dle - o - day, How - dy, dow - dy did-dle - o - day.

2. "Hi," said the blackbird, sitting on a chair,
"Once I courted a lady fair;
She proved fickle and turned her back,
And ever since then I've dressed in black." *Refrain*

3. "Hi," said the woodpecker, sitting in the grass,
"Once I courted a bonny lass;
She proved fickle and from me fled,
And ever since then my head's been red." *Refrain*

4. "Hi," said the greenfinch as he flew,
"I loved one that proved untrue;
And since she will no more be seen,
Every spring I change to green." *Refrain*

A Two-Part Song
Watch the dynamics in this song. They help tell the story.
Farmer Jacob
12
9
Hungarian Folk Song
Melody
f
mf
Farm - er Ja - cob had a bil - ly goat, 'Till a wolf de - voured him, sil - ly goat! Then he ate farm - er's old nan - ny goat, Now the farm - er has - n't a - ny goat!
Bil - ly goat, sil - ly goat! Then he ate the farm - er's nan - ny goat, Now the farm - er has - n't a - ny goat!

# CONDUCTING $\frac{3}{4}$

Can you sing and conduct at the same time?

## Farewell to Tarwathie

Folk Song from Scotland

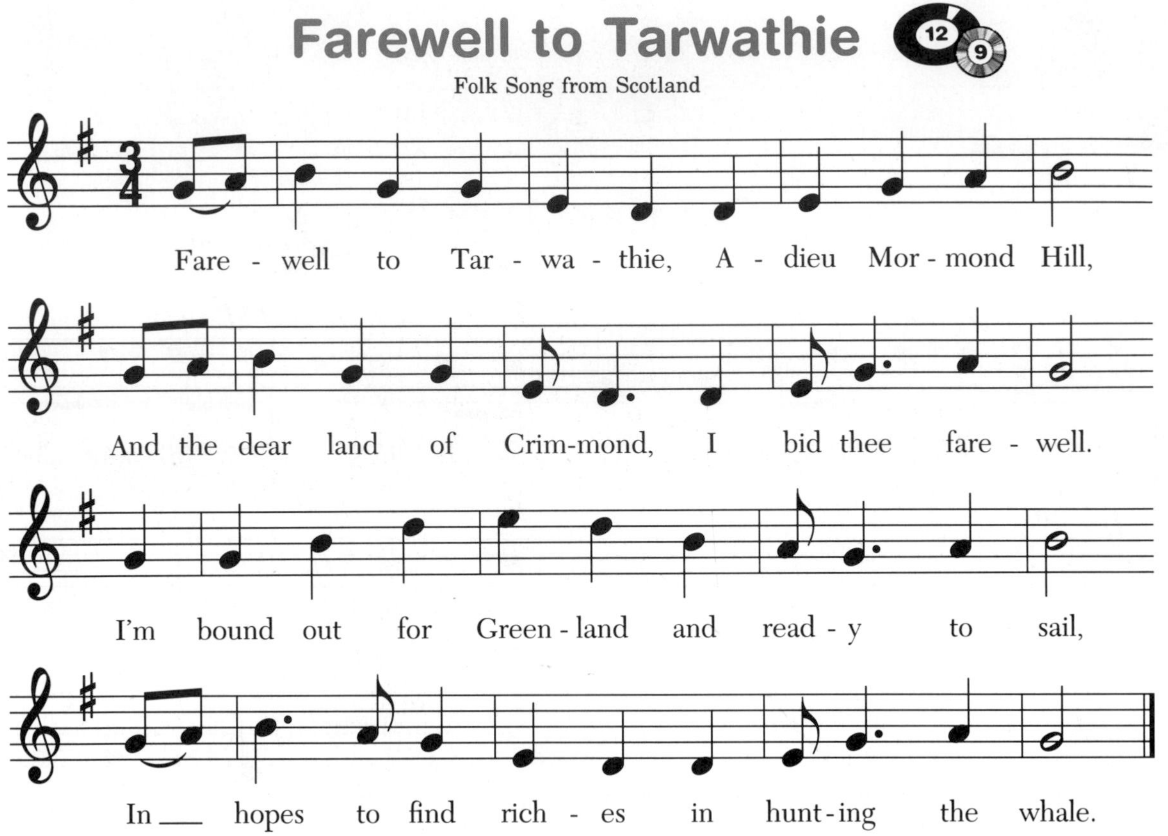


2. Farewell to my comrades for a while I must part,
And likewise the dear lass who first won my heart,
The cold coast of Greenland my heart will not chill,
The longer the absence the more loving she'll feel.

3. Our ship is well rigged and she's ready to sail,
The crew, they are anxious to follow the whale.
Where the icebergs do float and the stormy winds blow,
Where the land and the ocean is covered with snow.

4. The cold coast of Greenland is barren and bare,
No seedling nor harvest is ever known there,
And the birds here sing sweetly in mountain and vale,
But there's no bird in Greenland to sing to the whale.

# A Ballad from England

Here is a story of a fox and his family.

## The Fox

Folk Song from England

2. At last he came to a farmer's yard,
Where the ducks and geese were all afeared.
"The best of you all shall grease my beard,
Before I leave the town, oh!
Town, oh! Town, oh!" *(repeat lines 3 and 4)*

3. He took the gray goose by the neck,
He laid a duck across his back,
And heeded not their quack! quack! quack!
With the legs all dangling down, oh!
Down, oh! Down, oh!" *(repeat lines 3 and 4)*

4. Then old mother Slipper Slopper jumped
out of bed
And out of the window she popped her head,
Crying, "John, John! The gray goose is dead,
And the fox is over the down, oh!
Down, oh! Down, oh!" *(repeat lines 3 and 4)*

5. Then John got up to the top of the hill,
And blew his horn both loud and shrill,
"Blow on," said Reynard, "your music still,
Whilst I trot home to my den, oh!
Den, oh! Den, oh!" *(repeat lines 3 and 4)*

# A Sad Story

**Do the words of this song make any pictures in your mind?**

## Barb'ry Allen

Folk Song from Great Britain

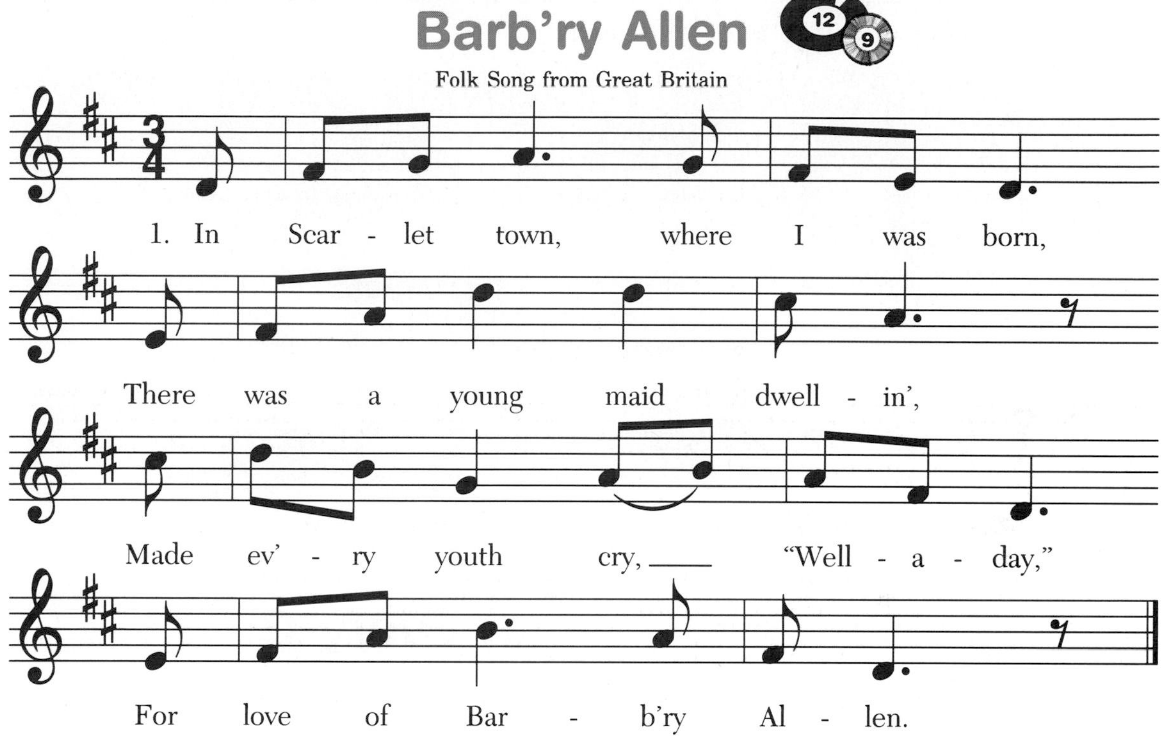


2. 'Twas in the merry month of May,
When green buds they were swellin',
Sweet William on his deathbed lay,
For love of Barb'ry Allen.

3. He sent his servant to the town,
To the place where she was dwellin',
Cried, "Master bids you come to him,
If your name be Barb'ry Allen."

4. Then slowly, slowly she got up,
And slowly went she nigh him,
And when she pulled the curtains back
Said, "Young man, I think you're dyin'."

5. "Oh, yes, I'm sick, I'm very sick,
And I never will be better,
Until I have the love of one,
The love of Barb'ry Allen."

6. Then lightly tripped she down the stairs,
She trembled like an aspen.
'Tis vain, 'tis vain, my dear young man,
To long for Barb'ry Allen.

7. She walked out in the green, green fields,
She heard his death bells knellin'.
And every stroke they seemed to say;
"Hard-hearted Barb'ry Allen."

8. "Oh, father, father, dig my grave,
Go dig it deep and narrow.
Sweet William died for me today;
I'll die for him tomorrow."

9. They buried her in the old churchyard,
Sweet William's grave was nigh her,
And from his heart grew a red, red rose,
And from her heart a brier.

10. They grew and grew o'er the old church wall,
Till they could grow no higher,
Until they tied a lover's knot,
The red rose and the brier.

## Singing a Round

You can sing this song as a round, or as a **quodlibet,** each group repeating one line over and over.

## Welcome, Welcome, Every Guest

Traditional Round

Wel-come, wel-come, ev - 'ry guest, Wel-come to our mu - sic fest,

Mu - sic is our on - ly __ cheer, Fills both soul and _ rav - ished ear,

Sa - cred muse, _ teach us the road, Sweet-est notes to __ be ex-plored,

Soft - ly swell the trem - bling _ air, To __ com-plete our _ con - cert fare.

Courtesy of Sacred Harp Publishing Co., Inc.

# THE GYPSY LIFE

**Why did the lady run away with the gypsies?**

## The Wraggle-Taggle Gypsies

Old English Ballad

3. It was late last night when my lord came home,
   Inquiring for his lady, O!
   The servants said on ev'ry hand,
   "She's gone with the wraggle-taggle gypsies, O!"

4. "Come, saddle to me my milk-white steed,
   And go and seek my pony, O!
   That I may ride and seek my bride,
   Who is gone with the wraggle-taggle gypsies, O!"

5. Then he rode high, and he rode low,
   He rode through wood and copses, too.
   Until he came to an open field,
   And there he espied his a-lady, O!

# Two Versions of a Song

Both these versions are **parodies** of a well-known song.

## Little Tommy Tinker

Traditional Round

### Version 1

Ti - ny Tom-my Tink-er was en-sconced up - on a clink-er and com-

menced to lac-ri-mate, "Ma-ter! Ma-ter! See me in my poor, pa-thet-ic state!"
May-tehr May-tehr

## Little Tom Tinker

Traditional Round

### Version 2

bus-tive, did la-ment, "Fe-male par - ent! I'm such a pit-e-ous gent!"

# A Song About a Soldier

Why are some of these notes in a different color?

## One Morning in May 

Folk Song from the Appalachian Mountains

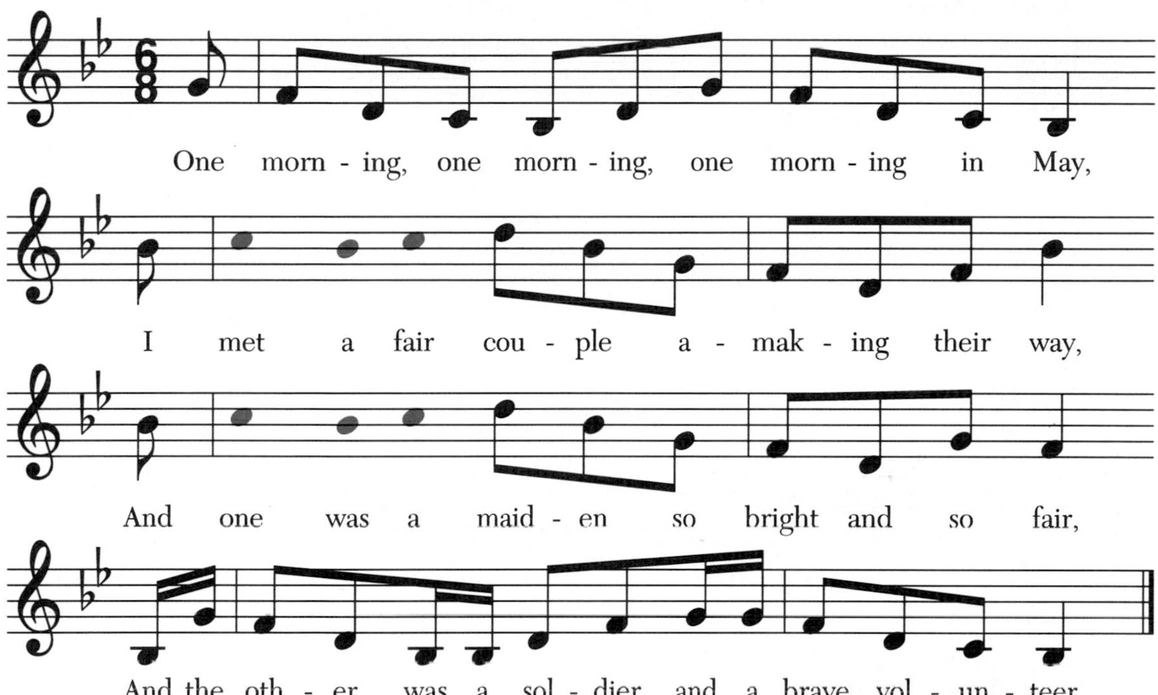


2. "Good morning, good morning, good morning to thee,
O where are you going my pretty lady?"
"O I am a-going to the banks of the sea,
To see the waters gliding, hear the nightingale sing."

3. We hadn't been standing but a minute or two
When out from his knapsack a fiddle he drew,
And the tune that he played made the valleys all ring,
O see the waters gliding, hear the nightingale sing.

4. "Pretty soldier, pretty soldier, will you marry me?"
"O no, pretty lady, that never can be;
I've a wife in old London and children twice three;
Two wives and the army's too many for me."

5. "I'll go back to London and stay there one year
And often I'll think of you, my little dear,
If ever I return, 'twill be in the spring
To see the waters gliding, hear the nightingale sing."

# A Song of the Sea

Follow the "road map" of this song.

# OPPOSITES

Can you find things in this song that are opposites?

2. I rode a gray horse that was called a gray mare,
With a gray mane and tail, green stripe down her back,
Gray mane and gray tail, green stripe down her back,
There was no hair on her that wasn't coal black.

3. She stood so still, she threw me to the dirt,
She tore my hide and bruised my shirt,
From saddle to stirrup I mounted again
And on my ten toes I rode over the plain.

4. Met the King and the Queen and a company more,
A riding behind and a marching before;
Come a strange looking drummer a-beating a drum,
With his hands in his pockets come marching along.

# A Sailor's Song

Keep a strong steady beat while you sing this song.

2. As I was a-walkin' down Paradise Street, To me weigh, . . .
   A pretty young lady I chanced for to meet, Give me, . . .

3. I hailed her in English, she answered me clear, . . .
   "I'm from the Black Arrow bound to the Shakespeare." . . .

4. But as we were going she said unto me, . . .
   "There's a spankin' full-rigger just ready for sea." . . .

5. But soon as that packet was clear of the bar, . . .
   The mate knocked me down with the end of a spar. . . .

6. And as soon as that packet was out on the sea, . . .
   'Twas dev'lish hard treatment of every degree. . . .

7. So I give you fair warning before we belay; . . .
   Don't never take heed of what pretty girls say. . . .

# A NEW RHYTHM

Is this wind fierce? Is it gentle? Can you find the new rhythm?

# Keeping Watch

Play this song on recorder. Will you have to learn any new notes?

## Little Boy of the Sheep

Folk Song from the Hebrides Islands English Words by Alice Firgau

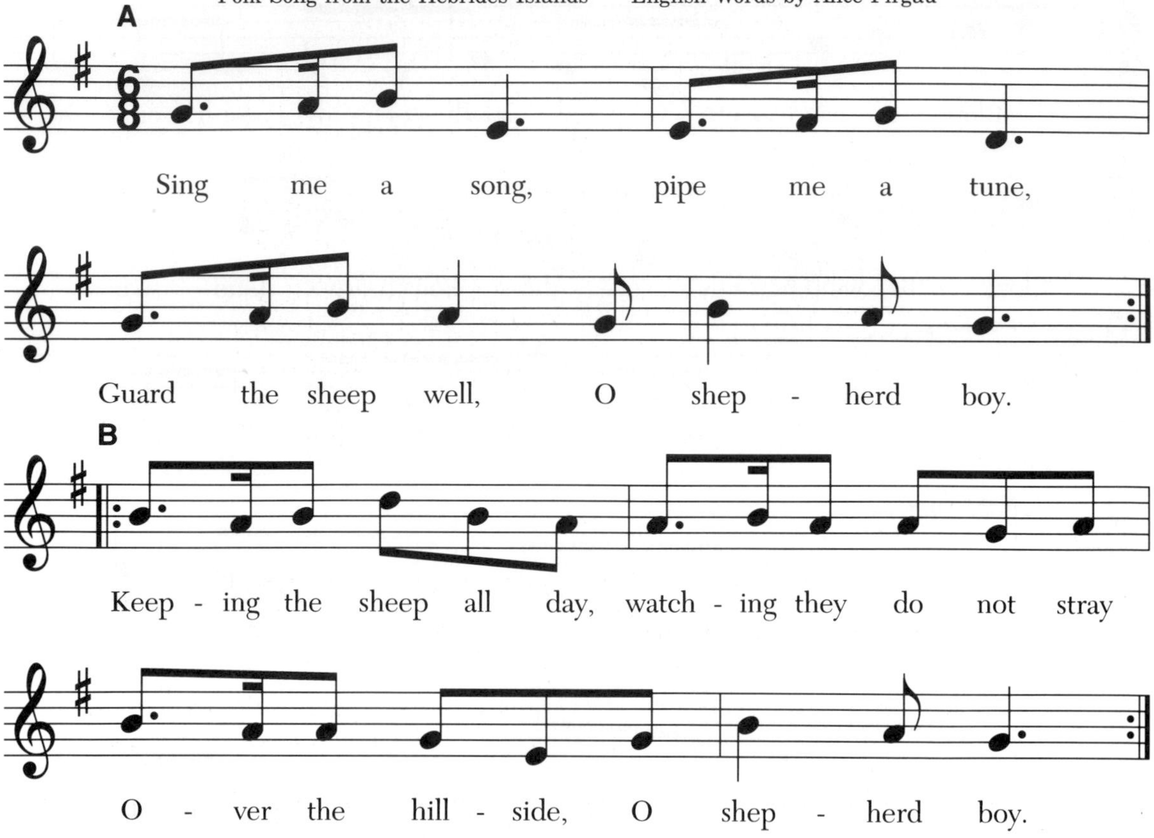
A
Sing me a song, pipe me a tune,
Guard the sheep well, O shep - herd boy.
B
Keep - ing the sheep all day, watch - ing they do not stray
O - ver the hill - side, O shep - herd boy.

From FOLKSONGS AND FOLKLORE OF THE SOUTH UIST. Used by permission of Margaret Fay Shaw.

## Sonata in A Major

Wolfgang A. Mozart

m f m s s r m r f f d d r r m s f m r
m f m s s r m r f f d r m s f m r d

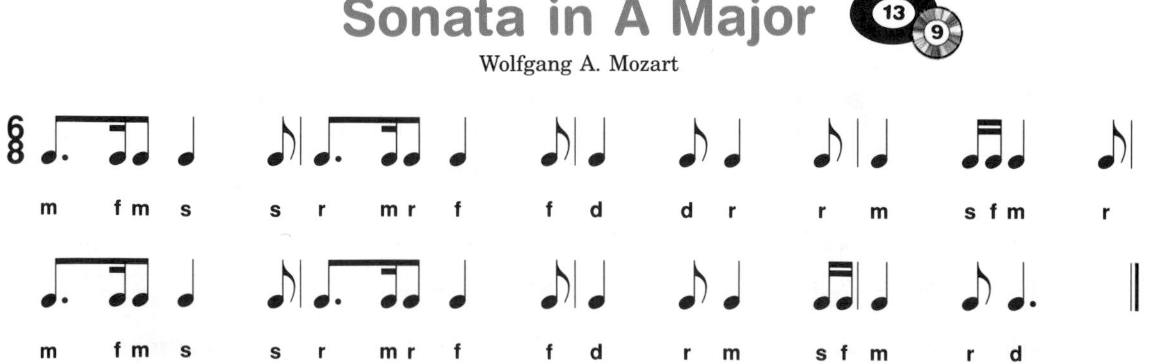

# A Song About a Lady

This melody has been well-loved for a long time.

**THE MUSICIANS** *Michelangelo Merisi da Caravaggio*

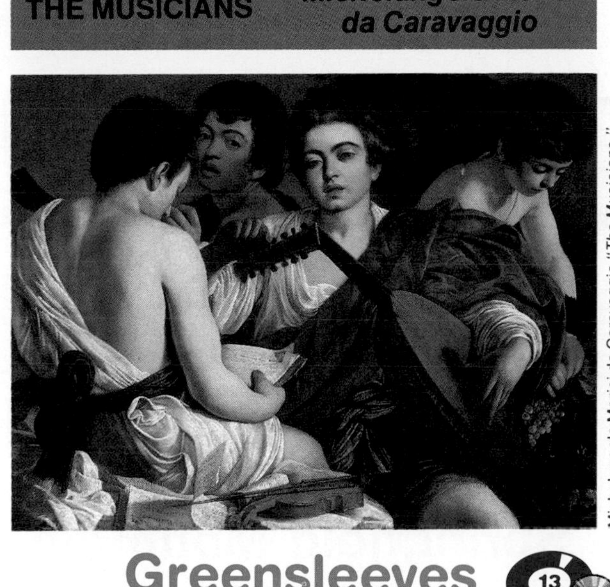

Michelangelo Merisi da Caravaggio *"The Musicians,"* The Metropolitan Museum of Art, Rogers Fund, 1952.

## Greensleeves

16th Century Folk Song from England

## Two Folk Songs from America

## SINGING FOR JOY

Create a performance of this song. Add as many parts as you can.

### Rock-a-My Soul

13 9

African-American Spiritual

I

Rock - a - my soul __ in the bo - som of A - bra - ham,

$V_7$

Rock - a - my soul __ in the bo - som of A - bra - ham,

I

Rock - a - my soul __ in the bo - som of A - bra - ham,

$V_7$ I

Oh, rock - a - my soul.

2. So high, you can't get over it,
So low, you can't get under it,
So wide, you can't get around it,
You gotta go in at the door.

# Playing Chords

Choose a key that suits your voice.

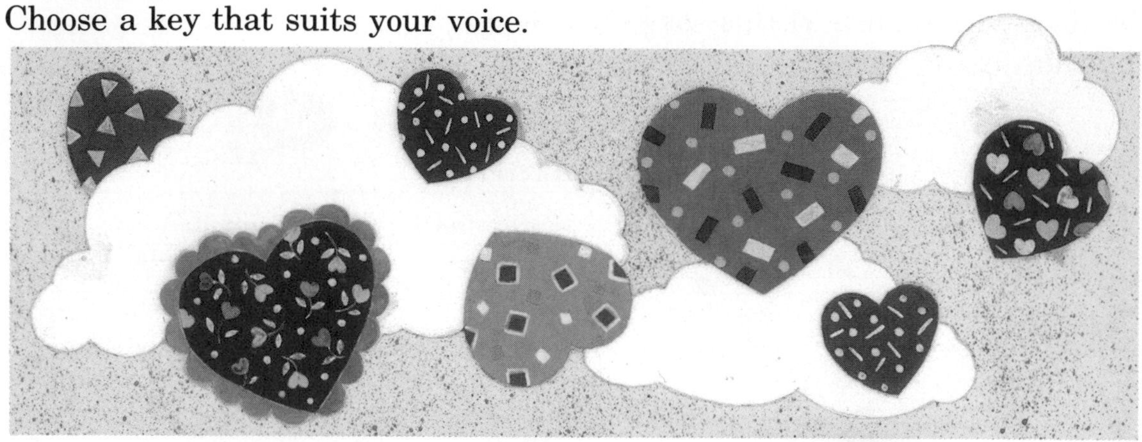

## Love Somebody

American Folk Song

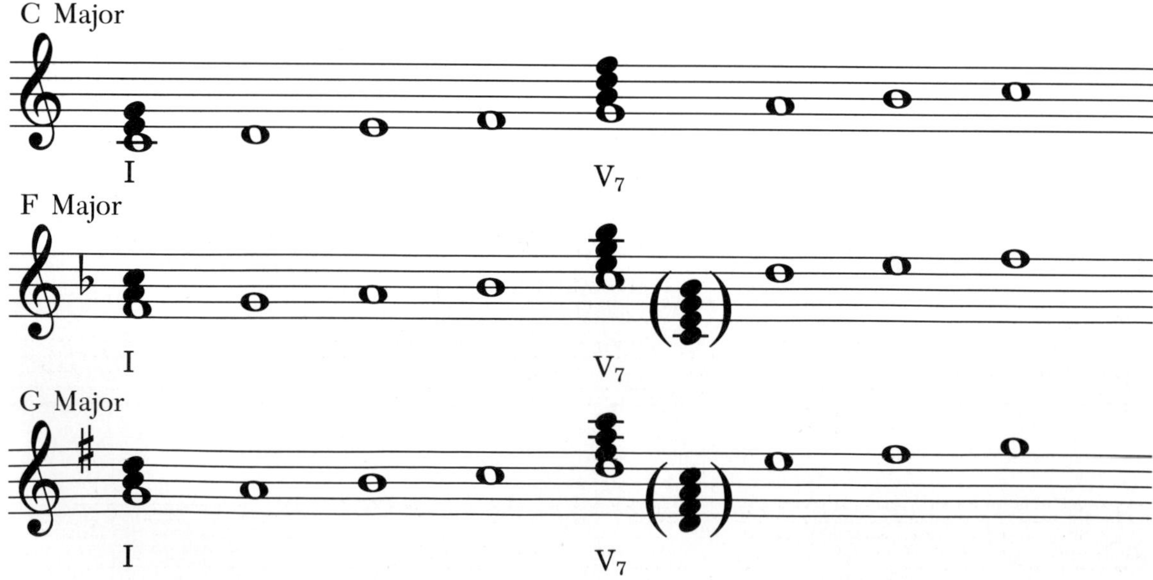

## Two Familiar Songs

Can you remember the words to these songs?

### Old Texas

Oklahoma Cowboy Song

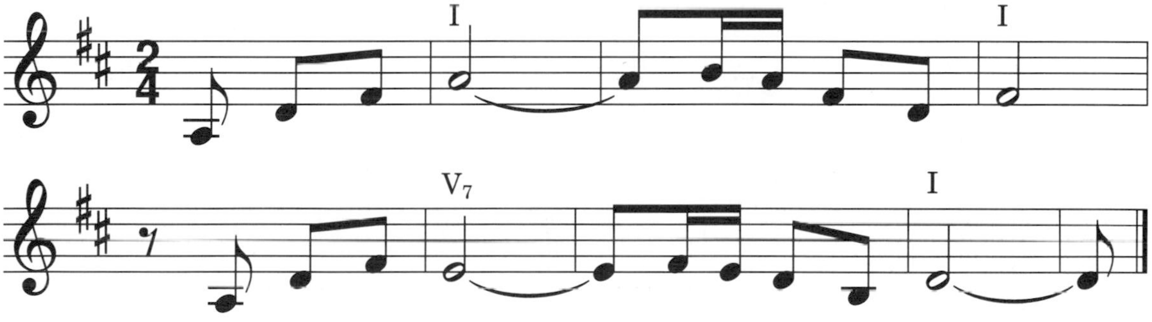

I I V7 I

### Springfield Mountain

American Folk Song

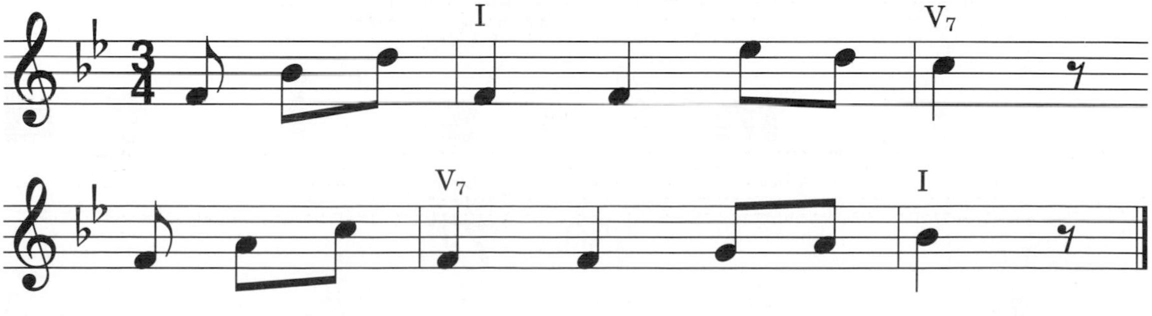

I V7 V7 I

# INTERVALS

You can count up or down—the interval is the same.

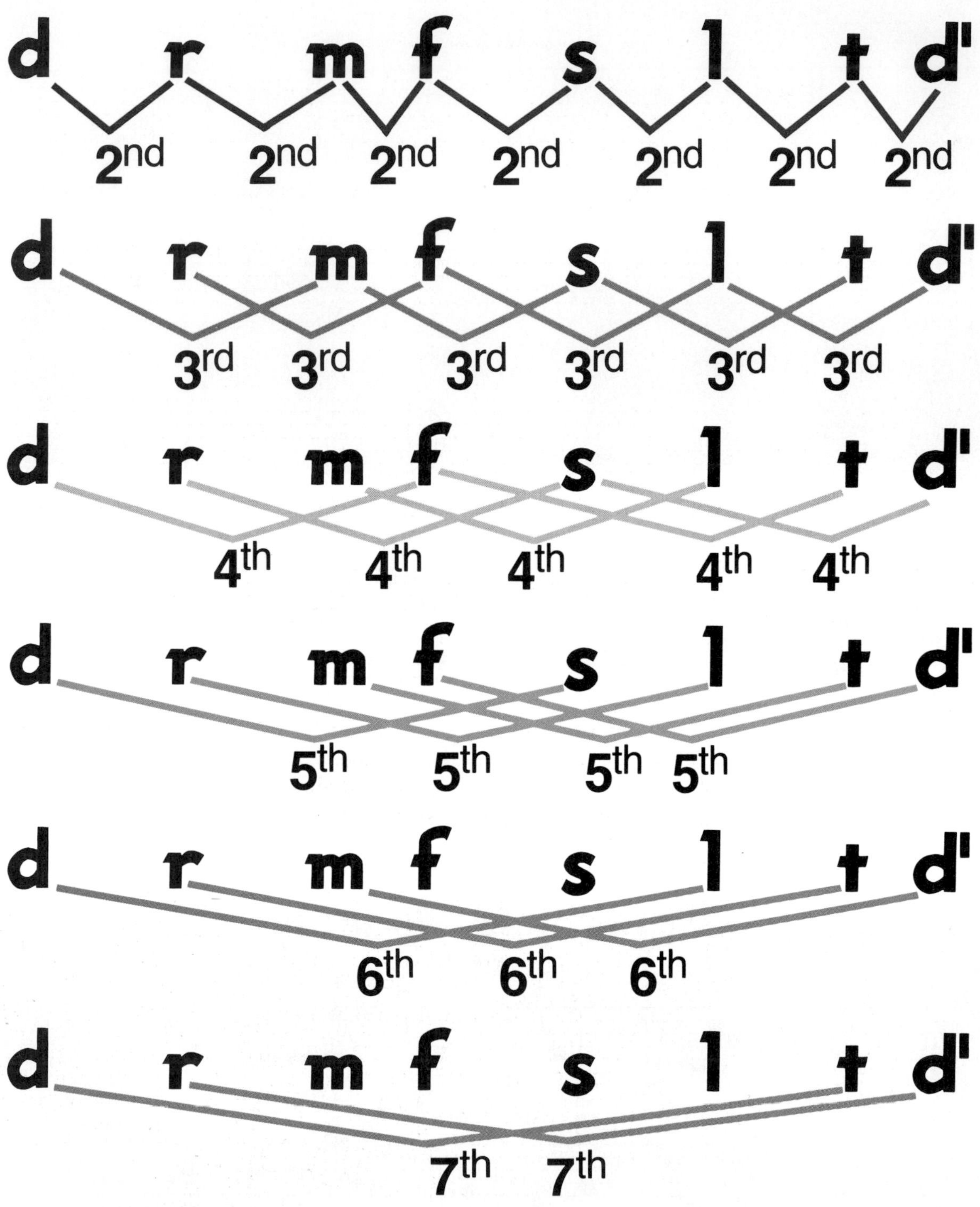

# Practicing Chords

How many chords do you need to play this song?

## When the Saints Go Marching In

13 9

African-American Spiritual

F

1. Oh, when the saints ___ go march-ing in, ___ Oh, when the

F C7

saints go march - ing in, ___ Oh, Lord I

F B♭

want to be in that num - ber ___ When the

F

saints go march - ing in.

2. Oh, when the stars refuse to shine,
Oh, when the stars refuse to shine,
Oh, Lord, I want to be in that number
When the stars refuse to shine.

3. Oh, when I hear that trumpet sound, . . .

# Under the Stars

This song tells about a very special event.

## I Wonder As I Wander

Collected by John Jacob Niles

1. I won - der as I wan - der out un - der the sky,
How Je - sus, the Sa - vior, did come for to die,
For poor on' - ry peo - ple like you and like I.
I won - der as I wan - der out un - der the sky.

2. When Mary birthed Jesus, 'twas in a cow's stall,
With wise men and farmers and shepherds and all.
But high from the heavens a star's light did fall,
And the promise of ages it then did recall.

# Two Songs About Friendship

We'll take a cup of kind - ness yet, For auld lang syne.

# A Melody from Africa

What do you think the Roman numerals mean?

## Kum Bah Yah

Traditional Song from South Africa

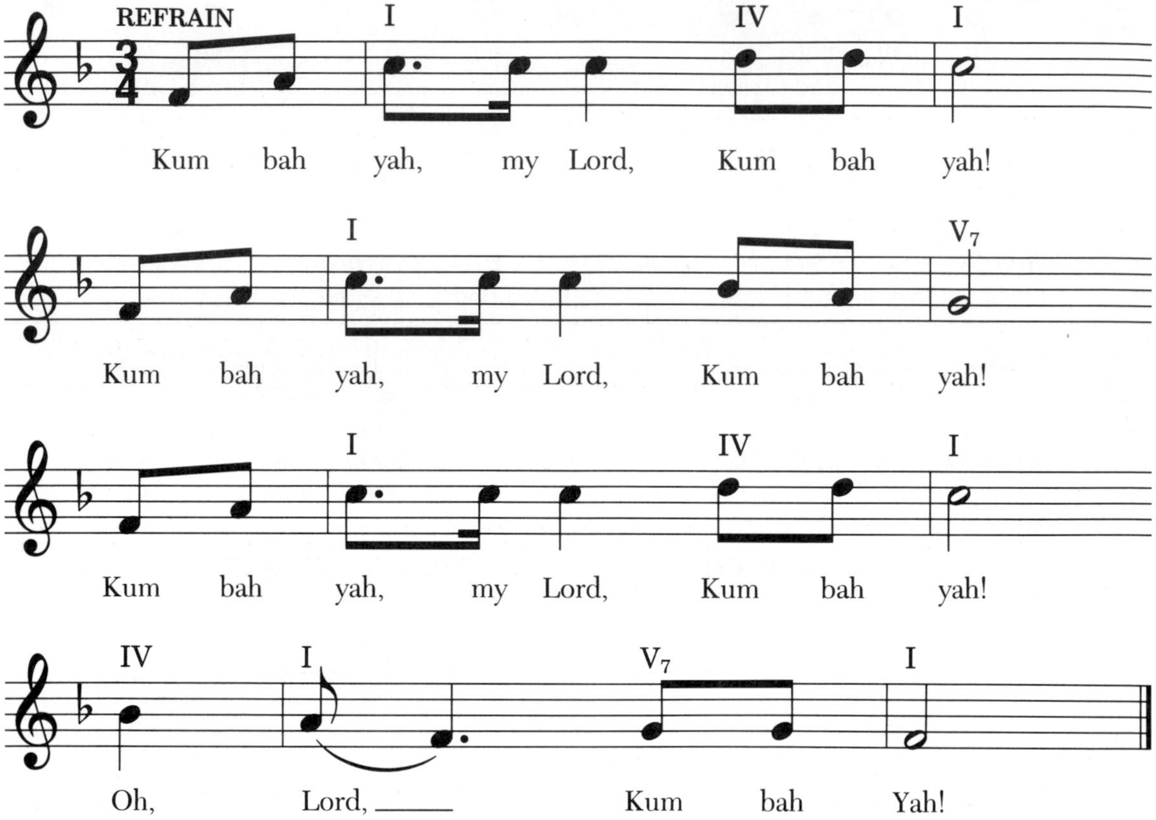

**REFRAIN**

I IV I

Kum bah yah, my Lord, Kum bah yah!

I $V_7$

Kum bah yah, my Lord, Kum bah yah!

I IV I

Kum bah yah, my Lord, Kum bah yah!

IV I $V_7$ I

Oh, Lord, _____ Kum bah Yah!

1. Someone's singing, Lord, . . .
2. Someone's praying, Lord, . . .
3. Someone's shouting, Lord, . . .

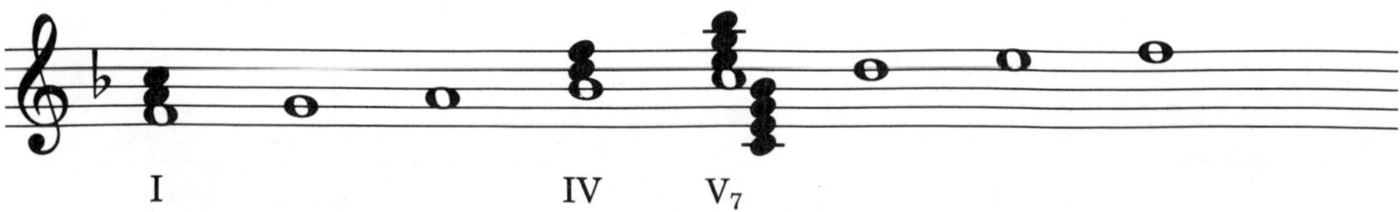

# A Cowboy Song

What instrument would you use to accompany this song?

# A Musical Description

Do you see any lines of music that look like other lines?

Words by June Hershey    Music by Don Swander

The stars at night are big and bright, Deep in the heart of Tex-as; ___

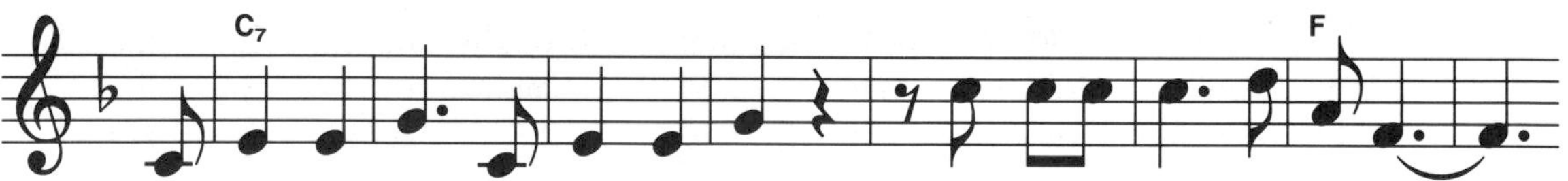


The prai-rie sky is wide and high, Deep in the heart of Tex-as. ___

The sage in bloom is like per-fume, Deep in the heart of Tex-as; ___

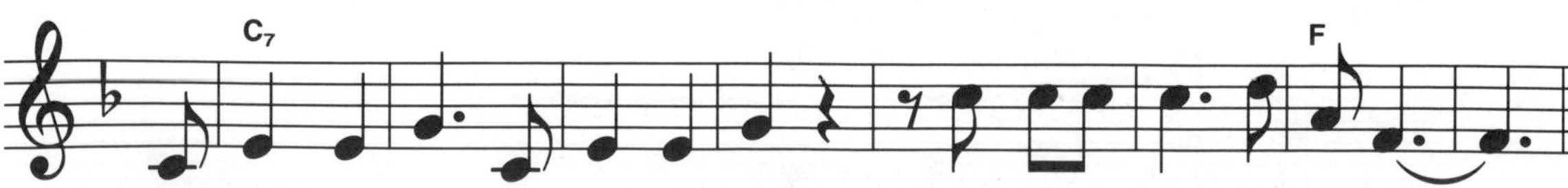


Re-minds me of the one I love, Deep in the heart of Tex-as. ___

## Get On Board

The Roman numerals tell you which chords to play as you sing this song.

# New River Train

American Folk Song

I

1. I'm rid - in' on that New Riv - er train,
2. Dar - lin', you can't love one,
3. Dar - lin', you can't love two,

I V7

I'm rid - in' on that New Riv - er train.
Dar - lin', you can't love one;
Dar - lin', you can't love two;

I IV

Same old train that brought me here
You can't love one and have an - y fun,
You can't love two and still be true,

I V7 I

Goin' to car - ry me back a - gain.
Oh, dar - lin', you can't love one.
Oh, dar - lin', you can't love two.

4. Darlin', you can't love three, . . .
You can't love three and still love me . . .

5. Darlin', you can't love four, . . .
You can't love four, make it up if you want more . . .

# Smaller and Larger

**Must songs sound different if they look different?**

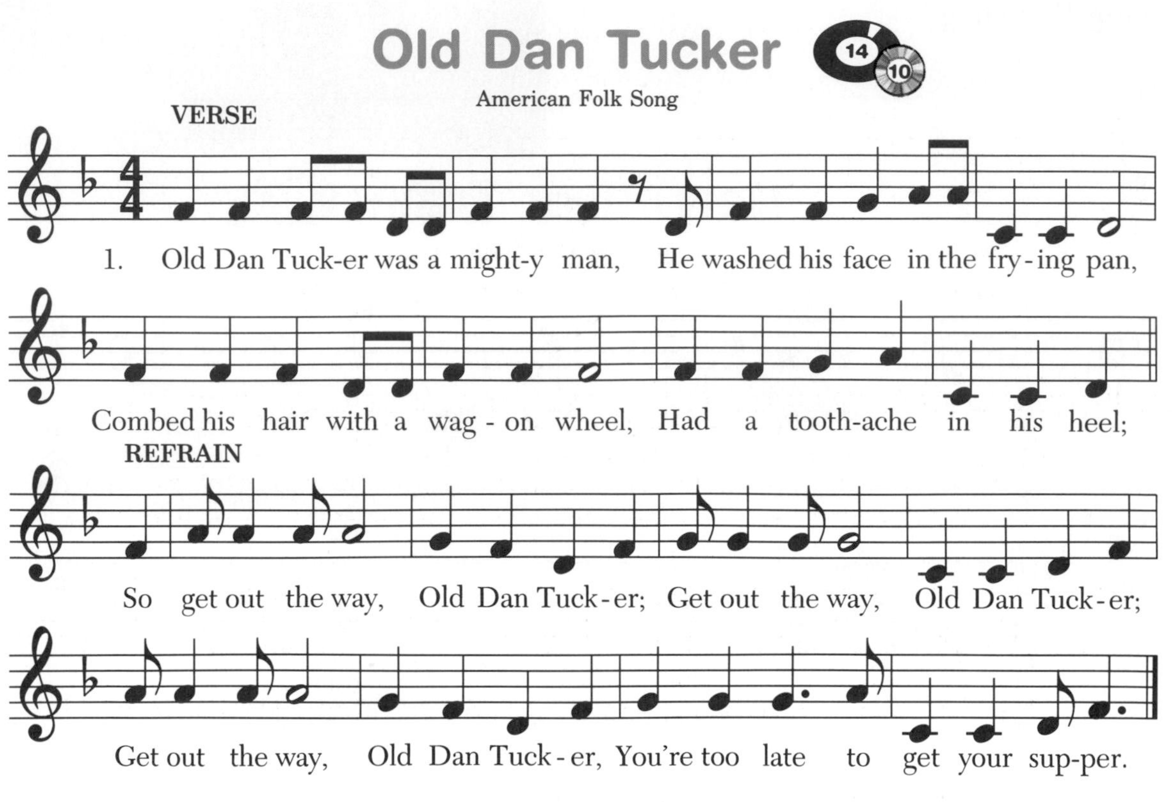


2. Old Dan Tucker came to town,
Riding a billy goat, leading a hound;
Hound dog barked, then billy goat jumped;
Dan fell off and landed on a stump; *Refrain*

## An American Shantey

Why would early sailors be so concerned about the wind?

### Blow, Ye Winds

American Folk Song

3. It's now we're out to sea, my boys,
   the wind begins to blow,
   One half the watch is sick on deck
   and the other half below.

4. The skipper's on the quarter-deck
   a-squinting at the sails,
   When up aloft the look-out sights
   a school of whales.

5. "Now clear away the boats, my boys,
   and after him we'll trail,
   But if you get too near to him,
   he'll kick you with his tail!"

6. Now we've got him turned up,
   we tow him alongside;
   We over with our blubber hooks
   and rob him of his hide.

7. Next comes the stowing down, my boys
   'twill take both night and day,
   And you'll all have fifty cents apiece
   when you collect your pay.

A Song for Recorder
Play this as a duet. Use recorders or any instrument you choose.
The Water Is Wide
14
10
Folk Song from England
Countermelody
Melody
The wa - ter is wide, I can't get
1. The wa - ter is wide, I can-not get o'er,
2. There is a ship sail - ing on the sea,
3. Oh, love is handsome and love is fine,
o'er, And I've no wings, No wings to
And nei - ther have I wings to fly,
She's load - ed deep as deep can be,
And love is charm - ing when it is true,

# A Lullaby

Why are thirds a good choice for adding harmony to a lullaby?

# Wheels

Can you find the notes of this song on the keyboard?

## Ezekiel Saw the Wheel

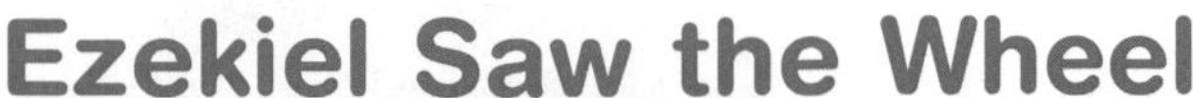

African-American Spiritual

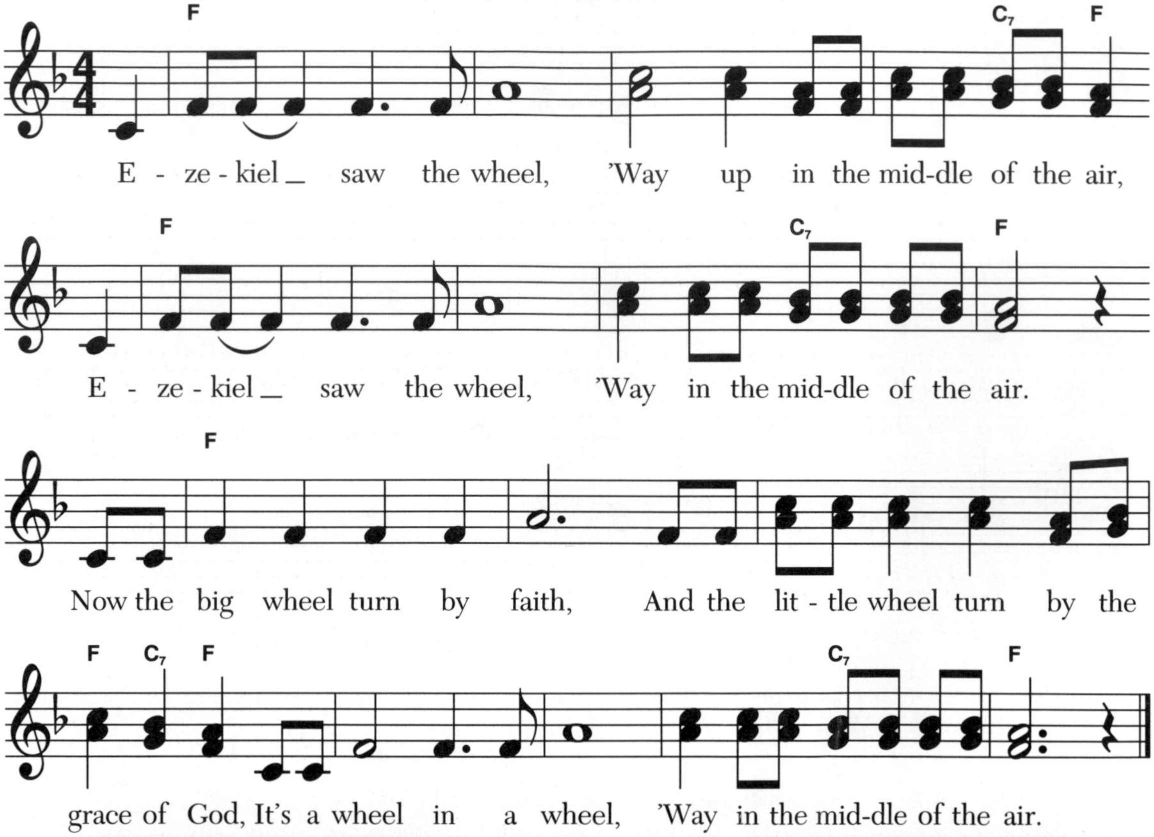

F C7 F
E - ze - kiel_ saw the wheel, 'Way up in the mid-dle of the air,
F C7 F
E - ze - kiel_ saw the wheel, 'Way in the mid-dle of the air.
F
Now the big wheel turn by faith, And the lit - tle wheel turn by the
F C7 F C7 F
grace of God, It's a wheel in a wheel, 'Way in the mid-dle of the air.


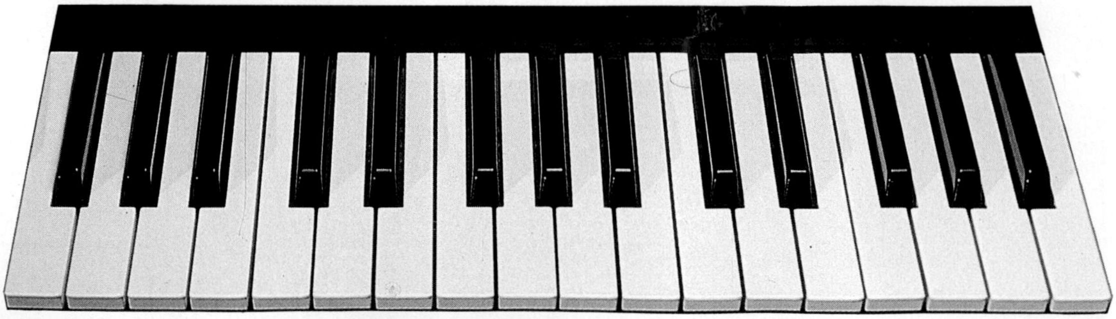

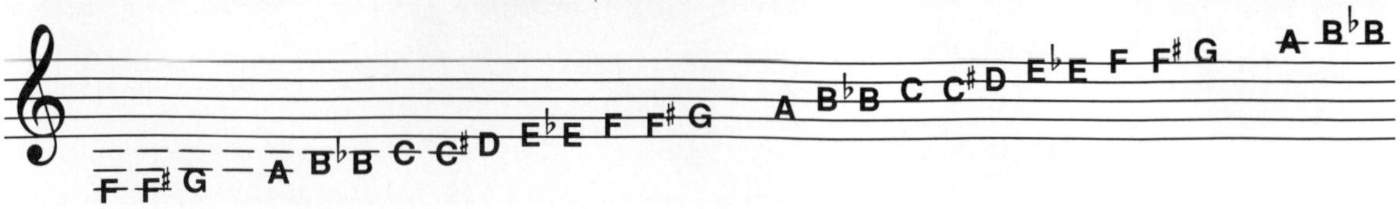

F F♯ G A B♭ B C C♯ D E♭ E F F♯ G A B♭ B C C♯ D E♭ E F F♯ G A B♭ B

# A New Note

Your ear will tell you what the missing notes sound like.

## Minka

Folk Melody from Russia    Words by Louise Ayres Garnett

## A Sweet Song

Does this song sound right to you? How should it sound?

# A Snow-White Bird

Folk Song from Flanders English Words by Jean Sinor

2. Oh, tell me, tell me, little bird,
Oh, tell me, tell me, little bird,
Is it my true love's song you've heard? Nonny, nonny no.
Is it my true love's song you've heard? nonny no.

3. More sadly sang the snow-white dove,
More sadly sang the snow-white dove,
For he was mourning for his love, nonny, nonny no.
For he was mourning for his love, nonny no.

# ACCIDENTALS

What do sharps, flats, and natural signs do?

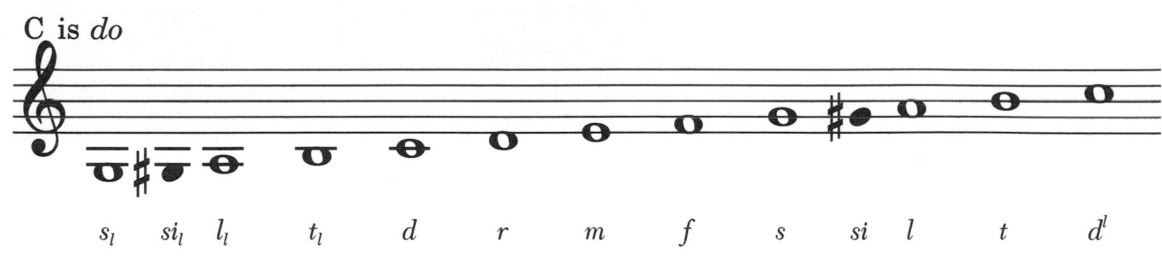


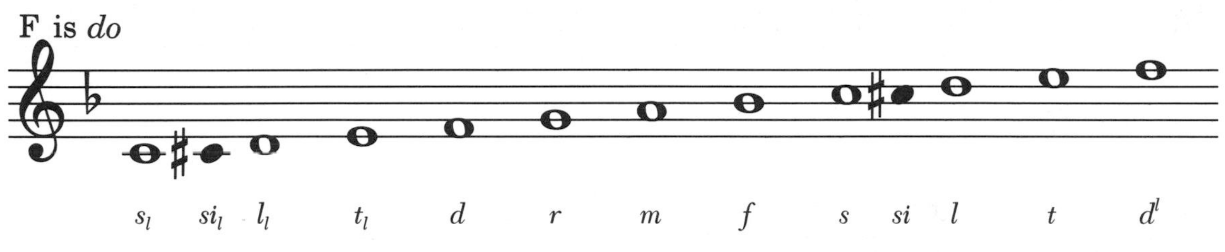


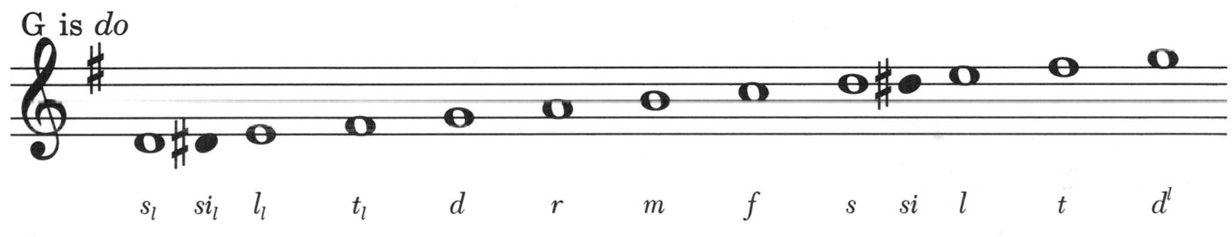


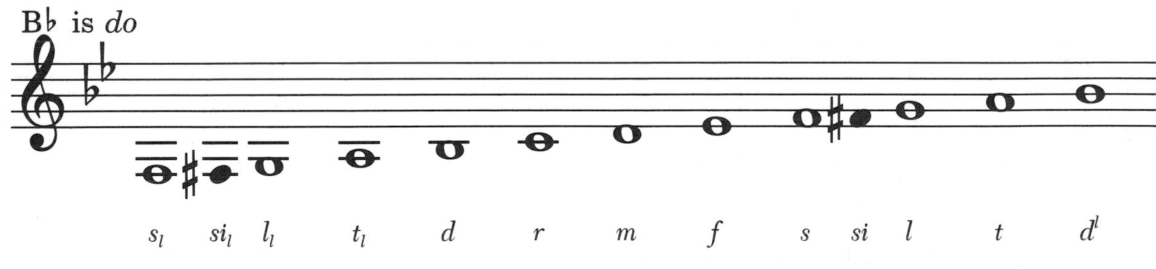


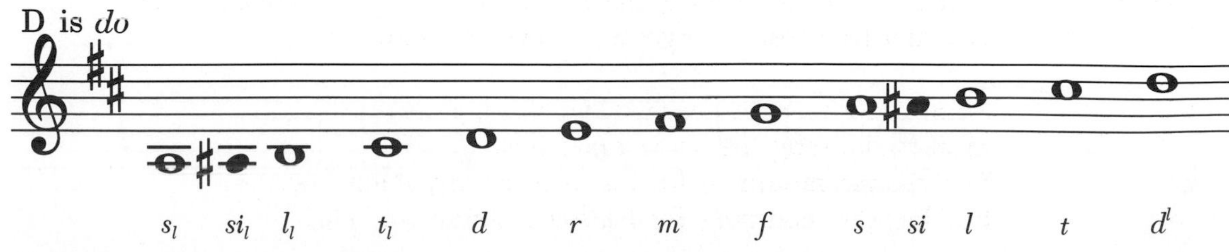

# A Lively Song

Try singing this as a round after two beats.

## Joshua Fought the Battle of Jericho

African-American Spiritual

**REFRAIN**

Josh - ua fought the bat - tle of ___ Jer - i - cho, ___

Jer - i - cho, ___ Jer - i - cho, ___

Josh - ua fought the bat - tle of ___ Jer - i - cho, ___

And the walls came tum - blin' down.

*Fine*

**VERSE**

You can talk a - bout your king of Gid - e - on, ___

You can talk a - bout your man of Saul, ___

But there's none like good old Josh - u - a ___

*D.C. al Fine*

At the bat - tle of Jer - i - cho.

# A Game Song

Can you play this song on recorder? Piano?

## Shake Hands, Mary

African-American Children's Song

## CHORDS

You can accompany this song using just two chords.

# The Miller of Dee

Folk Song from England

2. So let us his example take,
   And be from malice free,
   Let everyone his neighbor serve
   As served he'd like to be.
   And merrily pass the tray around
   And dance and sing with glee,
   If nobody cares a fig for us,
   Why not a fig care we.

# A Song About a Prince

Bonnie Prince Charlie is a hero in Scotland.

2. As he came marching up the street, the pipes played loud and clear,
   And the folk came running out to meet the young chevalier.
3. With Highland bonnets on their heads, and claymores bright and clear,
   They came to fight for Scotland's right and the young chevalier.

# A New Scale

Does this song sound mostly major or mostly minor?

## Carrion Crow

Folk Song from Nova Scotia

1. An ___ old car - rion crow was sit - ting on an oak,
Fol the rid - dle, all the rid - dle, hey ding doh,
Watch - ing a tai - lor cut - ting out a coat, Sing hey, Sing hoh, old
car - rion crow, Fol the rid - dle, all the rid - dle, hey ding doh.

**REFRAIN**

Ki - mi - lea - ro Kill my lea - ro Ki - mi - lea - ro Ki - mo, To me
hump, bump, bump, jump Pol - ly wol - ly lee, Lin - ko kil - ly cum Ki - mo.

2. Wife, oh wife, bring me my
   cross and bow, . . .
   That I may shoot yon carrion
   crow. . . . *Refrain*

3. Oh, the tailor shot and missed
   his mark, . . .
   And he shot the miller's sow
   right through the heart. . . .
   *Refrain*

## An Ancient Melody

This melody has been used by many composers.

### Greensleeves

16th Century Folk Song from England

1. A - las, my love, _ you do me wrong _ to cast me off ___ dis-cour-teous-ly;
2. My men were cloth - ed all in green _ And they did ev - er wait on thee;

And I have lov - ed you so long, _ De - light - ing in ___ your com - pa - ny.
All this was gal - lant to be seen, _ And yet _ thou wouldst _ not love _ me.

**REFRAIN**

Green - sleeves _ was all my joy, ___ Green - sleeves _ was my de-light,

Green-sleeves was my heart of gold, _ And who but my La - dy Green-sleeves?

# The Natural Sign

Can you tell what a natural sign shows?

# SHOWING DIRECTION

Do *fa* and *fi* show what the next note probably is?

# Naming a Song

What song do you think this is?

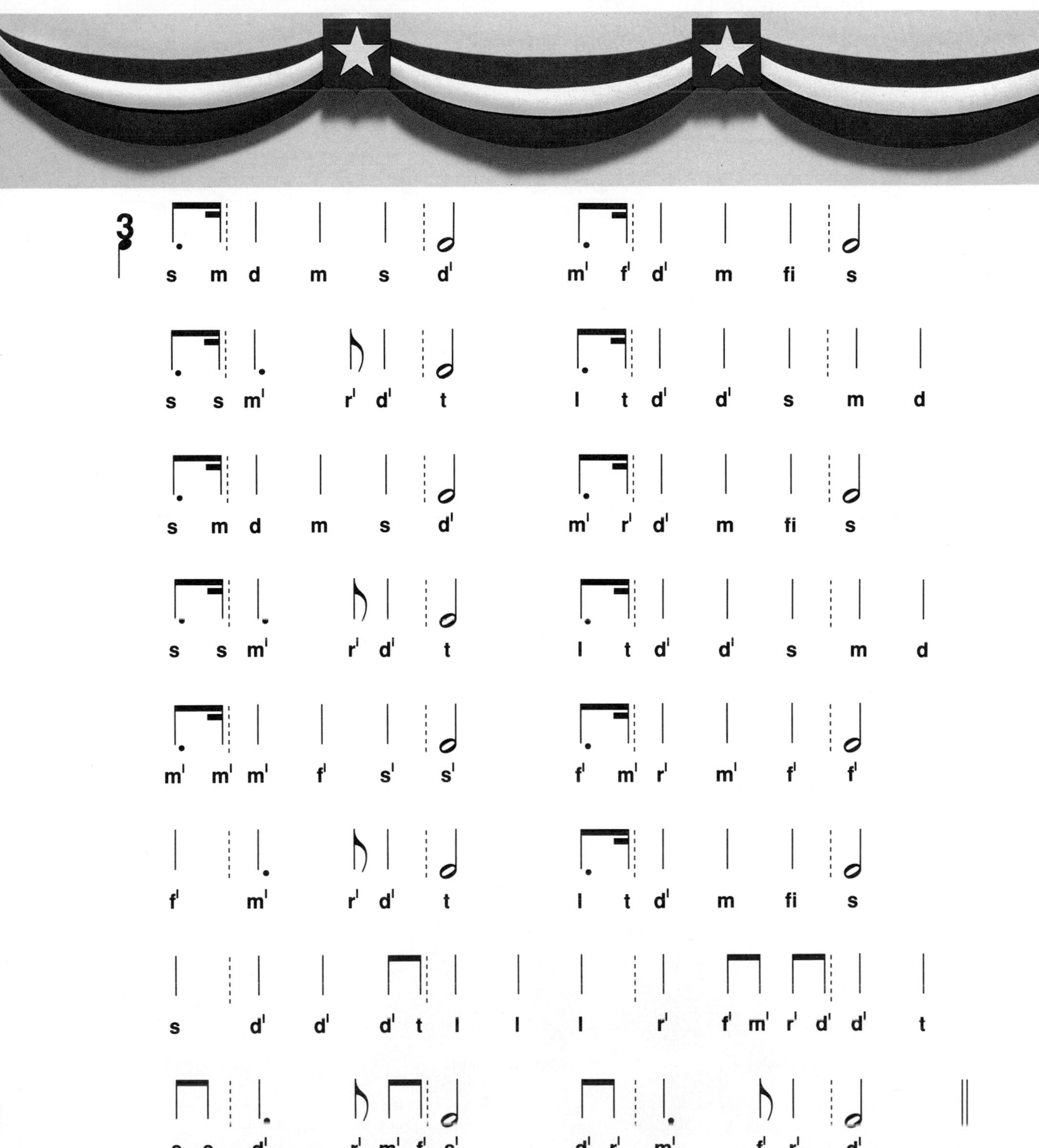

# An Old Friend

Where is the refrain of this song?

# In Praise of Beauty

What key is this song in?

## Yonder Stands a Handsome Lady

Folk Song from the United States

2. Madam, I have gold and silver
   Madam, I have house and land,
   Madam, I have a world of treasure,
   And all shall be at your command.

3. Madam, do not count on beauty,
   Beauty is a flower that will soon decay,
   The brightest flower in the midst of summer
   In the fall it will fade away.

## SINGING A MADRIGAL

The parts without words are meant for dancing. Will you dance as you sing?

# Now Is the Month of Maying

Words Anonymous Music by Thomas Morley

# A Great Composer

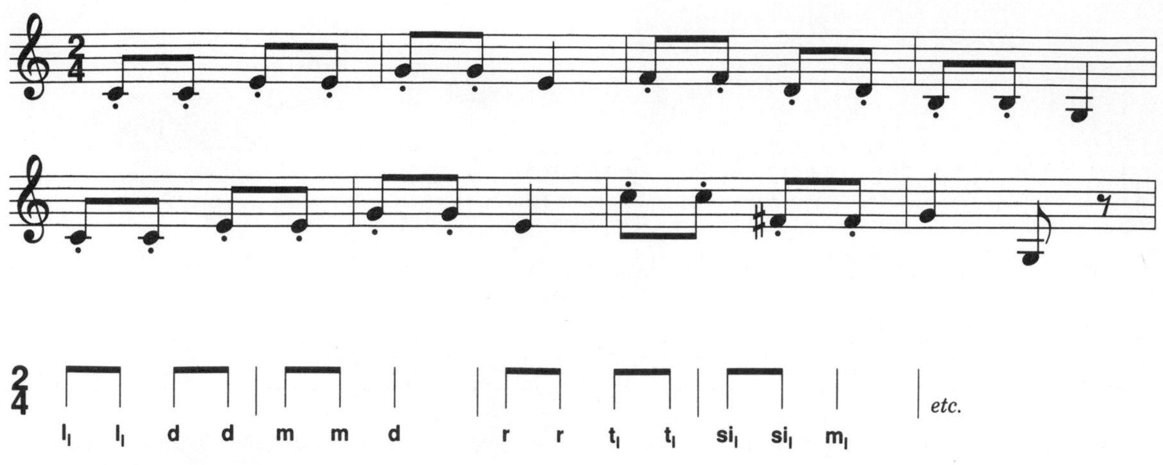

Franz Joseph Haydn was born in a small village in Austria. His father made wheels for carriages, and his mother was a cook in the household of a count.

When Haydn was a little boy, he would pretend to play the violin with two pieces of wood as he listened to his mother sing folk songs.

In 1761 a wealthy Hungarian nobleman named Esterházy hired Haydn to write music for his private orchestra. In those days, every castle had its own group of professional musicians. For thirty years, Haydn lived and worked at the Esterházy castle.

Although a musician living in a nobleman's house was just a servant, Haydn didn't mind. He was a simple man who was grateful for the opportunity to compose and perform music.

# ANOTHER MODE

Modes are scales. Let your ear tell you the mode of this song.

## Hold the Wind

African-American Spiritual

2. If you don't believe I been redeemed,
   hold the wind, . . .
   Just follow me down to the Jordan
   stream. . . . *Refrain*

3. My soul got wet in the midnight dew, . . .
   And the morning star was a witness
   too. . . . *Refrain*

Collected and adapted and arranged by Alan Lomax.

# A Well-Known Song

Is this song in major or in minor?

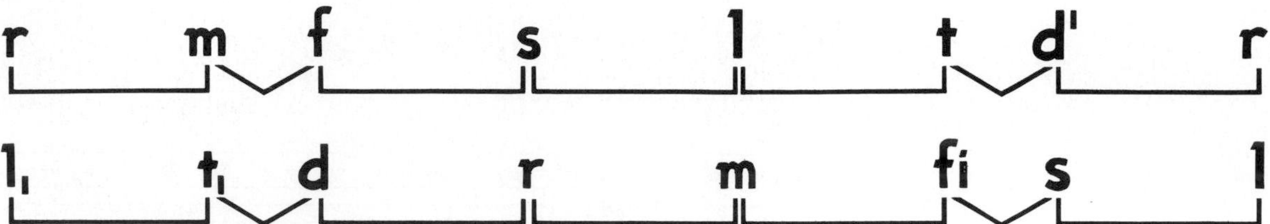

## Every Night When the Sun Goes In

Folk Song from the Southern Appalachians

1. Ev' - ry night, when the sun goes in, Ev' - ry
2. How I wish that ___ train would come, How I

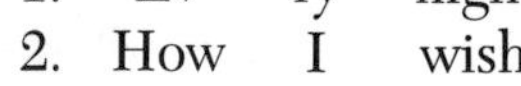

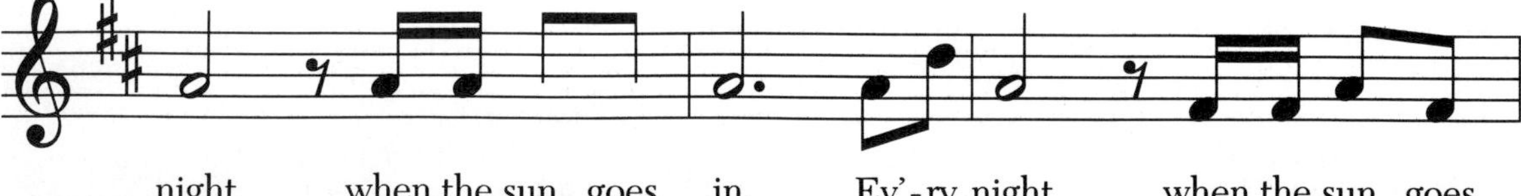

night when the sun goes in, Ev'-ry night when the sun goes
wish that ___ train would come, How I wish that ___ train would

in, I lay down my head and mourn-ful cry.
come, And take ___ me back where I come from.

## A New Song

What is a silkie? What notes should you sing at the question marks?

# The Great Silkie

Folk Song from Great Britain

1. I am a man up - on the land,
2. And it shall pass on a sum - mer's day,

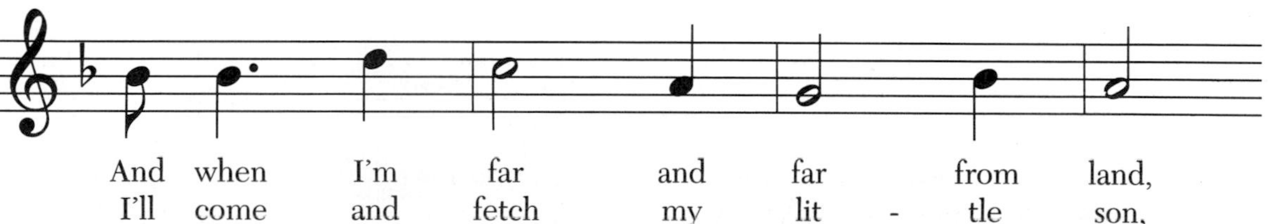


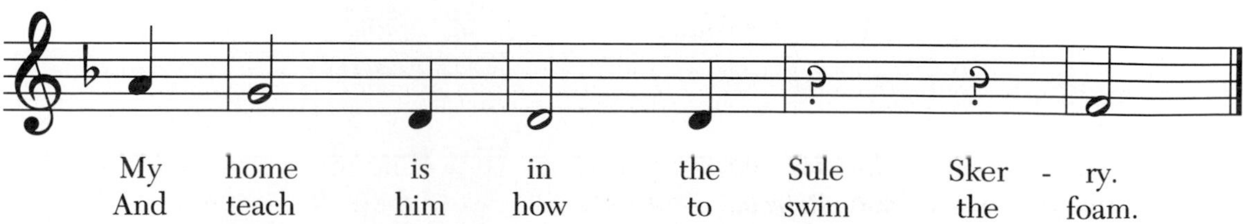

## An Old American Folk Song

Can you find anything wrong in the lyrics?

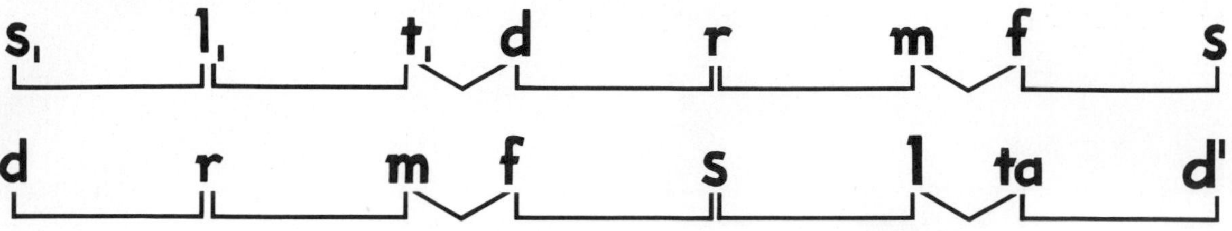


### Old Joe Clark

14 10

VERSE

Folk Song from the United States Words by Raymond Matthews

REFRAIN

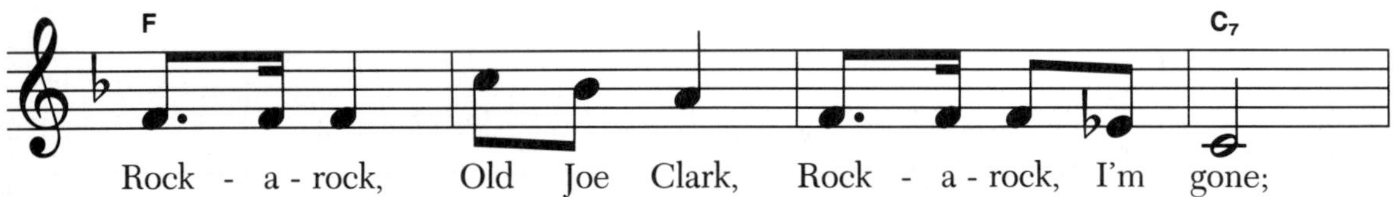

2. Old Joe Clark, he had a dog
Like none you've ever seen;
With floppy ears and curly tail,
And six feet in between. *Refrain*

3. Old Joe Clark, he had a wife,
Her name was Betty Sue;
She had two great big brown eyes,
The other two were blue. *Refrain*

# Notes You Know

Here are all the notes you have studied.

## Putting It All Together

Use this song to practice what you have learned.

# The Alphabet

Attributed to Wolfgang A. Mozart

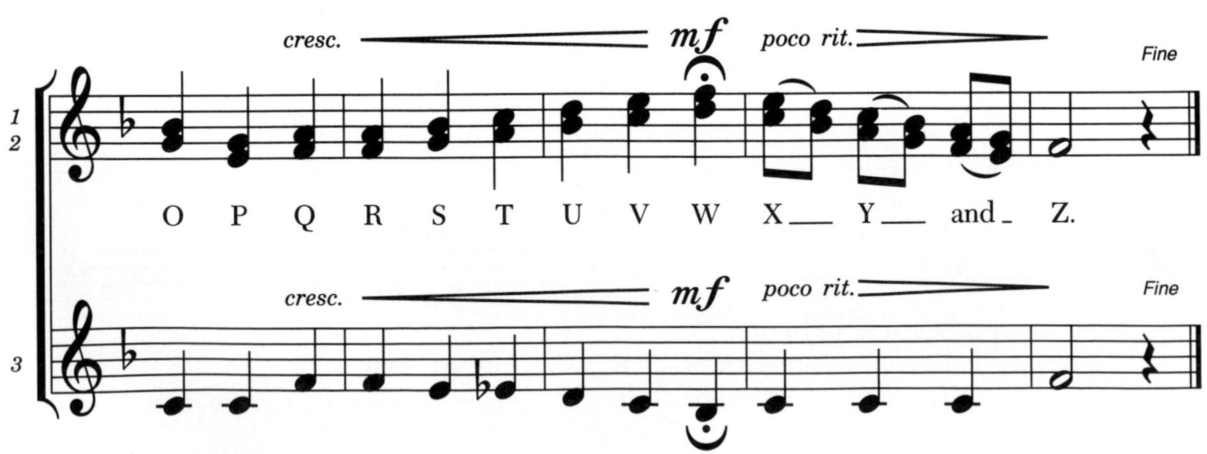

cresc.
A
B
C
D
A
B
C
D
mf
D.S. al Fine
E F G H I J K L M N O
E F G H I J K L M N O
cresc.
A B C D E F G H I J K L I J K L M N O
S
E
H

# Playing the Autoharp

## How to Hold the Autoharp

Hold the autoharp with the small end in front of your left shoulder. The large end rests on your left leg. Wrap your left arm around the autoharp, well below the pegs. Make sure you can press all the chord bars comfortably.

Your right elbow rests lightly on the front corner of the autoharp. When you strum the strings, do not move your upper arm. Let your wrist bend as you move your right arm freely over all the strings, close to the chord bars.

The girl in the photograph is playing the autoharp folk-style. This position gives you the freedom to develop right-hand accompaniments without crossing your arms.

Check your playing position in a mirror. Work toward varying the volume and toward control. Experiment. It takes time to be comfortable.

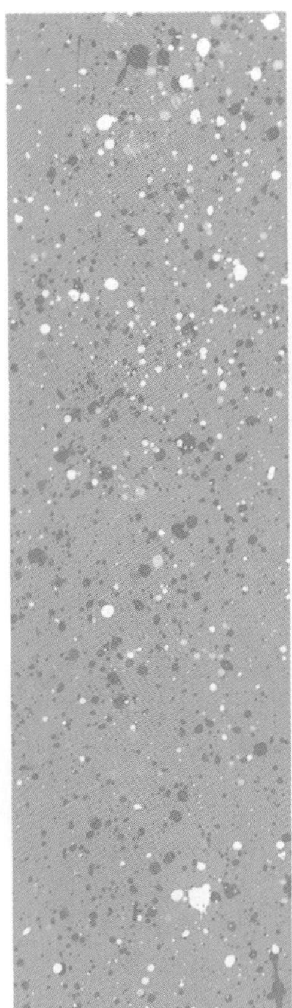

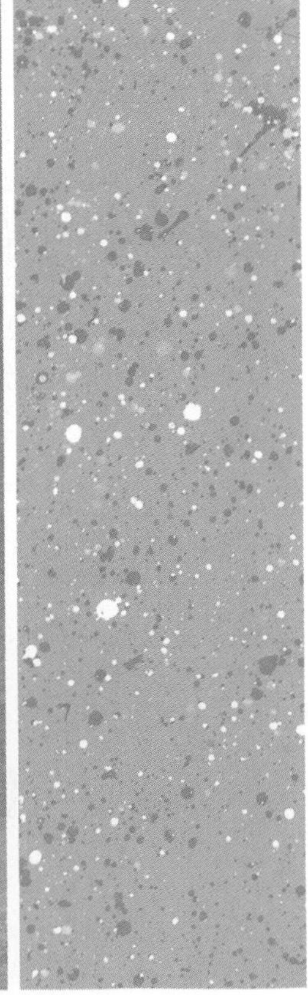

## How to Wear the Picks

Using picks provides greater volume and pitch control. Picks also help prevent damage to your fingertips. Most music stores sell both plastic and metal picks.

You will need a plastic thumb pick. It should fit snugly, covering most of your thumbnail.

You will also need one metal fingerpick with a gauge number between 15 and 25 (the higher the gauge number, the stiffer the metal). Put the pick on your middle finger and push it down snugly so it protrudes only about a quarter inch past the tip of your finger.

# Easy Thumb-Strum Accompaniments

## Thumb Strums

The strum patterns shown below provide good accompaniment patterns to the songs in your book. Strum on each beat with your right thumb, making long strokes when the arrow is long and short strokes when it is short.

Duple-Meter Thumb Strums

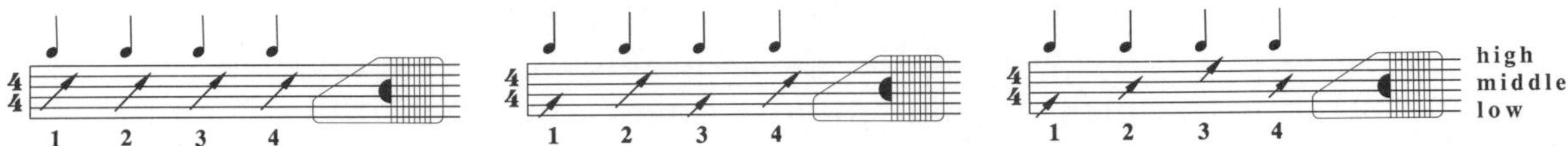


When you have mastered these strums, use them to accompany "Are You Sleeping?" p. 77. This song uses only one chord.

Here are more songs in duple meter you can play.

| | |
|---|---|
| The Twist, p. 199 | Jamaica Farewell, p. 26 |
| The Peddler, p. 17 | Early One Morning, p. 58 |
| Hold 'em, Joe, p. 24 | When the Saints Go Marching In, p. 87 |

Triple-Meter Thumb Strums

Try these songs in triple meter.

| | |
|---|---|
| Finjan, p. 18 | We Wish You a Merry Christmas, p. 230 |
| El charro, p. 23 | When the Chestnut Leaves Were |
| Las mañanitas, p. 22 | Falling, p. 92 |

## Left-Hand Finger Patterns

Most autoharp players use the index, middle, and ring fingers for playing three-chord melodies. Others use those fingers and add the ring finger when a fourth chord is needed.

Choose a different finger for each chord of the song. Rest each finger lightly atop its chord bar throughout the song.

## Fingerpicking Accompaniments

The middle-finger stroke always starts at or near the high strings and moves toward the low strings.

As you begin to use your middle finger, think of your right arm as a pendulum that swings steadily back and forth over the strings. When it swings from low to high, your thumb strikes the strings. When it swings from high to low, your middle finger strikes the strings.

Count out loud as you play; "One and two and three and four and . . ." Your thumb plays as you say each number. Your middle finger plays when you say *and.*

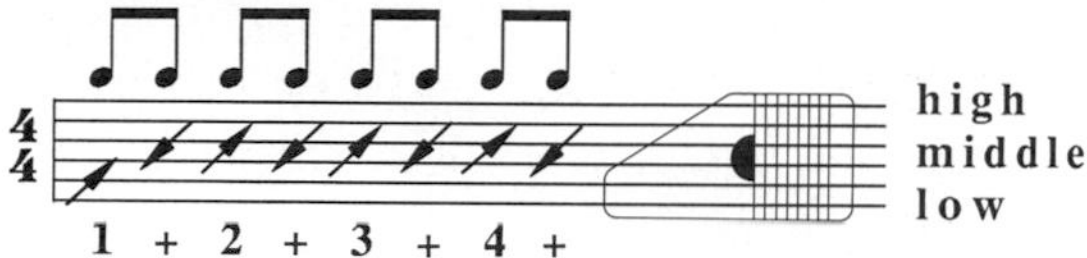


Next, practice the following strum pattern. Do not strike the strings on the *and* after the first beat. However, your arm continues its steady pendulum swing over the strings, bringing your thumb back so it can play the second beat.

Use this new duple-meter strum pattern to accompany the duple-meter songs in your book, listed on page 316. Choose a different left-hand finger to play each of the chords.

Next, practice the following triple-meter strum pattern. Use it to accompany the triple-meter songs in your book listed on page 316.

You have made a good start in folk-style autoharp playing. You may eventually want to learn more intricate right-hand accompaniments. Most exciting of all, you already know most of what you need to know to play interesting accompaniments.

# Playing the Guitar

This is how the neck of the guitar looks when you are holding it in playing position.

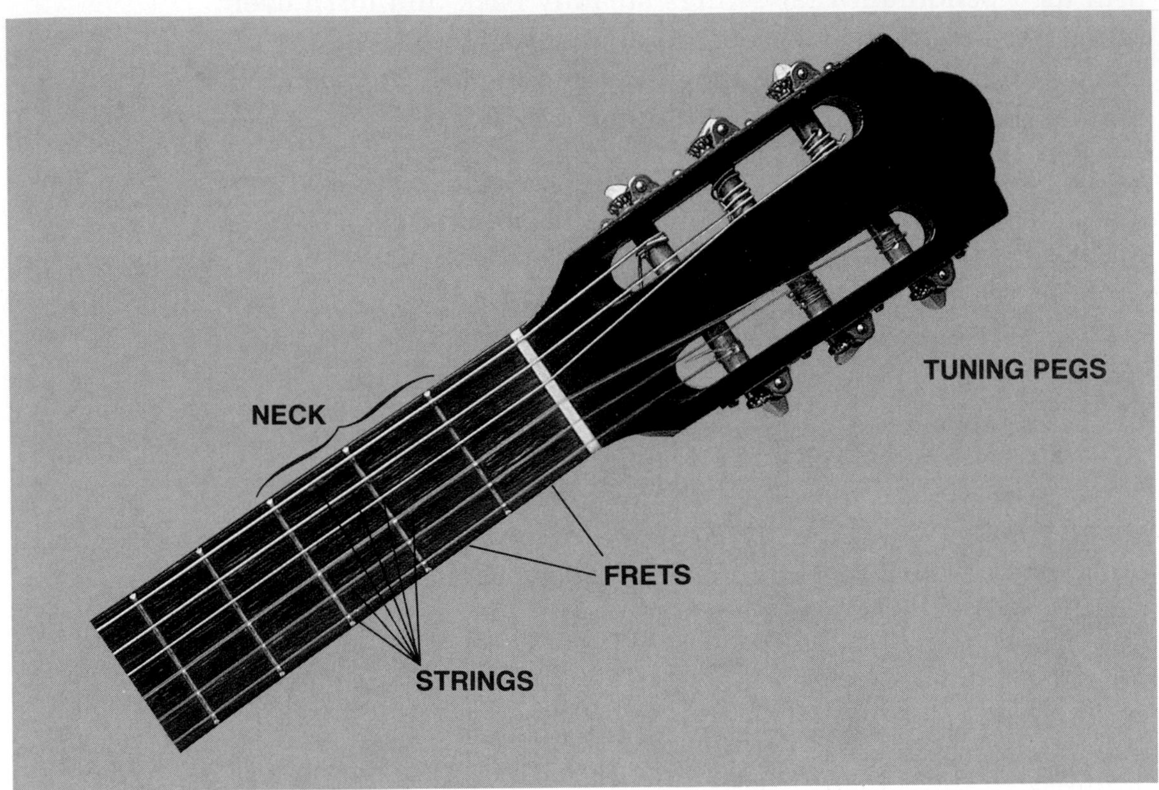


## The E-Minor Chord

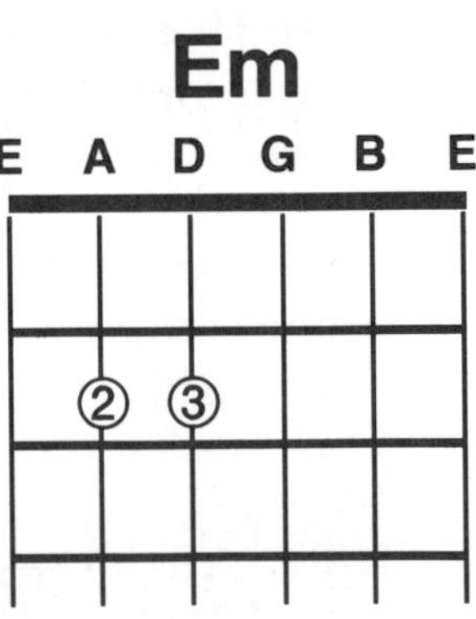


When you have learned to play the E-minor chord, you will be able to play an accompaniment for several songs in your book. The chord diagram shows you where to put your fingers on the strings. Press the strings and practice strumming with your thumb.

Using the fingering for the E-minor chord, strum the steady beat to accompany the following songs. These songs can be sung in E minor.

- Yibane Amenu, p. 19
- Circles, p. 67
- Wind and Snow, p. 235

## The C and $G_7$ Chords

These diagrams show simplified versions of the C and $G_7$ chords.

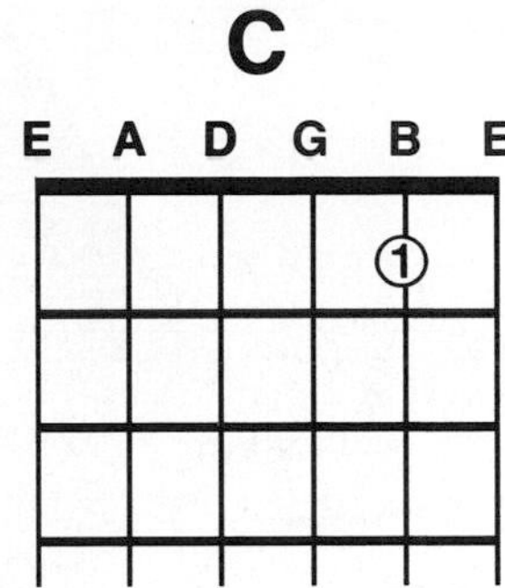


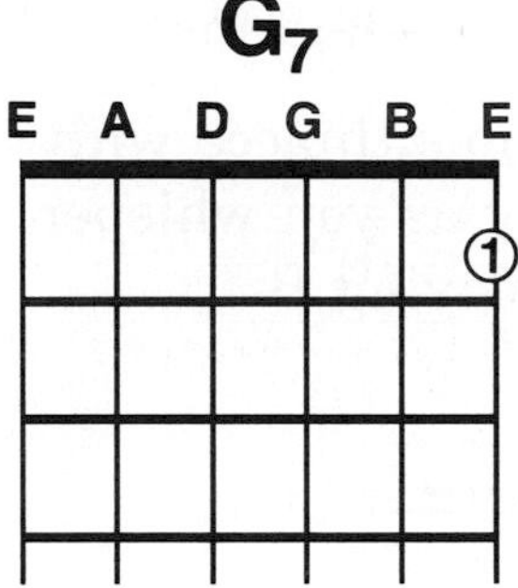


Use the C and $G_7$ chords to accompany "I Am a Great Musician," p. 120 and "The Holly and the Ivy," p. 238.

Try accompanying the round "Row, Row, Row Your Boat" by ear using the C and $G_7$ chords.

## The G and $D_7$ Chords

Practice changing back and forth from the G chord to the $D_7$ chord. Then try accompanying "Swing Low, Sweet Chariot," p. 32. Sing it in G Major.

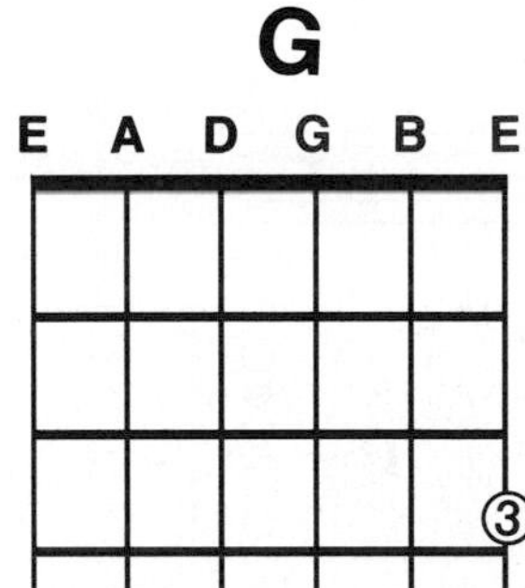


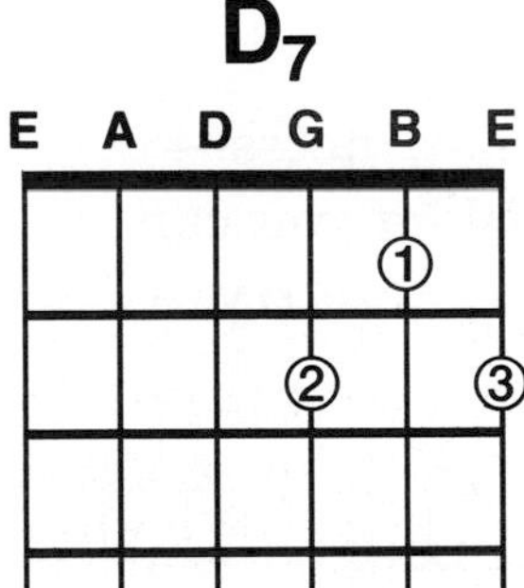


### Chord Family of G (G $D_7$ C)

You can use the G, $D_7$, and C chords to accompany the following songs in your book.

- Silent Night, p. 231
- Michael, Row the Boat Ashore, p. 108

# PLAYING THE RECORDER

Using your left hand, cover the holes shown in the first diagram.

Cover the top of the mouthpiece with your lips. Blow gently as you whisper "daah." You will be playing B.

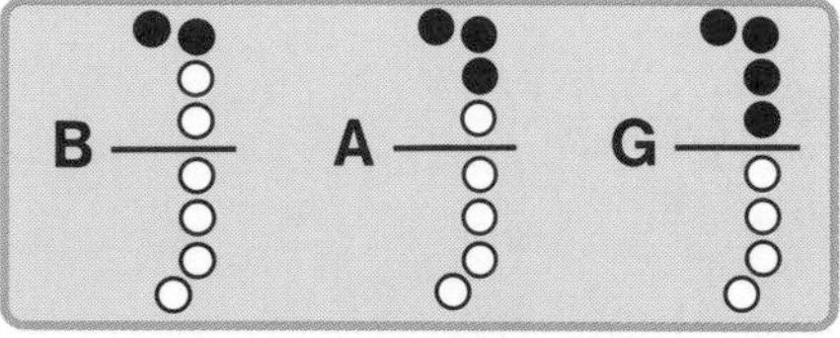

When you can play B, A, and G, you will be able to play melodies 1 and 2.

1. 

2. 

Practice playing two new notes—high C and high D. When you can play them, you are ready to try melody 3.

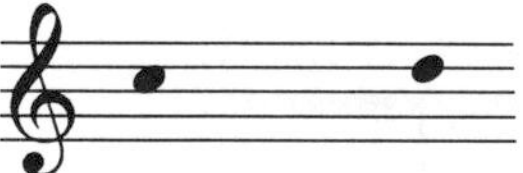

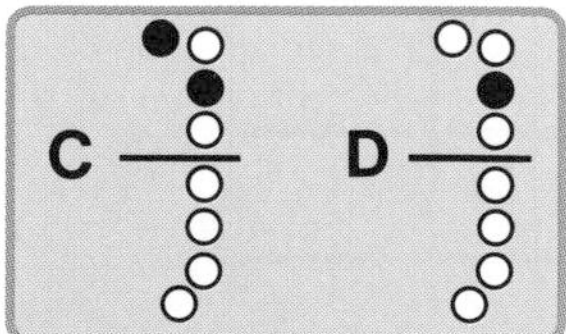


3. 

Here are four new notes to practice. When you can play them, you will be ready to try melody 4.

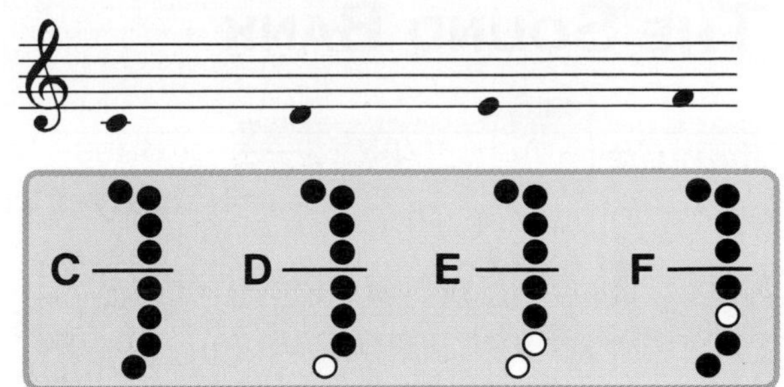

Here are two new notes to practice—F♯ and B♭. When you can play them, you will be ready to try the melody of one of the songs listed below.

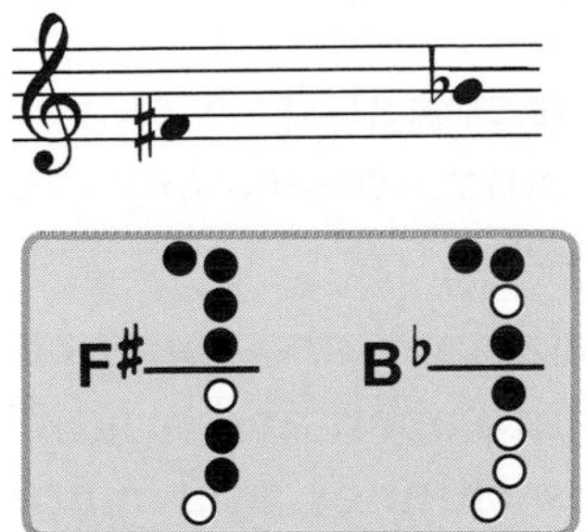


- In the Moonlight, p. 14
- El charro, p. 23
- Charlottetown, p. 162
- Peace Like a River, p. 164
- O Chanukah, p. 226
- We Wish You a Merry Christmas, p. 230
- Purim Day, p. 250

# The Sound Bank

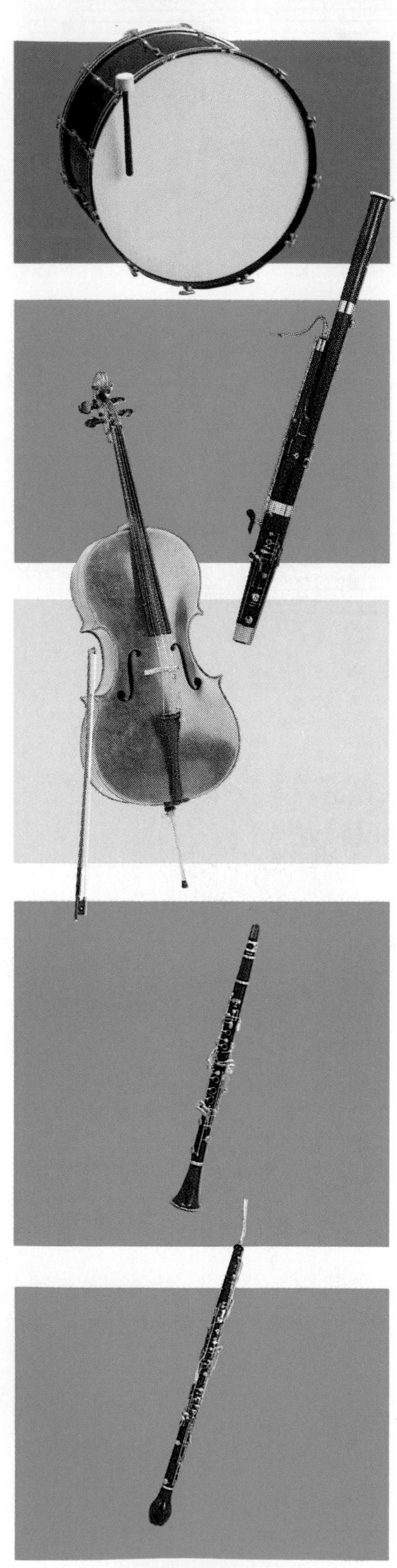

**Bass Drum** A large cylinder-shaped drum. The player can beat one or both sides with a large beater.

- The bass drum has a low "booming" sound, which can be soft and fuzzy or loud and demanding.

**Bassoon** A large tube-shaped wooden instrument with a double reed. The player blows into the reeds to make the sound and presses keys to change the pitches.

- Lower notes on the bassoon may sound gruff or comical. Higher pitches sound softer and more gentle.

**Cello** A large wooden string instrument. The player sits with the cello between the knees and reaches around the front to play. It may be plucked with fingers or played with a bow.

- The cello has a rich, warm voice that can sound quite low. Some of the cello's best notes are the ones sixth-graders sing.

**Clarinet** A cylinder-shaped instrument with a reed in the mouthpiece. It is usually made of wood, but may be plastic or metal. The player blows into the mouthpiece and presses keys to change the pitch.

- The lower notes of the clarinet are soft and hollow. The middle notes are open and bright, and the upper register is thinner and more piercing.

**English horn** A long wooden cylinder-shaped wind instrument with a double reed. There is a bulb-shaped bell at one end of the instrument. Pitches are changed by pressing keys.

- The sound of the English horn is similar to that of the oboe. However, it has a lower, warmer range of notes it can play.

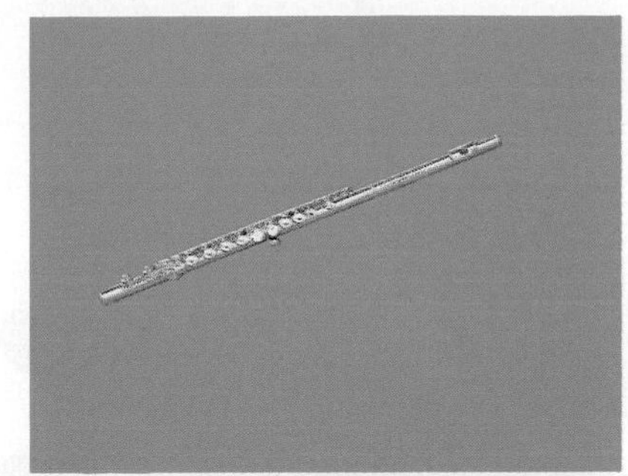

**Flute** A small metal instrument shaped like a pipe. The player holds the instrument sideways and blows across an open mouthpiece to make the sound. Pitches are changed by pressing keys and closing holes in the side of the instrument.

- The flute has a high voice, with a clear, sweet sound.

**French horn** A medium-size instrument made of coiled brass tubing. It has a large bell at one end, and a funnel-shaped mouthpiece. The player holds the horn in the lap, with one hand inside the bell. Valves on the side of the horn are pressed to change pitch.

- The sound of the French horn is mellow and warm.

**Guitar (acoustic)** A wooden string instrument with six strings. The player strums or plucks it with a pick or the fingers to play a melody or chords.

- When played softly, the guitar is gentle and sweet. It sounds lush and powerful when it is played more loudly.

**Guitar (electric)** Electric guitars are flatter and usually made of plastic. They must be plugged into an amplifier.

- Electric guitars are much louder than acoustic guitars. They can make many special sounds with the help of electronics.

**Harp** A large instrument with strings stretched over an open, triangular frame. The player plucks the strings and operates foot pedals to play chromatic tones.

- Present-day harps can play 6½ octaves. Rippling chords are characteristic of the instrument.

**Oboe** A small wooden cylinder-shaped wind instrument. The player blows into a double reed and changes pitch by pressing keys and covering holes in the side of the instrument.

- The sound of the oboe is thin, sweet, and often exotic. The higher notes are softer, the lower ones more noisy and edgy.

**Piano** A large keyboard instrument with 88 keys and many strings on the inside. The player presses the keys, and hammers inside the piano strike the strings to make sounds.

- The piano can play high and low. Many notes can be sounded at the same time.

**Piccolo** A very small flute.

- The piccolo's sound is like the flute's, but higher and more piercing.

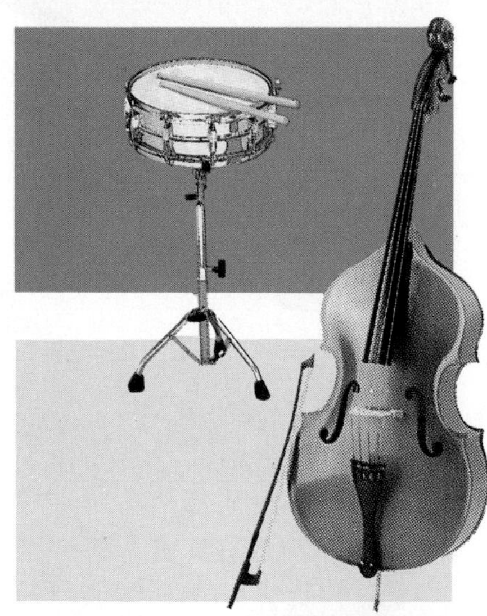

**Snare Drum** A small, cylinder-shaped drum with two heads stretched over the shell. Strings that have been wrapped with wire, called "snares," are attached to the bottom.

- Snare drums can make a long, raspy "roll," or a sharp, rhythmic beating sound.

**String Bass** The largest string instrument, so tall that the player must sit on a high stool or stand up to play it. The player reaches around the front of the string bass to pluck it or bow it.

- The voice of the string bass is deep, dark, and sometimes rumbling.

**Timpani** Large basin-shaped drums made of copper or brass, also called "kettle drums." The timpani can be tuned to specific pitches, and the player often uses several drums to play melodic patterns.

- The timpani can create dramatic effects, sounding like crashing thunder, a quiet heart-beat, or marching feet.

**Trombone** A large brass instrument with a bell at the end of the tubing. Pitches are changed by moving a long *slide* on the side of the instrument.

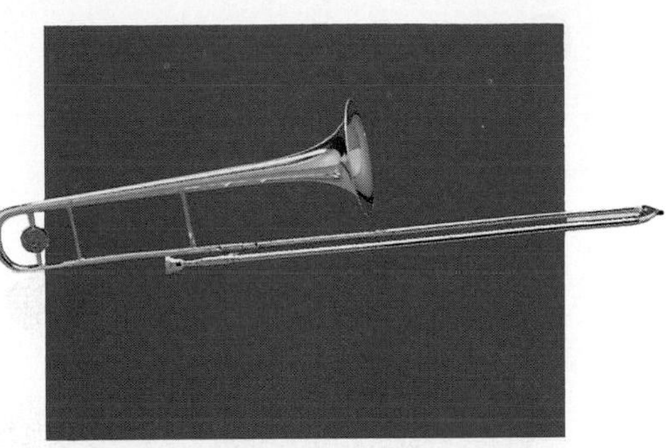

- One of the loudest instruments in the orchestra, the trombone may sound very noisy and aggressive. It can also sound very warm and mellow in its quieter moments.

**Trumpet** A small brass instrument with coiled tubing and a bell at one end. The player pushes three valves at the top of the instrument to change pitches.

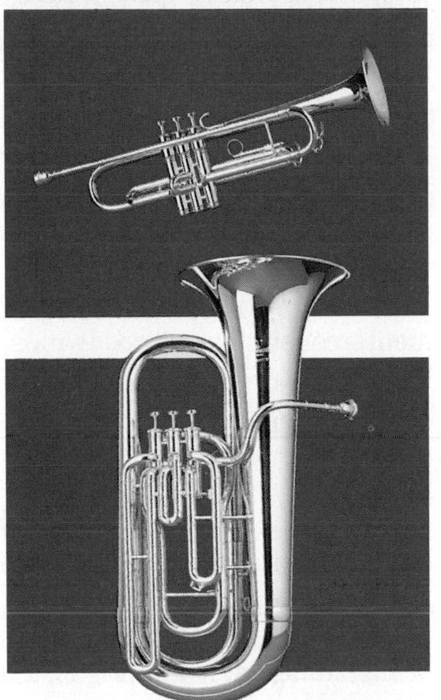

- The sound of the trumpet is bold and bright. On a lyrical melody it can sound sweet, even sad.

**Tuba** The largest brass instrument, with a very large bell that usually points upward. The player changes the pitch by pressing valves.

- The tuba's sound is very low, deep, and sturdy. When playing a melody, it can sound surprisingly rich and mellow.

**Viola** A wooden string instrument that is slightly larger than the violin. The viola is held under the player's chin and either bowed or plucked.

- The viola's tone is deeper and more mellow than the violin's, but very similar to it.

**Violin** The smallest orchestral string instrument. The small wooden violin can make a very large sound when plucked or bowed. It is held under the player's chin.

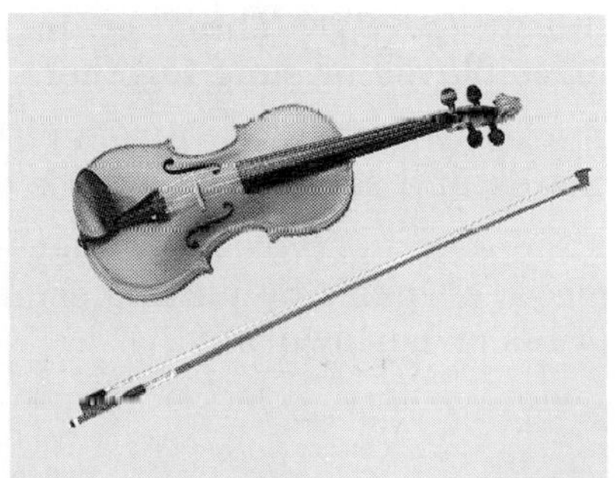

- The violin can make many different sounds. Its tone can be brilliant, warm, raspy, shrill, vibrant, harsh, or mellow, depending on the way the player uses the instrument.

# Glossary

**accelerando** *(p. 160)* Making the tempo, or speed of music, get gradually faster.

**accent** *(p. 60)* A single tone or chord louder than those around it (>).

**accompaniment** *(p. 107)* Music that supports the sound of the featured performer(s).

**antiphonal** *(p. 110)* "Sound against sound," one group echoing or answering another.

**band** *(p. 138)* A balanced group of instruments consisting of woodwinds, brass, and percussion.

**beat** *(p. 56)* A repeating pulse that can be felt in some music.

**cadence** *(p. 74)* A group of chords or notes at the end of a phrase or piece that gives a feeling of pausing or finishing.

**canon** *(p. 90)* A follow-the-leader process in which a melody is imitated by other voices or instruments, beginning at a later time in the music.

**chamber music** *(p. 38)* Music written for small groups, often having only one voice or instrument for each part, as in a string quartet.

**choir** *(p. 129)* Commonly used to mean a group of singers performing together. Also used to mean a group of instruments, as in a brass choir.

**chord** *(p. 94)* Three or more different tones played or sung together.

**chord progression** *(p. 95)* The order of chords in a segment of a piece of music.

**composer** *(p. 38)* A person who makes up pieces of music by putting sounds together in his or her own way.

**concerto** *(p. 48)* A piece for a solo instrument with orchestra, usually in three movements.

**contour** *(p. 82)* The "shape" of a melody, made by the way it moves upward and downward in steps and leaps, and by repeated tones.

**contrast** *(p. 84)* Two or more things that are different. In music, for example, slow is a *contrast* to fast; section A is a *contrast* to section B.

**countermelody** *(p. 17)* A melody that is played or sung at the same time as another melody.

**duet** *(p. 93)* Any two-part composition written for two performers.

**fanfare** *(p. 126)* A tune for one or more brass instruments, usually short and made of strong, accented passages; fanfares are often used to announce someone or something.

**form** *(p. 97)* The structure of a composition; the way its musical materials are organized.

**harmony** *(p. 86)* Two or more different tones sounding at the same time.

**interval** *(p. 75)* The distance between tones.

**jazz** *(p. 41)* An American musical style made of traditional Western music combined with African rhythms and melodic contours.

**lyrics** *(p. 34)* The words of a song.

**major scale** *(p. 75)* An arrangement of eight tones in a scale according to the following steps: whole, whole, half, whole, whole, whole, half.

**medley** *(p. 41)* A group of songs or parts of songs that are strung together to make one musical piece.

**melody** *(p. 37)* A line of single tones that move upward, downward, or repeat.

**minor scale** *(p. 76)* Several arrangements of eight tones in a scale, such as "natural minor": whole, half, whole, whole, half, whole, whole.

**opera** *(p. 46)* A musical play in which most of the speaking lines are sung.

**operetta** *(p. 174)* A musical play, often similar to an opera but usually less serious. In an operetta most of the dialogue is spoken.

**orchestra** *(p. 59)* A balanced group of instruments consisting of strings, woodwinds, brass, and percussion.

**ostinato** *(p. 19)* A rhythm or melody pattern that repeats.

**overture** *(p. 174)* A piece of music originally designed to be played before the beginning of an opera or musical play, often containing melodies that will be heard later.

**parody** *(p. 262)* A humorous imitation.

**pentatonic** *(p. 80)* Music based on a five-tone scale. A common pentatonic scale corresponds to tones 1, 2, 3, 5, and 6 of the major scale.

**phrase** *(p. 74)* A musical sentence. Each phrase expresses a thought.

**pitch** *(p. 72)* The location of a tone with respect to highness or lowness.

**quodlibet** *(p. 260)* Literally, "debate." Each voice sings its own line over and over, the lines harmonizing as in a round.

**range** *(p. 132)* In a melody, the span from the lowest tone to the highest tone.

**rondo** *(p. 99)* A musical form in which the main musical idea (A) is repeated, with contrasting sections in between (such as ABACA).

**round** *(p. 91)* A follow-the-leader process, in which all sing the same melody but start at different times. A round is a kind of canon but a round is usually repeated (with each voice starting over) a number of times.

**scale** *(p. 75)* An arrangement of pitches from lower to higher according to a specific pattern of intervals.

**score** *(p. 110)* Written music or notation of a composition, with each of the vocal or instrumental parts appearing in vertical alignment.

**sequence** *(p. 82)* The repetition of a melody pattern at a higher or lower pitch level.

**step** *(p. 75)* To move from one tone to another, upward or downward, without skipping scale tones in between.

**symphony** *(p. 124)* A large, usually lengthy piece of art music for full orchestra. The word is also sometimes used to mean "symphony orchestra."

**syncopation** *(p. 66)* An arrangement of rhythm in which prominent or important tones begin on weak beats or weak parts of beats, giving a catchy, "off-balance" movement to the music.

**tempo** *(p. 58)* The speed of the beat.

**tone color** *(p. 119)* The special sound of an instrument or voice.

**unison** *(p. 87)* The same pitch.

# Classified Index

## SONGS

## HOLIDAY AND SPECIAL-OCCASION SONGS

HALLOWEEN



THANKSGIVING



PATRIOTIC HOLIDAYS



SAINT PATRICK'S DAY



VALENTINE'S DAY



SEASONAL SONGS



UNITED NATIONS DAY



## POETRY



## THE LISTENING LIBRARY

# Song Index

# ACKNOWLEDGMENTS

Credit and appreciation are due publishers and copyright owners for use of the following.

"Barter" by Sara Teasdale, from ANTHOLOGY OF CHILDREN'S LITERATURE. Houghton-Mifflin, 1959, acknowledged to Macmillan
"River Fog" from JAPAN by Fukaybu Kiyowara. Translated by Arthur Waley. Used by permission of Allen and Unwin Publishers, England
"Velvet Shoes" from COLLECTED POEMS OF ELEANOR WYLIE, Copyright 1921, 1932 by Alfred A. Knopf, Inc.
The authors and editors of World of Music have attempted to verify the source of "Charlottetown," page 162 and "Yonder Stands a Handsome Lady," page 303. We believe them to be in the public domain.

# PICTURE CREDITS

**Contributing Artists:** Barbara Lanza 2–3, 236, 238, 276; David Wisniewski 4, 32, 33, 90; Glenna Hartwell 11, 224, 225; Jim O'Shea 18, 107, 156–157; Eulala Connor 19; Kathy Hendrickson 20, 272; Leslie Stall 21 *b.;* Nancy Munger 23, 79; Steve Schindler 25, 195; Jim Spence 29, 63, 204–205, 206–207, 210–211, 212–213, 214–215; Helen Davie 30, 31, 102, 103, 104, 105; Katherine Ace 39 *t.,* 41, 101, 117, 123, 147, 306. George Baquero 54–55; Ondre Pettingill 67; Wallop Manyam 71, 96, 97. Terry Foreman 82; Frank Ahern 88–89, 229, 231. Stephen Moore 142; Bob Dacey 191, 216–217, 219; Jim Cummins 217; John Holder 242; Marcus Uzilevsky 252–253; Gary Lippencott 254; Sharron O'Neil 255; Everett Magie 260; Laurie Jordan 261, 265, 289. Rae Ecklund 262, 305; John Gampert 263; Bill Finewood 273, 301; Andrea Vuocolo 274, 286, 308 *t.,* 310; Chuck Winter 282; Al Fiorentino 284–285, 307; Tom Cardamone 294; Julie Durrel 296; Linda Graves 303; Susan Dodge 313.

**Photographs:** All photographs by Silver Burdett & Ginn (SB&G) unless otherwise noted. Table of Contents: Photos Gene Anthony for SB&G, Scott Clemens/Sand Dollar Photography for SB&G. 6: *t.* Imagery; *m.* John Rocca/L.G.I.; *b.l.* Nick Elgar/L.G.I.; *b.r.* Martha Swope. 8: Brown Brothers. 9: E.R. Degginger. 10: G. Ricato, Shostal/SuperStock. 13: © 1984 Charlyn Zlotnik. © London Features INT/USA/LTD. 16: © Bradley Smith. 27: Pictorial Parade. 35, 36–37, 39 *b.:* Mark Philbrick for SB&G. 40: Ewing Galloway. 44: Culver Pictures. 47: © Beth Bergman. 56 *b.:* Ron Scott. 58: Gary Milburn/Tom Stack & Associates. 59: John Gerlach/Tom Stack & Associates. 61: Martha Swope. 65: *t.* Photo by SB&G, Courtesy St. Peter's, Morristown, N.J.; *m.l.* Shostal/SuperStock; *b.l.* © Noelle Bloom, Southern Living/Photo Researchers, Inc.; *b.r.* © Rigmor Mason/Photo Researchers, Inc. 85: Inset: John Rocca/L.G.I.; David Falconer. 86: All photos © Scott Clemens/Sand Dollar Photo. 87: Margaret Berg/Berg & Associates. 93: E.R. Degginger. 95 *t.l.:* Gene Anthony for SB&G. 98: Mark Philbrick for SB&G. 112: E.R. Degginger. 113: Erich Lessing/Magnum. 114: *l.* Steve Jennings/L.G.I.; *r.* Cheryl Griffin. 122 *b.l.:* Brownie Harris/The Stock Market. 138: Horst Shafer, Photo Trends/ Rangefinder. 140: Scala/Art Resource. 141: © Eunice Harris/Photo Researchers, Inc. 146: © Lawrence Migdale/Photo Researchers, Inc. 156, 157: Gene Anthony for SB&G. 159: Imagery. 161: Bob and Ira Spring. 162: Cheryl Griffin. 165: *t.* Merry Alpern/L.G.I.; *m.l.* © Beth Bergman; *m.r.* Nick Elgar/L.G.I.; *b.* Martha Swope. 174, 175, 176, 180, 183: Wilson Graham. 187: © David R. Frazier/Photo Researchers, Inc. 192, 193 *l.:* Culver Pictures. 193 *r:* Brown Brothers. 198 *b.:* The Bettmann Archive. 200, 201: Martha Swope. 221: E.R. Degginger. 249: Cheryl Griffin. 257: The Whaling Museum, New Bedford, Massachusetts. 271: Gene Anthony for SB&G. 275: © Bruce Kliewe. 280: Barney Nelson/Black Star. 281: Wolfgang Weber. 287: © Catherine Gehm. 288: Gene Anthony for SB&G. 290: Diane C. Lyell. 293: Gene Anthony for SB&G. 295: Scott Clemens/Sand Dollar Photo. 298. *l.* and *r.* Gene Anthony for SB&G; *m.* Lyn Elder. 302: The Whaling Museum, New Bedford, Massachusetts. 308 *b.:* David Ulmer. 309: © 1988 Hammond Photography.

ABCDEFGHIJ—RRD—96 95 94 93 92 91 90